Praise for *The Financial Times Guide to Finance for Non-Financial Managers*

'Jo Haigh is a master of translati... ...lan-
guage that even the numer... ...heard
Jo speak countless times, and witnessing the audience adore Jo's straight
talking speak – from young to old, rich to poor, start-ups to successful businesses – Jo is the darling of the owner/manager world.

The book is an extension of her renowned training courses and talks and
is a must for those that just need to understand the critical aspects of
numbers that then allows them to run their business efficiently. Having
graduated from INSEAD, this book should be on the compulsory reading
list for all MBA faculty. Jo's previous publications are a delight and this one
is no different!'

Charlotte Mason, founder SiliconIOM and INSEAD EMBA07

'As a Managing Director of a manufacturing business with a manufacturing
background I am indeed the ideal subject for a book like this.

A business is not something to be gambled with – just as we need to know
how to maintain our motorcar, we need to know how to keep our business in good financial health and input from Jo Haigh goes a long way to
focusing traditionally non-financial managers on the things that matter!'

Peter Holmes, Managing Director, Anchor Magnets Ltd

'Whatever your profession there is one certainty of business life: you will
never get to the top of any business, any public sector organisation or any
charity without a confident understanding of the financial figures. I work
with Boards and senior managers; I have worked with Jo. She is an impres-
sive business leader who knows her numbers and has practically translated
that knowledge into business success. Bottom line? She knows how to
inspire that confidence because she knows what she is talking about. Top
line? It may be what you do after the sums that matters, but if you don't
know your numbers you are not even in the game. If you want to get ahead,
do the sums and buy Jo's book!'

Squadron Leader John Peters, MBA MRAeS BSc (Hons) RAF Rtd.
***leadership and business coach, author of* Tornado** Down

'Business owners are brilliant at coming up with new ideas. But they don't always have the brains for budgets. This book "de-jargons" complex financial concepts and is jam-packed with practical tips. A must-read for entrepreneurs.'

Kate Bassett, editor of **Real Business**

'If you're looking for a book on finance for business, and you are NOT a finance person, then this is definitely the book for you. Jo Haigh is quite simply world-class in this space – thousands of business owners, CEOs, MDs will vouch for her; she has been there, done it (many times) and she can explain the subject in very practical terms. If only this book had been available thirty years ago when I started my first business! Whether you are a brand-new start-up, or an established business owner juggling the many different priorities and challenges of being CEO, this book should be in your office, on your shelf, on your desk or in your briefcase. Read it, scribble notes on it, refer to it, use the examples, follow its principles – it does what is says on the cover.'

Steve Gilroy, Chief Executive at Vistage (the World's largest CEO Network)

'Another rare gem of a book bringing together over 28 years of financial experience and the most comprehensive yet from Jo Haigh.

Jo provides a valuable and wonderfully clear insight into what numbers really matter. This book is extremely stimulating, takes out the complexity and gives you the framework to make informed financial decisions. A refreshing change. This book should be the first choice for any manager in business'.

Nigel Carlton, Managing Director UK, Fabricom GDFSUEZ

'Like so many things in life, finance is pretty straightforward once you realise that it's simple concepts dressed up in obscure language. In this book Jo explains accounting and finance in such a clear and easily understood way, that even for "finance-o-phobes" the penny will finally drop.'

Claire Madden, Partner at Connection Capital LLP

'I have no hesitation commending Jo Haigh's ability to communicate managerial skills. Jo's extensive experience in business allows the reader to admit their lack of financial knowledge, to understand in an uncomplicated way, the complexities that face them in business.'

Oliver Rothschild, CEO of Oliver Rothschild Corporate Advisors

'Jo Haigh's book is critical to business success. By explaining the jargon, demonstrating real case studies, and providing skill tests at every point, Jo demystifies finance and really empowers the non financial manager. I truly believe it is vital reading for owner/managers, entrepreneurs, middle managers, students and Angel Investors. Through this practical approach to financial intelligence, no one needs to feel a lack of confidence in interpreting the financial story. I wish this book had been available to me at the beginning of my career. It is certainly on the reading list for account managers within my sales & marketing team and my company will be the better for it.'

Deb Leary OBE, CEO of Forensic Pathways and National President of BAWE (British Association of Women Entrepreneurs)

PEARSON

At Pearson, we believe in learning – all kinds of learning for all kinds of people. Whether it's at home, in the classroom or in the workplace, learning is the key to improving our life chances.

That's why we're working with leading authors to bring you the latest thinking and the best practices, so you can get better at the things that are important to you. You can learn on the page or on the move, and with content that's always crafted to help you understand quickly and apply what you've learned.

If you want to upgrade your personal skills or accelerate your career, become a more effective leader or more powerful communicator, discover new opportunities or simply find more inspiration, we can help you make progress in your work and life.

Pearson is the world's leading learning company. Our portfolio includes the Financial Times, Penguin, Dorling Kindersley, and our educational business, Pearson International.

Every day our work helps learning flourish, and wherever learning flourishes, so do people.

To learn more please visit us at: www.pearson.com/uk

The Financial Times Guide to Finance for Non-Financial Managers

Jo Haigh

PEARSON

Harlow, England • London • New York • Boston • San Francisco • Toronto • Sydney • Auckland • Singapore • Hong Kong
Tokyo • Seoul • Taipei • New Delhi • Cape Town • São Paulo • Mexico City • Madrid • Amsterdam • Munich • Paris • Milan

Pearson Education Limited

Edinburgh Gate
Harlow CM20 2JE
Tel: +44 (0)1279 623623
Fax: +44 (0)1279 431059
Website: www.pearsoned.co.uk

First published in Great Britain in 2012

Pearson Education is not responsible for the content of third-party internet sites.

ISBN: 978–0–273–75620–0

British Library Cataloguing-in-Publication Data
A catalogue record for this book is available from the British Library

Library of Congress Cataloging-in-Publication Data
A catalog record for this book is available from the Library of Congress

ARP Impression 98

Typeset in 9pt Stone Serif by 3
Printed in Great Britain by Clays Ltd, St Ives plc

This is dedicated to
Annie, my old university friend,
who reminded me of late that she was surprised
I had written a book on finance as I
struggled to balance my bank statement at university!

Contents

About the author

Jo Haigh is a Partner and Head of Corporate Finance for Corporate Finance Services, with bases in London, Birmingham and Yorkshire, and a partner in the fds Group, a specialist training and development business.

An experienced dealmaker, Jo specialises in putting together the right deal at the right time and in the right format for growing businesses throughout the country. She has bought and sold over 300 companies in the last twenty years, specialising in owner-managed companies.

She is a regular presenter for the Institute of Directors on corporate governance and mergers and acquisitions.

As Partner of fds, a highly successful training and consultancy organisation she founded at the start of the 1990s, she has held more than forty non-executive roles over that period in companies across the country and helped many businesses through successful transactions. She has sold three of her own companies and undertaken two personal MBOs.

She is a Visiting Fellow at the University of Leeds where she delivers the Corporate Governance development programme for all academic staff wishing to hive off new companies, in addition to training and developing non-executive directors appointed to university companies whose role is to represent university interests.

She is currently Non-Executive Director of five companies: Anchor Magnets Ltd, Sticky Content Ltd, Talent Training and Talent Services Holding Ltd, TPD Corporate Finance and Imperative Training Ltd. She also sits on the board for the Angelus Advisory Group.

Awards/titles/achievements

- Runner up for the 2011 IoD Awards in the Business Advisor Category
- Finalist in the 2011 Sue Ryder Women of Achievement Awards
- RealBusiness.co.uk columnist
- On the advisory board of the Angelus Advisory Group
- Part of the judging panel for the Growing Business Awards 2010
- Shortlisted for the Forward Ladies Women in Business Awards 2010 in the Corporate Leader category
- Named in the Yorkshire Post top 100 entrepreneurs 2010
- Shortlisted in the Women of the Future Awards – Mentor of the Year category 2009
- Winner of IoD Business Advisor of the Year 2009 and 2006
- Nominated for Financial News' Top 100 Most Influential Women in Finance 2009
- Entered into the 2008 edition of *Who's Who of Britain's Business Elite*
- Shortlisted finalist in the First Women CBI Awards 2007, in the Finance category
- Voted 'Star Speaker' and 'Outperforming Speaker' at the Vistage Annual Speakers Awards 2008, 2007, 2006 and 2005
- An Ambassador of Huddersfield, along with Joanne Harris
- Selected as a 'woman of achievement' at the prestigious Women of the Year lunch, which brings together outstanding women from all walks of life, in 2006
- One of the first corporate financiers in the country to receive a new qualification based on her past experience alone: the prestigious advanced diploma in corporate finance awarded by the Institute of Chartered Accountants England and Wales
- Recipient of a 2006 Woman of Achievement Award by the American Biographical Institute
- Yorkshire Businesswoman of the Year 2005
- Her first book, *The Business Rules*, published 2005 and 2006, was such a success that a foreign rights deal has been confirmed with a publisher in China. Jo's second book, *Buying and Selling a Business: An Entrepreneur's Guide*, was published in March 2007 and her third book, *Tales from the Glass Ceiling: A Survival Guide for Women in Business*, was

published in June 2008 and sold out of its first reprint after five days. It was best-selling business book of the year 2008, selling over 500,000 copies.

Testimonials from some past clients

Jo is a pleasure to work with. She really cares for her clients and works hard to achieve the best results for them. Her energy and enthusiasm are infectious and drive a deal through. She delivers!

Edward Persse, Partner, Irwin Mitchell

I've seen both sides of Jo in action; the authoritative yet motivational speaker, and also the Corporate Financier. In either role she is superb. Her knowledge, coupled with her ability to impart it to others in terms that are easily understood and her practical and pragmatic approach places her in a unique position – an advisor who walks the talk!

Grant Ellis, Executive Chairman, Broker Network Group

Jo is a real 'hot-shot' corporate financier and what she doesn't know about deal making ... is very little! She negotiates strongly to get the best deal for her clients, whilst ensuring a 'win-win' position for all parties. As a Vistage and IoD speaker, she is recognised as a leading light in her field and is always engaging to hear and see. She is a polished presenter and she is also great fun to spend time with.

Paul Luen, MD, Martek Marine Ltd

Jo is providing some independent thinking and challenging our Executive Board along with bringing valuable networking contacts.

Peter Holmes, Anchor Magnets

We engaged Jo as a non-executive director in 2009 with a view to providing us with guidance from a corporate governance perspective and to use her corporate finance expertise to further the growth of our company. It is very evident that she will move us towards our goals very swiftly and far more quickly than had she not become involved. All input has been very positive.

Neil O'Keefe

As a business coach, I often have need to find someone in corporate finance to advise my clients whom I can trust implicitly to do a good job. Jo is just such a person for whom I have the highest regard and whose name is always top of the list when it comes to recommendations.

David Adams, Group Chairman, Vistage International

Jo is working with me as a non-executive director and has been supportive and highly focussed on a number of key business planning decisions that we have needed to make as the company moves forward. Jo is great fun to work with and her experience is invaluable.

A. Davidson, MD of Hayes Davidson

From our very first meeting with Jo it was clear that she has immense experience in the selling of owner managed businesses. Jo gained a thorough understanding of our business, the market sector and the acquirer which ensured a professional and competent approach through to completion.

The negotiation process had several areas of contention which required a firm but common sense approach to ensure we were adequately protected from excessive risk and that any unreasonable terms within the sale and purchase agreement were removed. This was achieved to the satisfaction of all parties.

It was a pleasure working with Jo, who fully understood our personal and business requirements and ultimately delivered fully on what we set out to achieve.

S. Ashton, Hallmark Fire Limited

Acknowledgements

For most authors it goes without saying that the writing process, although solitary, in many ways requires numerous people to bring it to a completed manuscript. My journey has been a similar one. If you are not mentioned in the list it's not because you haven't been there for me in one guise or another, but because I only have one page allocated to these acknowledgements.

Chris Cudmore, my Editor, has moved from debit to credit and back again in my own personal balance sheet (thankfully for both of us!) as he put me through my paces to get to the well constructed book you are about to read. I was pleased when he said he had learnt much from reading the book but I will acknowledge it was no one-way traffic and would like to say a very great personal thank you.

My wonderful and fabulous PAs, Steph and Arlene, who struggled with my hand-written papers composed on dodgy trains, planes and taxis: ladies, the book is here only because of you both.

My sensational colleague Martin Venning, who checked my chapters for technical accuracy, and my beautiful and talented daughter Jessica, who corrected my less than adequate grammar.

This is my fourth book and so I would like to say thank you to Angel and Coco, who kept me sane with their unconditional love, provided of course I kept feeding them doggie chocs!

Introduction

Decisions, decisions: every day we are making decisions. Some are made without any thought of the consequences; others are considered like those of a champion chess player, reflecting on the consequences of moving this way or that way or not moving at all.

In our global economy with its rapidly changing markets, we see new and successful players enter the business game, and economies that previously seemed robust falter and fail. The ability to make sound financial decisions is more important than ever before.

Of course bad decisions will always be made and hindsight is a wonderful thing, as Decca Records know all too well after turning down the Beatles.

But Decca are by no means alone. In 1876, a Western Union internal memo read

This 'telephone' has too many shortcomings to be seriously considered as a means of communication. The device is inherently of no value to us.

Even well respected decision makers don't always get it right. Winston Churchill is on record as saying

I do not believe there is the slightest chance of war with Japan in our lifetime. The Japanese are our allies ... Japan is at the other end of the world. She cannot menace our vital security in any way ... War with Japan is not a possibility which any reasonable government need take into account.

What could be further from the truth than Thomas Watson, then IBM Chairman, saying in 1958 *'I think there is a world market for about five computers'*, or, as Bill Gates allegedly said as recently as 1981, *'640K ought to be enough for anybody'*? The question is whether these statements were made on the back of a sound understanding of the financial consequences, or were they business hunches or simply business ignorance?

Clearly it would appear to be nothing to do with intelligence or business acumen. Perhaps it could be just the lack of intelligent data.

Making financial decisions

Business is more complex than ever before, partly as a result of the global economic meltdown. And even though things are now improving, these events together with more and more regulations and relentless and increasing competition mean it is essential to react swiftly to ongoing changes in the business environment, and to be certain of your reactions. It is critical that managers, owners and directors alike must be able to read and understand the numbers. Poor quality data, or an inability to understand data quickly, will always severely affect your performance and career progression or the performance of your business or department.

Through the various chapters I will not only explain seemingly complex financial concepts but provide you with practical business tools to help improve the financial quality of your business or department.

I have tried to take a practical approach to the contents and order of this book by first of all setting the scene in Chapter 1 with an overview of what data is needed in the financial decision making process and why.

Chapter 2 follows logically as it concerns who uses the data and what they do with it. Chapter 3 provides you with an insight into financial terminology and its various nuances so is appropriate to understand before we look at the main financial paper of profit and loss, cash flow and balance sheet covered in Chapters 4, 5 and 6 respectively. Having established a current status position with the above, Chapter 7 looks forward to how we use budgets and forecasts to predict and manage the future business opportunities.

In Chapter 8 we bring the main accounting paper of the profit and loss account and the balance sheet side-by-side with the budget in the management accounts pack and in Chapter 9 we look into the less frequently required area for the non-financial manager to understand, that of capital appraisal and investment appraisal.

I have concluded the book in Chapter 10 with a business health check which provides you with an insight into the well-being of your organisation and gives advice and suggestions on how to tackle and identify issues before they become unsurmountable.

Finally, the sample documents at the end of the book are there to help you see first hand how standard documents are presented, and the glossary is an alphabetical guide to act on as and when a manager is faced with an issue that needs further clarification.

Chapter guide

Chapter 1 will consider the general financial decision making process, what you should consider specifically before committing to something and some general principles that you need to be aware of in relation to how choosing a particular route could alter the future destination of your organisation.

Chapter 2 looks at the people that use financial and accounting information, how they may view data provided to them, or sourced directly, and the ramifications of that information being manipulated.

Chapter 3 looks at the peculiar language of finance and at the nuances in its translation. It considers how the language has changed over the years and the issues related to not being able to speak or understand 'accountant'.

Chapter 4 considers how the choice of profit over service levels, for example, can alter the face of your business from a financial perspective. Such business decisions may not be your choice but any manager, and particularly a business owner, needs to fully understand the consequences of their decision.

In Chapter 5 we will consider why understanding the difference between profit and cash can mean the difference between success and failure. They are not the same although commonly believed to be so. Absolute clarity on the difference and why it is so will be provided with easy to navigate templates.

Of all the financial statements readily available the balance sheet is often the most difficult for a non-financial manager to understand. Chapter 6 takes the reader through an easy to navigate template and so addresses the concerns that someone unfamiliar with this document generally experiences. It also explains how it is possible to depress or enhance assets' apparent value without anything of substance being changed.

All but the most modest of businesses should understand budgeting processes and how a budget differs from a forecast. Chapter 7 looks at these two strategic management documents, analyses how you should create them and looks at how third parties view such data. It also summarises the risks attached to inflating and deflating budgets when there is an apparent desire to satisfy a third party, whether that be a bank, a shareholder, another department or the board.

In Chapter 8 we will consider that all-important monthly management account pack, de rigueur in most businesses, and identify what is required for compliance purposes, what it should contain and, importantly, what it shouldn't. How should it be compiled, how issued and to whom? Chapter 8 will consider all these issues, leaving the reader better informed and more confident in their understanding of this critical management tool.

Chapter 9 will give the reader an insight into the whole process of capital expenditure (Capex) and investment approval. It will provide example of ratios used and why one return is desirable to some parties and completely undesirable to others. It will provide navigation tools to allow a non-financial manager the best opportunity to put forward a Capex request in the most advantageous manner.

Finally, Chapter 10 provides practical health checks for businesses and departments which will ensure the non-financial manager is ready and able to take preventative action or, at worst, understand the consequences.

A glossary of financial terms is provided at the end of the book.

Although no book can turn you into a financial wizard *The Financial Times Guide to Finance for Non-Financial Managers* will give you some straightforward instructions that will take the mystery out of the financial data we are all presented with on a daily basis.

1

Data and Decisions

A few key lessons

In this chapter we will explore how a decision made without a full and proper understanding of the ramifications can affect your business performance and how, with some basic processes and techniques, you can take a business action with much more confidence and in the knowledge that you have considered the effects of the activity.

Making a decision about business based on financial data is, for the most part, based on historical data, forecasts and budgets. The trouble with this is it is not feasible to assume that what happened previously will be what *should* happen in the future.

So how do you as a savvy professional make use of financial numbers without spreadsheet purgatory and analysis paralysis? What is there to rely on in the non-financial manager's box of tricks?

The first thing to realise is that all financial data is fundamentally flawed. There is no such thing as 100% accuracy. Much financial information is based on guesstimates and assumptions. Therefore the effort to get anything 100% correct is quite fruitless. It's much better to concentrate on getting the information where it needs to be in a timely manner with the best degree of accuracy available than to produce late data that may only be marginally more correct. Remember that delay in making a decision nearly always means targets are missed.

Presentation

As an astute manager wanting to make the most of all financial data available, you may also like to consider the format in which it is presented.

Non-financial people, by and large, find a graph or pie chart easier to understand than a list of numbers.

Consider the difference between Figures 1.1 and 1.2 and Table 1.1.

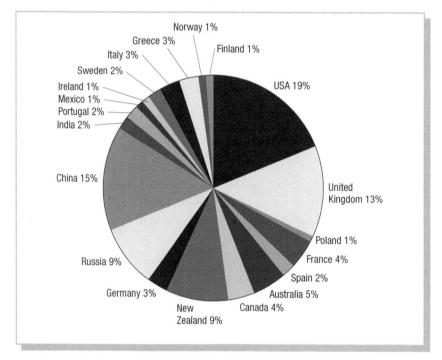

 Sales percentages shown as pie chart

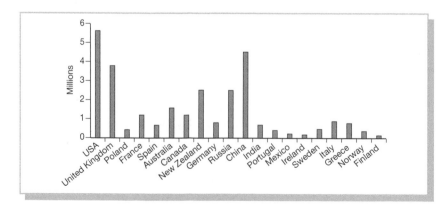

Figure 1.2   Sales figures shown as graph

Table 1.1   Table of sales figures and percentages

Country	Sales (£)	Percentage
USA	5,700,050	18.86
United Kingdom	3,870,500	12.81
Poland	450,870	1.49
France	1,257,000	4.16
Spain	685,147	2.27
Australia	1,587,940	5.25
Canada	1,256,789	4.16
New Zealand	2,578,946	8.53
Germany	870,458	2.88
Russia	2,578,900	8.53
China	4,573,569	15.13
India	748,960	2.48
Portugal	500,100	1.65
Mexico	258,979	0.86
Ireland	235,980	0.78
Sweden	568,700	1.88
Italy	987,500	3.27
Greece	856,120	2.83
Norway	450,239	1.49
Finland	204,870	0.68
	30,221,617	100.00

The impact of the graph and the pie chart is obvious. If your data isn't presented in this way this is something you should definitely consider. And if **you** are thinking this is preferable almost certainly someone else will be thinking the same. The majority of the best business decisions are made on the availability of **high quality**, **timely**, and most importantly **concise** information.

What data do we need to make a robust decision?

High quality and timely information includes critical success factors (CSFs) and key performance indicators (KPIs). These are those things which will turn the gas up and down on your business's success. Examples of KPIs (to evaluate the process of a particular activity on an ongoing basis) are

- Gross profit percentage
- New customers acquired per month
- Turnover growth
- Debtor and creditor days
- Return on equity.

Critical Success Factors (CSFs) can be defined as those things that are necessary for an organisation or project to achieve its mission. Examples might include

- New CEO appointed
- Market share percentage goal realised
- IT system integrated across the business.

All CSFs need to be SMART, i.e. specific, measurable, attainable, realistic and time-framed.

Clearly these may change or evolve over time; the important thing is that they should be contained, i.e. kept to a minimum. If a project or business is tracking more than half a dozen of each of the KPIs and the CSFs then the manager has gone too far as not only can this slow down the decision making process but, worse still, it could create indecision.

For more detailed use of these KPIs and CSFs, see Chapter 10.

A view from inside the finance department

Some decisions are outside the remit of the non-financial manager and remain firmly in the finance department (whether it is with the finance director and his/her team or the external auditor). However, as a non-financial manager you need to have an awareness of the impact on business, even if at first sight you won't be able to directly influence the decision in the first place. Let's look at some key things you'll need to be aware of.

Borrowing/debt versus equity

When a business or department needs funds for growth or recovery the money available to them is usually either debt or equity. Debt is borrowed money and is largely secured funds which have a defined capital repayment and interest programme. On the other hand equity is an unsecured investment in the business itself, sometimes with no defined exit or return. Which of these options is chosen can make a serious difference to the financial performance of the organisation.

When an equity investment is made it is done, in the first instance, on a high risk basis, in the hope of high reward. When someone, or an organisation, acquires shares in a business (which is what an equity investment is), they do so on the basis that if the business performs well they will get a proportion of that profit. That payment is called a dividend, or a division if you like, of the profits. Clearly such investments have variable success rates and a dividend could be substantial if profits are high or zero if the business does not make sufficient profit to make a distribution.

Conversely with a debt provision the interest is payable by the company to the funder whether the business makes a profit or not and of course there will almost certainly be a capital redemption required – in other words the business has to pay interest on the debt and has to repay the capital sum borrowed against an agreed timescale.

These payments are not dependant on profit though of course they may practically be dependant on the business having the **cash** available.

An example

Company A borrows £10,000 secured against its debtor book (invoices receivable) or those monies outstanding from customers to whom goods or services were supplied. The terms are a £2,500 per year capital repayment with interest at 5% above base rate (i.e. bank rate), assumed to be 1%.

The **profit and loss (P&L) account** is a financial statement that summarises the financial transactions for a business over a given period of time. This statement shows the revenue (sales or income), expenses (costs) and the NET difference between the two being profit. (For more information on the profit and loss account see Chapter 4.) The impact of Company A's borrowing on its P&L account is £600 interest (a cost) which reduces the business profit in its first year.

The **balance sheet** is a financial statement of assets (things a business owns or is owed less liabilities (things a business owes), the net difference being called net assets. (For more information on the balance sheet see Chapter 6.) The impact on Company A's balance sheet will be a liability of £10,000 which will reduce the net asset value of the business, although it will be matched by the increase in the cash position (an asset, but only until the cash is spent).

Externally, in companies a charge (a legal document which gives the organisation that requested it the right of control over the sale of particular assets to satisfy an unpaid debt) is registered at Companies House. This reduces the company's ability to borrow against that asset and, even if no external charge is taken, clearly the lender, even if it's another department within the company, will take this into account when looking at future funding requirement.

Cash flow is the amount of cash generated by a business in a specific period. In order to fund this loan the company or department within the company must find £3,100 of cash in its first year to service the interest and capital repayments. Of course this can come out of the £10,000 borrowed, but that was not the original purpose of the loan.

Company B on the other hand takes an equity or share investment of £10,000. The lender would like a 30% return on its investment but, of course, as it is likely it will take that by way of a dividend it will only get this return if the business is profitable.

The impact on Company B's **profit and loss account** is zero. Although if the company does make a profit it will be a dividend out of its post-tax profits, it could be more or less than 30% as the way in which the investment is made will determine how the payment is made.

Company B's **balance sheet** will be strengthened as shareholder funds will increase, and permanently so, until shares are redeemed or sold.

Externally, mostly an external investment in a business by way of an equity stake is seen as a positive by third parties who see it as a business that is seen by others as worthy of investment.

Company B's **cash flow** in the first instance will increase by the £10,000 and no repayment to the equity investment may be needed unless and until the business makes a profit. Even if it does make a profit in the first year and the investor gets the maximum return at 30%, this £3,000 would be less than the debt funding costs of £3,100 referred to above.

Clearly, though, unlike the debt-based deal, the cost to cash flow would be the same year on year for a profitable business, whereas for the debt-based deal the cost of interest accruing, if base remains static, will come down as capital repayments reduce the loan.

The question of whether debt is preferable to equity is an impossible question to answer. Each case must be looked at separately and reviewed on its merits. Equity can ultimately be far more expensive to the person or organisation seeking it but as this is unsecured finance it may be the only option available. Equally limits on the availability of debt against a secured asset may mean that this choice of finance will restrict the growth of the business.

But of course it is not only funding routes that affect financial performance. It could be the choice of percentage or method of depreciation on an asset purchased. (For more information on the difference between cash and profit, see Chapter 5.)

What else can affect the financial statements?

Depreciation

Depreciation is the accountancy tool used to calculate the expected value of an asset at any given point in its life.

There are essentially two types of depreciation: straight line and reducing balance. In relation to percentages used, the choice is one to be agreed between the directors (including the finance director) and the auditors.

The first thing to note is that depreciation has no effect either on cash flow or on taxable profit calculations. It does, however, affect profits on which dividends are paid and on which certain analytical ratios are calculated. It also affects the net book worth of an asset and so the net worth of a business.

For example, if you acquired a desk at a cost of £500 and expected it to last you four years, after which point you would throw it away, you would depreciate the asset using the straight line method at 25%. The effective result on the profit and loss account would therefore be as follows:

Year	Reduction to profit
Yr 1	£125
Yr 2	£125
Yr 3	£125
Yr 4	£125

The net book value of the desk would appear in the balance sheet as follows:

Year	Net book value
Yr 1	£375
Yr 2	£250
Yr 3	£125
Yr 4	£0

Conversely, if you bought a desk for £500 and expected it to last for four years but anticipated being able to sell it for at least something at the end of the period, you would use the reducing balance method of depreciation at 25%.

This method of depreciation calculates the percentage cost based on the reducing value rather than the initial capital value. The effect on the profit and loss account would be:

Year	Reduction to profit
Yr 1	£125
Yr 2	£93.75
Yr 3	£70.31
Yr 4	£52.73

and the net book value would appear in the balance sheet as:

Year	Net book value
Yr 1	£375
Yr 2	£281.25
Yr 3	£210.94
Yr 4	£158.21

The effect of both the choice of percentage and method of depreciation is quite clear. In the first example, the business or department had its profits reduced over the four-year period by £500; in the second example, they were reduced by £341.79. In other words, the second business is £158.21

more profitable than the first, and in addition has a higher asset value on its balance sheet.

As a non-financial manager, even though depreciation policy may not be within your remit, when looking at capital budgets you need to, at the very least, understand the impact on your accounts or budgets. (See Chapter 7 for more information on budgets, and Chapter 9 for capital investment appraisal.)

Indeed depreciation is just one financial policy that can affect business performance; another will be how you choose to value your stock or work in process.

In choosing either straight line or reducing balance as a method of depreciation, you should consider the validity of the method in relation to the expected end value of the item being depreciated. The straight line approach suggests that at the end of the depreciation process the item in question will have zero value and should be disposed of, so an example of this may be IT equipment. Likewise, when you use reducing balance as a method of depreciation you are doing so in the knowledge that the item in question will always have some residual value, however small – say for example a motor vehicle.

Stock and work in progress (WIP)

The accounting convention for the valuation of stock and work in progress, WIP, is 'the lower of cost and net realisable value'. The issue, of course, is what the finance department defines as the cost. Is the actual cost the latest cost, the average cost, the weighted cost or the moving average cost?

Stock valuation techniques

The main stock valuation techniques in common use are FIFO, LIFO and average cost.

FIFO stands for first-in, first-out, meaning that the oldest stock items are assumed as being sold first.

LIFO stands for last-in, first-out, meaning that the most recently produced items are assumed as sold first.

These are just stock valuation techniques. They do not necessarily mean that the actual physical objects have been individually tracked as they were sold.

Under the **average cost method**, it is assumed that the cost of stock is based on the average cost of the goods available for sale during the period.

Weighted average cost takes the cost of goods available for sale and divides it by the total amount of goods from beginning stock and purchases. This gives a **weighted average cost per unit**. A physical count is then performed on the ending stock to determine the amount of goods left. Finally, this amount is multiplied by weighted average cost per unit to give an estimate of ending inventory cost.

To calculate **moving-average cost**, assume that both beginning stock and ending stock cost are known. From them the cost per unit of beginning stock can be calculated. During the year, multiple purchases were made. Each time, purchase costs are added to beginning inventory cost to get the cost of current stock. Similarly, the number of units bought is added to beginning inventory to get the current goods available for sale. After each purchase, the cost of current stock is divided by the current goods available for sale to get the current cost per unit of goods. Also during the year, multiple sales happened.

The current goods available for sale is deducted by the amount of goods sold, and the cost of current inventory is deducted by the amount of goods sold times the latest (before this sale) current cost per unit on goods. This deducted amount is added to cost of goods sold.

At the end of the year, the last cost per unit on goods, along with a physical count, is used to determine ending inventory cost.

The question for the non-financial manager is what does such a decision do to the value of the balance sheet or the profitability of the business?

In the first instance the answer is simple. If you choose a method that creates a higher stock value, and of course the nature of the product or service will be relevant in making this choice, then the net asset value of the business will be greater (see Chapter 6 for more information on balance sheets and net assets). This is clearly only at that point of time but that may be very relevant dependent upon what the business's or department's aims are.

Conversely when stock has been valued high, when it comes to selling it, unless sale prices have also been enhanced proportionally, profits will be less (see Chapter 4 for further information on the effect of these choices).

How external forces affect financial decisions, accounts and policies

There are generally accepted accounting principles (GAAP) which are guideline rules and procedures used in recording and reporting accountancy information and in audited financial statements, but these do not necessarily apply to management information for internal use, and nor are they law. They are good practice principles and are by and large used universally by the accountancy profession, but there is a choice and it's vital that a non-financial manager understands the implication of such choices.

Notes to published financial statements are considered essential for all but the smallest of businesses, and those notes describing the accountancy principles utilised by a company are a **must** read when attempting to interpret financial accounts. They would generally be the first place to start when looking at accounts in the public domain.

Management accounts and financial accounting policies are often within the finance team's remit but will clearly affect a business and its financial performance, and so understanding the implications is something you need to be aware of.

Shareholder requirements and actions

Dividends are a share of the profits of the business that are attributed to shareholders proportionate to their percentage stake in the business and in line with any specific rights attached to their shareholding.

Of course a shareholder is generally looking for a return on their investment. The value and frequency of such a distribution lies in the hands of the directors, who recommend to the shareholders a dividend payment. Once this is approved it becomes a debt due and payable to the shareholders.

When a dividend is paid it affects cash flow (see Chapter 5 for what does and doesn't affect cash flow), which, in turn, affects the availability of cash for other corporate needs – be it investment or recovery requirements. The question therefore is one of balance. If you don't make an acceptable return to your shareholders they have, certainly in a quoted company, a choice. They can sell their shares and invest in something that gives them a more acceptable return or, of course, hang on in there.

In a private company, when there is no real market in selling shares, 'bailing out' may be more difficult, but that will not stop a disgruntled shareholder causing other problems. The 2006 Companies Act in particular has created a very powerful tool for a disgruntled shareholder called a derivative action. Such an action allows any shareholder to bring an action against a specific director, or the board as a whole, where they believe such people have been negligent, in default, breached a duty or breached trust.

These actions can be brought about for so-called 'ordinary mistakes' or non-fraudulent lapses in duties, and there is no requirement to prove the director being sued has had any personal benefit – and, of even more concern, when such breach occurred the shareholder now bringing the action does not need to have been a shareholder at the time of the breach. This means that someone could choose to buy shares just to cause trouble and it provides scope for almost any decision by a director to be challenged.

Strategic forces

Cost savings

As a non-financial manager you could be involved in a much broader decision, for example, closing down a department or a division or, even worse, a whole company.

Any decision of this nature will impact on cash flow. The ultimate plan may be to save money; the question to address initially, though, is what the cost is in the short term, both to cash and profits. Nearly always these are underestimated, so here are some headings to consider:

- Legal costs
- Redundancy costs
- Site clearance
- Professional costs such as liquidation
- Loss on sale of stock and assets which never achieve full value particularly in a 'fire sale'
- Leases that may have to be serviced even though the business or department is no longer using the facilities or equipment
- Legal action from affected staff e.g. unfair dismissal
- Removal or relocation costs
- Ongoing rates and service charges if property is left unattended and unsold

▦ Security services

▦ And unquantifiable management time and the distraction therein.

Interest rates

There are also the issues of funding costs and interest rates. Currently, as I write, in the UK interest rates are at a lifetime low but, conversely, funds remain very difficult to access, and there are questions that occupy many business people's minds: Should we borrow? Can we borrow? What will the rate be? How long will it remain relatively low if we are able to negotiate a deal?

As a result decisions may have to be made by the finance team on 'hedging'. For the non-financial manager a 'hedge' is more likely to mean something green and leafy that surrounds a field or specific area to protect it from trespassing or to keep those inside the hedge from getting out. In finance a 'hedge' has in fact some similarities with the green leafy variety; in at least that it is a financial tool used to manage fluctuations and exposure to risk.

In effect it wraps around a known cost of borrowing. This can sometimes be described as a cap and collar so if the finance department cap and collar a rate, it means they have agreed with the lender that if interest rates go down or up a certain percentage, the borrower will not either benefit or be penalised.

Of course there is an element of risk for both parties as if rates drop below the bottom rate agreed, the borrower will not benefit; then again, if they get above it, they won't have to pay an increased rate.

It would be rare in a market where rates are at 0.5% that such a collar comes for free, so the cost of the tool being utilised to secure the hedge is also part of the total financial cost.

For heavy borrowers (i.e. those who borrow large sums on a regular basis) hedging a rate is usually a sensible option if the initial cost can be managed as, if nothing else, it gives a degree of certainty in terms of fixing the cost of borrowing.

International currency management

Because we operate in a global market, many businesses are at risk from currency fluctuations as rates, by and large, have, of late, been affected internationally. The finance team may therefore find it prudent to buy forward. A forward contract is an agreement between parties, one of whom may be a currency dealer, to carry out a particular transaction (by currency) at a pre-agreed price.

The alternative is to buy at spot rate i.e. today's rate.

The choice of buying spot or on forward will affect the business performance, although it will of course depend on how you have negotiated the 'on sell' price of the goods or services ultimately being traded, and the ability of the trader to adjust their sale price in line with currency peaks and troughs.

If your sale price is totally flexible, spot price is the best option but this flexibility, for most businesses, would be rare so buying forward is the more cautious approach. However, buying forward assuming currency movements will go upwards when, in fact, they drop means your sale price clearly becomes less competitive. This is something which few companies can afford – so which route should they take? Most forward contracts do not have a premium cost attributed to them and you could choose not to utilise the funds until rates change again in your favour but that assumes

1   You have the wherewithal to use the currency at a close date, whenever that is

2   You have sufficient additional funds to draw down monies at a more appealing rate in the meantime.

Business ethics

When things go wrong in business the ethics of the executive can be challenged and decisions are made that perhaps, in other circumstances, may not have been.

The directors of Enron, and lately any number of banking and financial institutions from RBS and Bank of Scotland to Lloyds, have made some decisions that have been severely criticised as being far from ethical.

Things like morals are a personal business position much in the same way as one person's terrorist is another person's freedom fighter. However, because for most commercial companies or departments the priority is profit, it can sometimes appear that an ethical approach will not render the profits desired, or indeed required, by the shareholders. When times are tough, an ethical or moral position can be sorely challenged as financial performance is more paramount for the non-financial manager who may not immediately see the financial implications of his or her ethical view on a decision, or indeed if they do understand, it can be a less than comfortable process.

Challenging the decision is best done using sound financial rationale when speaking with the financial team. Rather than debating what is ethical with regard to a particular decision, it is preferable to provide a financial view on the long-term impact of the decision. (See Chapter 4 for more information on profit drivers.)

No one gets it always right and the well known phrase 'those people who never get it wrong are most likely those that never do anything in the first place' rings true.

Some decisions will inevitably have a positive effect on financial performance, others less so. It is only hindsight – which is not yet available in a bottle – which helps the decision making process, as numerous publishers know to their cost after having rejected J. K. Rowling's first manuscript!

2

Who Uses Accounting Information and Why

In a world in which virtually any information is available online anyone in business needs to have an understanding of how financial and corporate data can be used by all their stakeholders. It's not only the varied sources of information but also the relative speed at which this can be accessed that is unprecedented.

As a manager you need a sound understanding of who accesses corporate data and the rationale behind data analysis, so as to avoid potential pitfalls.

Consider the following stakeholders as potential users of data:

- The customer
- The supplier
- The funder (private equity and asset-based)
- The shareholder
- The finance department
- Revenue & Customs
- Regulators
- Local and central government
- Employers and prospective employers
- The competition and prospective competition
- Trade unions
- Other departments in a business

- Prospective buyers of a business
- Accountants and auditors
- Lawyers.

Some of these people, groups or companies will be looking for a similar reason, for example, to assess the robustness of the business or department; others may be looking for highly speculative reasons or, of course, just out of sheer curiosity.

Mandatory requirements

Some information is in the public domain: this means anyone can look at it – albeit sometimes for a modest fee. At Companies House, the current fee is £4 for a document package or £1 for individual documents such as company reports. Other information is private and in-house so can only be reviewed either by those given access to it or those who have chosen to access it, not always with permission in some cases.

Information on companies can be divided into two clear categories: financial accounting data, which is public, and management accounting data (see Chapter 8), which is private.

Financial data is mandatory information required by regulators. Management accounting data is information created by executives for the purposes of managing the business.

So, why is it necessary to keep accounting information?

All companies must submit accounts to Companies House on their financial performance on an annual basis. This needs to be nine months after the year end for private companies and seven months for publicly listed companies.

Requirements for different sizes of company

In addition to this, different sized companies have different filing requirements. With regard to the quantity of data in the public domain, small and medium sized companies are exempt from issuing certain information, while larger companies have to make much more detailed information available.

Small and medium sized companies

Under the Companies Act 2006, a company is treated as small or medium sized if it does not exceed more than one of the criteria shown in Table 2.1

Table 2.1 Criteria for small and medium sized companies

	Small	Medium sized
Turnover	£6.5m	£25.9m
Net worth	£3.26m	£12.9m
Average number of employees (on a monthly basis)	50	250

Small companies have exemptions from the requirements to file full accounts, but the following documents need to be filed:

■ Auditors'/accountants' report (where necessary)

■ Balance sheet

■ Notes to the balance sheet.

Medium sized companies must include the following in their accounts:

■ A profit and loss account

■ A balance sheet

■ Notes to the accounts

■ Group accounts (if applicable)

■ A directors' report and business review

■ An audit report.

Large companies

Standard accounts will include the following:

■ Directors' report and business review

■ Auditors'/accountants' report or audit exemption details

■ Profit and loss account

■ Balance sheet

■ Notes to profit and loss account and balance sheet.

For more information on the balance sheet see Chapter 6.

Requirements for auditing

As well as having to submit information for public view, some companies have to have such information audited. Again, this is business size dependent, although it should be noted that while an audit is mandatory for certain companies, the shareholders of any company can elect to have an audit.

In addition, Limited Liability Partnerships (LLPs) need an audit unless they are exempt under the size definition as utilised for small companies as set out above. In addition, the definition of a small group may apply.

For designation as a 'small group of companies', a group must meet at least two of the following conditions:

- Aggregate turnover must be no more than £6.5 million net (£7.8 million gross)
- The aggregate balance sheet total must be £3.26 million net (£3.9 million gross) or less
- The average total number of employees of the group must be 50 or fewer.

So if you are involved in a small company or a small group, to qualify for total audit exemption, your company must

- Qualify as small; *and*
- Have a turnover of not more than £6.5 million; *and*
- Have a balance sheet total of not more than £3.26 million

and the directors must resolve not to have their accounts audited.

Sole traders and non-limited partnerships, whose accounts are not in the public domain, do not need to have an audit, but a non-statutory audit may, for instance, be required as part of a partnership agreement or by a funder.

A PLC always requires an audit.

The role of the auditor

It is perhaps at this point worth noting what constitutes the role of the auditor, as much myth and mystery surrounds just exactly what they are supposed to do.

Their duty is **not** to report to the directors. Their job is to report to the members or shareholders. Of course, a director and a shareholder (member) may be one and the same person but, by law, they have two completely separate legal personas.

The duty of the auditor is to review the financial statements as prepared by the board and to agree, partly agree, or not agree at all (a qualification) as to whether the information they have reviewed from an independent point of view represents a true and fair view (and materially accurate position) of the business at a point in time.

A financial audit, or, more accurately, an audit of financial statements, is the review of the financial statements of a company or any other legal entity (including governments and limited liability partnerships), resulting in the publication of an independent opinion on whether those financial statements are relevant, accurate, complete and fairly presented.

An audit is a spot check of information and by no means serves as an exhaustive review of all the financial transactions. It is widely perceived by non-financial directors and senior management that auditors check **all** transactions in arriving at their report, and therefore the accounts are 100% accurate. This is not and will never be the case.

Auditors are not, as is commonly thought, specifically charged with uncovering fraud although, of course, should they uncover anything suspicious they are bound to make appropriate reports.

Non-mandatory information

Having covered what legally must be in the public domain, let's look at which information may be requested that isn't necessarily in the public domain and indeed why such a request may be forthcoming.

Requests for information may include the following:

- Management accounts
- Budgets and forecasts
- Business plans
- Aged debtors and creditors
- Loan agreements
- Capital expenditure plans
- Investment agreements
- Bank covenants

- Auditors' management letters
- Insurance and other claims history
- Contingent liabilities analysis
- Non-published key performance indicators (KPIs) e.g. credit notes raised
- Risk registers and policies
- Health and safety records
- Management's and directors' CVs and qualification verification
- Hire purchase and leasing agreements.

Just because information isn't legally mandatory does not mean it is not essential to comply with a **covenant** (a promise to carry out a particular requirement – e.g. produce management accounts by the 15th of each month) from an investor.

You need to remember that the information which you provide will have an effect on all sorts of business issues. These might include things such as securing a new supply line, engaging a prospective employee, retaining a credit line or, even more importantly, getting one – whether that be from an internal or external source.

The Interpretation of information in the public domain

Although all information is liable to different interpretations it is important to know how accountancy information is considered. This is so that you can at worst prepare, or at best pre-address any issues in a proactive manner.

Publicly available accounts can be either

1   Full accounts (see the sample full accounts in Appendix B)

or

2   Abbreviated accounts (see the sample abbreviated accounts in Appendix C).

Full accounts generally include:

- A profit and loss account.

▪ A balance sheet signed by a company director or by a designated member of an LLP. The copy of the balance sheet must also state the name of the director or designated member of an LLP who signed it on behalf of the board.

▪ An auditor's report, unless the company or LLP qualifies for small companies' audit exemption. If the accounts have been audited, it is also a requirement to disclose the amount of remuneration paid to the auditor (including any benefits in kind) in the notes to the accounts. The copy of the auditor's report must state the auditor's name. Where the auditor is a firm, the auditor's report must state the name of the auditor and the name of the person who signed it as senior statutory auditor on behalf of the firm.

▪ A directors' report. This is a report signed by a director or the company secretary that usually describes the company's principal activities, a review of the business and an indication of future developments. The Companies House copy does not need to be signed but, if it is signed, it must state the name of the officer who signed it. Since 1 October 2007, the directors' report must also include a business review. The review must provide information on the company's performance and future prospects. This applies to all companies, except small companies and LLPs.

▪ In the directors' report of a PLC the names of the directors and any share interests or share options in the company must be included as well as details of dividends and details of research and development as well as political and charitable gifts given during the year.

▪ Notes to the accounts must be attached, or Companies House may reject the accounts.

▪ Group accounts, if applicable, must also be submitted.

The company or LLP name and number should appear on one of the composite documents if the business is eligible and chooses to submit any abbreviated accounts.

Submitting abbreviated accounts, even if legally allowed, may well affect the credit rating of the business. This is because when a particular area is not clear negative conclusions may be drawn, on such things as profit or sales (neither of which are published in abbreviated accounts).

In a business which is performing well the advantage of submitting full accounts is entirely positive as the numbers will speak for themselves. Even for a business not performing well it is sensible to submit full accounts because this gives the directors an opportunity to provide explanations for declines.

Management data

Most other financial data is not publicly available but management data (see Chapter 8 for more information on the management acccounts data) may be requested by both internal and external stakeholders. This may be for a number of reasons: agreeing credit terms; funding; supplier terms; employment roles; shareholding; capital expenditure; pricing agreements.

Management information, by its very name, suggests it's for management which, in the first instance, it may well be. However, as it is this data that provides so much more of an insight into a business's or department's performance, it is something that is more and more frequently required by external users.

So what may a customer, or even a potential customer, request and what would and could they use it for?

In addition to general commercial issues a **customer** may want to review a number of things about a business:

1 What your gross margin is compared to other possible suppliers – this may tell them if you are more or less price competitive

2 Debtor collection days to see how generous you are in giving credit

3 Stock holding days to assess if you will be able to meet their demand

4 Other customer details to assess if you are supplying the competition

5 Whether the business is sustainable, i.e. whether the supply chain can be maintained

6 Staff turnover.

Of course no financial data is robust enough to provide certainty but in a general scenario these questions can be answered on the strength of a series of numbers.

Business health check tools

For more information on the health check process, including a suggested health check list and report format, see Chapter 10.

Profit

This is relatively easy to assess from full published accounts, but remember that these may be out of date: private companies have nine months from their year end to file details at Companies House. If the company does not have to file full accounts it is not possible at all to assess profit accurately.

Management accounts (see the sample management accounts pack in Appendix A) are generally more up to date (usually prepared monthly in arrears) and clearly show the profit, gross and net for the month and for the year to date. Of course, this is for all sales and so may not be sufficient to satisfy a potential customer about pricing. But it is a good start if comparing it to a competitor, and a savvy customer may even ask for detailed costings (this so called 'open book' accounting, i.e. sharing costings with both buyer and seller, is becoming more and more common).

Debtor collection

Although credit terms may well be as stated in the company's terms and conditions, in reality enforcing these is often a different matter. It is possible, by various financial equations, to at least gauge the ferocity of the credit controller. You can do this by calculating, for instance, average debtor days. This is calculated as follows (assuming you are working on annual accounts):

$$\frac{\text{Trade debtors}}{\text{Sales}} \times 365$$

So an example would be

$$\frac{1{,}500}{12{,}150} \times 365 = 45 \text{ days}$$

This is a generic figure but if your terms of business for the company are 30 days and debtor days work out at 45 then it is not too difficult to draw a conclusion.

Stock days

An experienced business person knows it is important to hold just the right amount of stock: enough to make a sale, but not so much that you tie up precious working capital.

The customer, however, has a lot less concern for working capital. Instead, what they care about is if their orders can be fulfilled. The calculation can be done swiftly on full accounts. On abbreviated accounts it is not possible, but if management accounts are made available then the formula (assuming you are working on annual accounts) is:

$$\frac{\text{Stock}}{\text{Cost of goods sold}} \times 365$$

An example would be

$$\frac{900}{8,000} \times 365 = 41 \text{ days}$$

i.e. the business holds approximately 41 days' worth of stock.

Business sustainability

For a 'business to consumer' (B to C) supplier, or a 'business to business' (B to B) supplier, it's very interesting to know just who else is being supplied and, even preferably, at what rate.

Although the latter point may be a fiercely protected commercial position the former may be a mandatory revelation for a prospective customer. This data is rarely, if ever, available anywhere except in management data.

In view of the recent catastrophic corporate failure rate in 2009/10 (over 50,000 companies went into liquidation in this period – this compares with circa 20,000 in 2008 which was an increase of 50% on 2007) continuation of business in terms of certainty of supply remains fairly important for all but the most basic of commodity dealers.

Of course no one can be wholly accurate in predicting business failure or explaining why a business has failed but there are a number of warning signs:

- Liquidity
- Gearing
- Return on equity
- Interest cover
- Return on capital employed (ROCE)
- Bad debt percentage.

– to name but a few.

The formula and minimum desirable requirements for these are as follows.

Liquidity

The current ratio is considered to be an indicator of a company's level of liquidity. It is calculated as follows:

$$\text{Current ratio} = \frac{\text{Current assets}}{\text{Current liabilities}}$$

Two to one would be regarded as a good credit risk because, should a default on an agreed payment by the borrower occur, the lender whose liability is due (e.g. a bank overdraft, which is considered a current liability because the definition of current in accounting terms is due in the next 12 months) can draw some comfort from the fact that in order to enforce a payment they do not have to administer the sale of a fixed asset such as a building but can rather seize more available assets such as stock to cover outstanding debt.

Therefore where a business has twice as many current assets as liabilities then a lender has substantially more comfort in terms of security.

Gearing

$$\text{Debt equity ratio} = \frac{\text{Long-term debt}}{\text{Total capital}}$$

Anything over 50% is considered highly geared **by a lender** but the following example shows that high gearing, i.e. where there is more debt (borrowing) in the business compared to equity (shareholders' funds), may in fact give a good return to an investor over a period of time, even taking into account the non-profitable years.

However, for the lender (i.e. the debt provider) as soon as the business moves into a position where it is not making sufficient operating profit to pay the bank their interest then the funder becomes unable to recover its charges. Any subsequent increases in interest rates would make this even more risky for the lender.

Low financial gearing

Shareholders' equity		16,000	
Long-term debt (10%)		4,000	
Total capital		20,000	

	Yr 1	Yr 2	Yr 3	Yr 4	Yr 5
Operating profit	4,000	3,000	**2,000**	1,500	1,000
Interest	400	400	**400**	400	400
PBT	3,600	2,600	**1,600**	1,100	600
Tax (25%)	900	650	**400**	275	150
PAT	2,700	1,950	**1,200**	825	450
Shareholders' return	16.9%	12.2%	**7.5%**	5.2%	2.8%
Average	8.9%				

High financial gearing

Shareholders' equity	4,000
Long-term debt (10%)	16,000
Total capital	20,000

	Yr 1	Yr 2	Yr 3	Yr 4	Yr 5
Operating profit	4,000	3,000	**2,000**	1,500	1,000
Interest	1,600	1,600	**1,600**	1,600	1,600
PBT	2,400	1,400	**400**	(100)	(600)
TAX (25%)	600	350	**100**	-	-
PAT	1,800	1,050	**300**	(100)	(600)
Shareholders' return	45%	26.3%	**7.5%**	(2.5%)	(15%)
Average	12.3%				

Return on equity (ROE)

$$\text{Return on equity \%} = \frac{\text{Net profit after interest and tax}}{\text{Total equity}}$$

It is difficult to give an accurate figure here as different equity investors have different and forever changing requirements but certainly for an institutional investor it would be at least 35%.

Interest cover

$$\text{Interest cover} = \frac{\text{Operating profit (profit before interest and tax)}}{\text{Interest charge}}$$

Banks require a minimum of three times more operating profit than interest. This gives them plenty of scope to ensure they get their interest every month even if profits decline.

ROCE

This ratio indicates the efficiency and profitability of a business's capital investments. In other words it demonstrates how well a company is utilising capital to generate revenue.

ROCE should normally be higher than the rate at which the business borrows, otherwise any increase in borrowings will reduce shareholder earnings.

The difference between ROCE and ROE (see above) is that ROE means the amount of profit a business generates with the money invested by shareholders and ROCE means the return made on money from shareholders and debt funders.

$$\text{Return on capital employed} = \frac{\text{Operating profit (profit before interest and tax)}}{\text{Total capital}} \%$$

A ROCE figure of 25% is generally deemed to be acceptable but this is often also dependent on just who is the equity investor and what their requirements are.

Bad debt percentage

It is difficult to quantify a level of bad debt that should cause concern, but anything over 1% of turnover may be considered problematic.

Relationships

A final point for customers – business is often about a personal relationship. Continuation of products is one thing but what about that all-important invaluable customer/client relationship?

Staff turnover

Companies that have a high staff turnover may not necessarily be inherently flawed, it could be a symptom of the industry e.g. holiday companies, catering businesses, seasonal companies and the like, but one may assume a savvy customer would be aware of this so a high staff turnover could be a negative when assessing a business. What is really important is staff turnover consistent with the industry.

The formula for staff turnover is:

$$\frac{\text{Total number of people in the year}}{\text{Current number of employees}} - 1 \times 100$$

For example, if the total number of people employed over the year was 75, and there are 50 employees now, we get:

$75/50 = 1.5$

$1.5 - 1 = 0.5$

$0.5 \times 100 = $ **50% turnover.**

You can only get this data if the company shares its management information.

Access to information: stakeholders and interested parties

Suppliers

Suppliers, or would-be suppliers, have not too dissimilar requirements. Certainly, continuation of businesses and how quickly will they get paid is critical for most suppliers. For the latter they can perform a simple creditor days calculation as follows:

$$\frac{\text{Trade creditors}}{\text{Cost of goods sold}} \times 365$$

An example would be:

$$\frac{700}{10,000} \times 365 = 26 \text{ days}$$

If the company being reviewed has terms of 30 days but trade creditor days are 26, once again they will perhaps make an unacceptable conclusion in that they assume they will be paid earlier than terms!

A supplier may also want to know whether they can secure a solid relationship with the buyer and what is the policy and spend requirement for such a position. This sort of information is only ever likely to be available in a business plan or strategy document, neither of which are, generally, publicly available.

Business had moved more to partnering the old relationships of an unequal nature that were all about cost. It has now moved much more towards managing risk, product development and, above all, maintaining relationships.

The funder

Bear in mind that most funders prefer not to be the sole source of support. By and large fund raising is not a simple task. It is often ongoing and takes time and effort so getting, and keeping, financial data in an accessible and clear place is essential to the success of most funding requests.

As part of their research, any external funder will have looked at anything and everything in the public domain. What they now want is the up-to-date management data, e.g. payback plans and projections (see Chapter 7 and Chapter 9 for more information).

In undertaking any funding relationship, whether it is with internal or external providers, the first and most important thing to understand is where the funder is coming from in terms of their expectations.

There are, undoubtedly, the famous five Ps: preparation prevents particularly poor performance. Apply this principle rigorously to all data you give to any funder. In this market you are lucky to get one chance to present, rarely will a second chance be on the table.

A funder is going to ask for a plan. Whether that is a business plan and budget or a cost benefit plan will depend on the nature of the requirement but what is important is that, in some cases, you may not have any personal relationship with the finance provider and, therefore, you may be subject to a box-ticking exercise where two plus two must always equal four.

It is best to look at the exact needs of different breeds of funders. There are some generalisations, as mentioned above, but, more importantly, there are some very specific requirements related to the nature of the funder and what the fund would be used for. **External funders** include banks and private equity firms, angel investors and asset lenders.

Banks

A bank has two main requirements:

1 To have sufficient security against a debt so that, should it need to, it can recover unpaid sums due, in order to de-risk their position

2 Interest to cover the cost of the lend. This is how they make their own income (see interest cover ratio earlier in this chapter).

In order to make their calculations, banks need to appraise technically the value of the assets. The way they do these appraisals will depend on what the asset is.

Security

For example, if a building is to be offered as security, the bank will need to make an assessment on its value using a bank-approved surveyor. Although this is technically an open market value, by and large, the bank surveyors tend to provide a less attractive valuation than if you are using an estate agent's value for a property sale.

On the issue of what percentage lend may you expect, a maximum of 'up to' 75% is about reasonable – but watch for the words 'up to'.

If the asset being used as security is the debtor book then a bank is very unlikely to lend more than 60% of debtors under 90 days old.

Other assets used as security may include stock and WIP (work in progress or goods being produced that are only partially complete or services rendered but not billed to the customer as yet). Generally banks attach no value to these at all, whatever their nature, due largely to the difficulty in selling them post-failure. The same applies to fixtures and fittings and, with only some exceptions, plant and equipment can be largely discarded as being worth very little in terms of security.

Established businesses with proven profitable track records are clearly much easier to assess in terms of risk and therefore are generally more attractive to a bank but if there is any perceived shortfall, a funder may ask for personal guarantees from the directors.

What to do and not do in negotiation for a personal guarantee (PG)

A personal guarantee means that should the business prove unable to satisfy a debt then the individual or individuals giving their guarantee will be forced to make good any difference.

Giving a personal guarantee is very serious and should only be considered as a last resort. There are, however, some practical tips that can limit the risks attached to such a guarantee.

Firstly, never sign a joint and several guarantee, only sign a several. This ring fences your proportion of the debt if there are a number of people involved in providing the security. For example, if three people provide a joint and several guarantee for £300,000 it does not mean that each is responsible for one-third of that, rather that any one of the three may have to pay all the £300,000 should the debt be called in. However, if the security is only several then the most any one of the three could be asked to pay is £100,000.

Secondly, avoid guarantees unlimited in time (an indefinite period that a funder can hold the security), as once a bank has such a security they are generally reluctant to return it and asking for it back can change the bank's view of the customer adversely.

Avoid guarantees unlimited in amounts.

If the security requirements are as stated then the interest position is as follows:

■ Rates will vary depending on a number of things, including the age of the business, the amount borrowed, the security available and even the industry type.

■ Rates are based on either a percentage above base rate or LIBOR (the

London Interbank Offer Rate, or the rate at which banks offer to lend the money to one another in the City of London).

■ It is possible to negotiate cap and collars (see Chapter 1) or even fixed rates but this negotiation will be based on the perceived robustness of the business proposition.

Bank covenants

Banks may also require the maintenance of one or more covenants. A covenant is a promise or agreement backed by a legally binding contract that could be enforced in court if breached. It may cover, for example, an agreement not to take a pay rise for a given period. If covenants are breached, the bank may even have recall rights, i.e. the right to call for early redemption.

Covenants can have reference to, for example,

■ Interest cover

■ ROCE

■ Asset ratio

■ Acid test ratio

■ Gearing.

These have been explained above.

Private equity firms/venture capitalists and angels

These equity investors have a different view on how they invest in a business or venture and of the perceived risks. Because of this they inevitably need different information in order to make an investment.

In addition to the information required by a bank, these people will need to have a business plan with a defined exit route: most of these funders need to know how they will exit the investment, usually within a three to five year period. This exit can be achieved by a refinancing exercise or, better, a sale either to the trade or to the public.

Invariably this exit will need to be at a premium, the amount of which will be variable but will be a minimum of double the investment and generally much more.

In the meantime the investors will require a return on their investment and this, added to the fact that equity investments are largely unsecured, will not be modest, ideally at least 30% to 40% per year. In order to deliver this sort of return, budgets and forecasts are best constructed with some ability to manipulate the data dependent on 'what if' scenarios (see Chapter 7).

There will be a lot of not strictly financial data such investors need before investing, including market data, competitor information, management data and product/service information to name a few.

Be aware that sometimes these investors take a more hands-on role in the business once a transaction is completed including, for example, taking a role on the board.

Asset lenders

These significant funders lend against the security of a discrete asset, whether that be a building, plant, equipment, fixtures and fittings, stock and WIP or debtors, and are therefore interested specifically in the perceived value of the asset, whether the business can service the loan and interest payments attached to the lend.

They need to validate any value the business attaches to the asset and, like banks, they will inevitably use their own valuers or specialists. The difference with these funders is the level of lend against the asset which tends to be much higher than with funding from a bank.

The reason is the way security is taken. For the most part, these funders own the asset as opposed to just taking a charge on it and, therefore, have more control over its sale and proceeds should the borrower default.

In order for lends to be assessed against assets, business plans will need to include cash flows, generally for the period of the lend (see Chapter 7 on budgeting and cash flows).

Shareholders

Shareholders may be considered as a sort of a funder, and their intentions or characteristics come in a variety of shapes and sizes from large pension funds to 'Ma and Pa' investors.

There are a number of reasons why someone would invest in a business but the two main financial ones are capital growth and income generation. For certain investors both are desirable.

Shareholder funding is an equity investment and therefore nearly always 100% at risk in that, unlike bank and asset funds, if the business fails the shareholder will only be paid out of any residual funds after all other debt is cleared.

In deciding whether to make such an investment from a purely financial point of view, historical performance has to be analysed, perhaps in comparison to other investment options, and, of course, future prospects assessed.

This will be done using publicly available accounts and, where made available, business plans as well as actuarial analysis where a large investment is being made.

These investors may require regular updates on company performance and prospects. If the investment is in a public company certain information is available as a matter of course, as allowed and required within the stock exchange rules. In a private company it may be part of an investment agreement that such information is provided.

The finance department

The finance department may often be the arbitrator of a decision related to a funding request, but they are equally likely to be part of a team putting together a proposal, possibly to an internal group such as a board of directors or an external body such as a bank.

For internal information the finance department will have access to most, if not all, financial data. However, when you are asking the finance department to act as an arbitrator on a decision you may well need to reconsider your position versus theirs. They will perhaps need those requiring funds to support a project, to provide market intelligence on risk and market share, or even competitor and supplier pricing and sale prospects.

The board

Very often the board are overwhelmed with financial data and are asked to make decisions on all of it. Clearly a board has the right to ask for anything at all from its executives, but the directors are often given information they don't need and, sometimes, that they do not require. Often they are not given really critical information for many reasons including time and internal politics.

When providing information to a board you should remember the duties of directors: principally, to promote the success of the company for the benefit of the shareholders. They also have a duty to act with skill and care.

Because of this they need to have information in a format that allows them to consider various 'what if' scenarios (see Chapter 7).

Boards are very busy and often for a large project approval (see Chapter 9 on Capex approval) need to allocate both time and resources to suit the task.

Non-financial people and non-board members in particular need to be aware of the fact that often their request/requirement will be one of many issues being considered and need to manage their proposals alongside this.

To assist your case present information clearly, concisely and with a selection of options and recommendations stating clearly the pros and cons.

HMRC

HMRC (Her Majesty's Revenue and Customs) have considerable powers and influence over businesses and will be examining data in the public domain as a matter of course. In particular, they can look at a company's accounts to examine such things as margins and other KPIs (see Chapter 10) in order to ascertain if they are in line with similar businesses in their sector. Should this not be the case, it may trigger an investigation, so should your business not follow a general trend, it may be important to point this out.

Should a business be investigated, HMRC have considerable powers and co-operating with them is essential. This includes the provision of information as swiftly as possible.

In terms of financial information they require it may include all business records but, in general, they will examine bank statements, management accounts and budgets, VAT and PAYE records, employee files, cheque book stubs and deposit account details.

You will nearly always be personally interviewed and you may choose to do this with a professional advisor present.

You are obliged, by law, to keep proper accounting records though the standard is hugely subjective and thus variable.

Omission or unavailability of data is rarely positive in these cases.

Regulatory bodies

From the Advertising Standards Board to utility regulators and everything else in between, regulators cover every aspect of business. A few of the most well known and their roles are shown in the list of regulators in Appendix D.

Some of these regulators have more relevance to different businesses and departments than others. These bodies will assess relevant publicly available information but may make specific requests and if you fail, or are unable to comply, you could find yourself subject to numerous penalties or even forfeit your trading rights.

Bodies such as the Committee of Advertising Practice are self-regulating. Others, such as the Financial Services Authority (FSA), have mandatory membership in terms of business practice for certain businesses and business functions.

In terms of financial data the FSA can certainly ask for client records, and query and review how you have advised and communicated with clients. And so the content of such documents needs to mirror other relevant data.

Local and central government

A government body or department, whether central or local, has no more right to request financial data than anyone else external to a business, but if that body is providing such a thing as grant support, they will require certain other data from the business management information system.

This may include business plans, employment procedures for new staff, utilisation of grant money, explanation of eligibility, and availability of your own funding (most grants require a matched funding route). As these funds are in high demand and generally in short supply, expect the application process to be a time-consuming job where every element of an application will be scrutinised.

Employees and prospective employees

Assuming they are not directors, employees are only entitled to see financial information that is in the public domain but, of course, that does include company accounts and information about directors and shareholders in terms of their shareholding and, in the case of public company directors, their salaries.

Some businesses take a more transparent position on what they share with their staff, including sharing monthly management accounts, KPIs and business plans. On the other hand, others work on a mushroom-growing principle. If you fall into the former category it's not likely that the employees will be able to fully understand detailed financial management information and a sensible approach would seem to include FAQ sheets and team briefings. This is to prevent employees misreading the numbers and making unnecessary and often negative assumptions.

For example, just because your business has made a profit, this does not mean it is cash rich. In fact it may be quite the opposite (see Chapter 5 on the difference between profit and cash) if you have invested heavily in capital items so an explanation of the difference between cash and profit, at the very least, would seem sensible.

Cash is cash and, as such, is a liquid asset of a business – the inflow of money into a bank account (i.e. actual money received, not what's promised). Cash of course flows out of the business through paying bills for supplies and for buying capital equipment, but of course not all bills are paid by cash, many being on credit terms.

Profit, on the other hand, is measured by taking all costs and expenses away from sales. It is different from cash because profit is money earned by the business as represented in the accounts. There are many things that affect profit that don't affect cash, such as depreciation and capital expenditure.

The competition

Your competitors can access Companies House data like everyone else, but they may also use a number of other analytical tools including Plimsoll reports (see www.plimsoll.co.uk) which provide analysis on company performance against other businesses in the sector with all sorts of interesting assumptions and conclusions such as financial security and future risks to help you decide, for example, whether you should be doing business with them, and whether they are likely to be taken over. Plimsoll data have predicted nine out of ten company failures in the last 25 years so what a competitor reads from the information is worth knowing.

Of course there are lots of other organisations that provide competitive data and the like on businesses including Experian (www.experian.co.uk) and Dun and Bradstreet (www.DNB.co.uk).

In all these and many other cases, the analysis is taken largely on the back of data available in the public domain and any other industry intelligence they can gather. Either way what's in the public domain is what is mostly used to ascertain risk and credit ratings.

Unions

In terms of information that a union may access they generally have no right to more than what is in the public domain. However, some firms have taken a more open-book approach to information-sharing. This may happen when both sides feel this will help with settling disputes in relation to wages and indeed any employment issue.

Alternatively, under the ACAS guidelines it would be preferable to share requested information on an ongoing basis. If that information is against the interests of national security or would contravene a statute etc., then disclosure is not needed but, in other instances, it is best to comply with reasonable requests.

Interdepartmental issues

Information may be shared openly and willingly or, alternatively, kept highly confidential. Much would depend on the nature and size of both the company and the department in question. What is important to realise is that such information may have high internal political value and those in charge of its inception and distribution can hold immense power in terms of their ability to influence decisions one way or another.

Certain departments, principally the finance department, have control over more politically sensitive information than others. Making friends with the authors of this data will certainly assist your ability to access data and understand the rationale behind its unavailability.

Some companies and departments operate an open-book policy on information though some areas remain that of the sacred cow, not least wages and salary information. Others operate on a need to know basis. It's a common myth that directors are allowed access to all corporate information whereas, legally, they are only allowed access to information to carry out their role.

Finally, of course, you may well be the purveyor of information rather than a recipient so be aware how data can be interpreted. As any savvy sales director will tell you, hitting sales targets is great, not meeting them is not quite so pleasant, and as such they learn very quickly in their career to hold some sales back for those rainy days.

Prospective acquirers

When someone is interested in your business with a view to an acquisition, sharing information is vital, albeit with appropriate non-disclosure agreements (NDAs) in place. What you say and how you say it can be interpreted in different ways by various recipients.

Stick to facts and don't shy away from flaws or problems as in a due diligence exercise these will result in one of only two things: deal failure or price chipping.

Vendors are, inevitably, cautious, and rightly so, of sharing very commercially sensitive information, for example customer names, price, formulas etc., particularly if the buyer is a competitor; but in all cases, sight of such information will be required to complete a deal so timing is as important as the NDA. If not providing or hiding information is an issue, then overegging the facts is, conversely, just as damaging. So, again, the motto is stick to the facts and heavily caveat any possible upsides as may be perceived by the buyer.

Professional advisors

Professional advisors, including accountants, auditors and lawyers, need as much information as necessary to do their job, though the latter two categories may use legal jurisdiction to obtain certain privileged information. Auditors, for instance, are allowed to see the directors' minute book and, as they are effectively working for the shareholders, could insist on sight of anything to allow them to report properly. The auditors' job is to report on the business and state if the information they have been provided with by the directors is true and materially accurate and, finally, whether the business is capable of continuing to trade. If there is any doubt on these areas they will qualify their reports which, inevitably, will affect the credit rating of the business.

Failure to co-operate with the auditors may, certainly, be seen as an offence. Developing a relationship with the auditors will help you, and them, to understand the 'softer' side of your business, and this helps them produce a more robust report for the business. So learn to speak 'auditor' and be prepared to give full compliance and explanations for any actions you take that they challenge or do not understand.

In summary, financial data touches many, many people. How they interpret this may often be outside your control but at least you should now be more aware of just what they may see and how this will affect your department, you or your business and take care to prepare for any eventualities.

3

The Language of Finance

In this chapter we'll explore the importance of financial and accounting language. As with all languages, the basics of grammar can be taught, but local dialects are inevitably more difficult to grasp.

Foreign language students spend a good part of their degree programme living and working in the country whose language they are attempting to learn. This is because a language can only be fully grasped when you become immersed in it.

As a non-financial manager you won't be immersed in the world of finance, but you will touch on it on a daily basis. The more senior your role the more important it is quickly and coherently learn to speak this very special language.

To start with, a reality check

There is a very old joke about a well respected accountant who, like many in his profession, was stereotypical being quiet, reserved and methodical but frankly, a bit boring.

Each day his habits included looking at a small laminated card he kept in his locked top drawer. He never shared this wisdom with anyone but was faultless in his habit.

Everyone speculated on what was on that card – perhaps a motivational doctrine, perhaps a precious love note.

On the day of his retirement his colleague saw him carefully place the laminated card in his top pocket and so felt compelled to ask 'Can I see what's on the card?' To everyone's surprise the accountant said 'Of course' and handed over the card. The two lines read:

Debits on the left

Credits on the right

The moral of this is, however complicated accountancy looks it is actually very simple. Behind all accountancy processes is a concept called double entry bookkeeping. This means that each and every entry must have an equal and opposite entry in order to balance.

Some basics

Long before the advent of computerised or mechanical accountancy systems all accounts were kept in basic manual ledgers. If you imagine this in the form of a T, to the left is a debit and to the right is the complementary credit.

Provided you always record in this way your books are sure to balance; now all you need to grasp is the language behind the process.

So you'll see that the language of finance can be taught.

Key financial statements and their language

There are a number of standard financial statements you will regularly encounter in a set of accounts. Principally these include the balance sheet, the profit and loss account and the cash flow statement. It is appropriate, therefore, to start by covering the words you are most likely to see in these documents.

However, a problem for the non-accountant is that some items have several names yet all mean the same thing (see the Glossary which appears as Appendix G).

A principal document such as the profit and loss account may be referred to as an income statement, and a cash flow statement may be called a funds flow statement. These different titles don't change the content of these documents, or even their use, but the differing name tags could cause confusion even before you attempt to examine the more detailed content.

The balance sheet

A balance sheet is a statement of assets, net of liabilities. Assets are things that a business owns or is owed, and liabilities are those things that a business owes. A balance sheet is a statement of the position at a specific point in time. By this I mean that it does not consider potential liabilities or assets: it is not a statement about the future potential of the business. (See Chapter 7 on budgets and forecasts which covers this.)

Nor does it accurately value assets and liabilities in terms of market value. Although the term net worth is used (see later in this chapter), in a balance sheet this is unlikely to be anything to do with the actual market worth of the assets but rather what we call net book value (NBV), i.e. the difference between the purchase price and the depreciation to date.

Fixed assets, tangible assets

When something is called a fixed asset this would refer to an asset the business has acquired that it does not intend to resell in the near future. It is required within the infrastructure, to assist with the running of the business. Such an item may be a car, a desk, an item of plant and equipment, a computer or a building.

When we talk about the value of such an asset in the balance sheet this NBV refers to the purchase price less the depreciation charged against such an asset to date.

Depreciation means the writing down of an asset over its expected useful life. For instance if you purchased a piece of equipment at a cost of £20,000 and expect it to last four years, after which you anticipate it having no value at all to the business, you would charge depreciation over a four year period so that your balance sheet and your profit and loss account would be affected as follows:

	Balance sheet NBV (£)	Profit and loss account Expense (£)
Year 1	15,000	5,000
Year 2	10,000	5,000
Year 3	5,000	5,000
Year 4	–	5,000

As you can see, the profit and loss account is being charged £5,000 per year depreciation. This reduces the profit whilst the balance sheet reflects the declining value of the asset being used.

What has been described above concerns tangible fixed assets i.e. things you can touch and see but most businesses would like to consider that they have a further kind of fixed asset which is not quite so visible. This is referred to as goodwill and it comes in two categories.

Intangible assets

1 **Inherent goodwill** is that which reflects the reputation of the business, its customer base, its brand. In the UK this is not shown in the balance sheet as it is difficult to value. Indeed it's a bit like 'looks' – ultimately they are in the eye of the beholder and its true value is only ever certain when it is sold.

2 **Purchased goodwill** is the excess of the purchase price paid by an acquirer for a business over the value of the net assets (i.e. the total sum of all the business assets, the things it owns or is owed, less all the business liabilities i.e. the things it owes).

Current assets

In addition to fixed assets most businesses have some form of current assets. The word current is an accountancy term which means assets which are expected to be used up and replaced within one year. Such assets may include stock, bank and cash, debtors and prepayments.

Stock

Inventory is another word for stock. It is common to break stock down into finished goods, raw materials and work in progress (WIP).

For example a manufacturer of carpet will have yarn (raw materials), partly finished carpets sat on a loom (WIP) and finished goods (rolls of carpet ready for distribution).

To further confuse the matter the word stock also means shares in a business, which has nothing to do with stock that another business may be buying and selling and would not be classed as a current asset but rather a fixed asset under the heading of Investments.

Bank and cash

This doesn't mean physical pounds and pence sitting in a petty cash tin and/or bank account, it means a reconciled figure. In other words the net figure that would be monies held in the bank if all payments and receipts were cleared, plus the petty cash.

Debtors

This term can be very confusing as it appears to indicate some sort of debt and furthermore we give credit to our debtors, and creditors are debt! So, to eliminate this confusion remember that if someone buys something from you, i.e. you make a sale (usually something a business wants to do) and you give the customer time to pay, that outstanding payment becomes a debtor which, provided the customer pays in time, is desirable – so debtors are desirable!

Normally where you may have concern that some of this debt will not be paid you would make a provision for such non-payment. This allowance is what we call a provision for doubtful debts and so reduces the debtors figures.

Prepayments

For non-accountants this term can be confusing because common sense would suggest this is something you have been paid for in advance. In fact it is entirely the opposite, as it refers to something **you** have paid for in advance of the goods or services being received. For example, business insurance premiums are usually paid for in advance for the following twelve months.

As an asset is not just something you own but something you are owed, the accounting position is that you would be entitled to reclaim this advance payment should you not choose to use the goods or services and therefore it must be treated as an asset.

The matching principle

There are a number of accounting principles. One of these is called matching. For example: your business is charged rent at £9,000 for three months, payable in advance (fairly typical). In month one you would not be honouring the principle of matching if you were to show three months of costs for rent in that period. Therefore the prepayment process effectively takes the two months that do not belong to that period out of the expenses and the profit and loss account and transfers it to the assets in the balance sheet.

Liabilities

The balance sheet divides these into current and long-term.

Current liabilities

For current liabilities the same principle applies as with current assets. A current liability is an amount owed within one year, for goods and services purchased on credit terms i.e. payment for such goods is due at a date later than the date of sale.

Trade creditors

These are amounts owed to suppliers. As referred to earlier, this term credit can be confusing as it is in fact a business debt. As no one really likes the idea of being in debt you may like to remember the mantra 'treat creditors with caution' to remind yourself they are a liability.

Accruals

In much the same way as we have prepayments in current assets for items we have paid for but not utilised, we equally have to provide for those liabilities we have incurred but haven't been charged for yet. For example it is widely accepted that utilities are charged retrospectively. As we prepare a set of accounts in the knowledge that we have used some service or product (e.g. electricity) that we have not, as yet, been charged for we must provide for these amounts; these are called accruals.

It is also usual to provide for *proposed* items such as a dividend (a dividend is a payment made to a shareholder which reflects their share of the profits that have been divided amongst all the members or shareholders); this means the amounts the business promises to pay in the coming year.

Bank overdrafts

Those amounts of money (reconciled) that the business is currently borrowing at that point in time from the bank.

Other creditors

Other items payable within the coming year such as National Insurance, PAYE and tax which are owed at that time would be classed as other creditors.

Net current assets

These can also be called working capital and represent the difference between total current assets and total current liabilities. They are called working capital because of the principle that these are the funds that the business uses on a day-to-day basis.

Long-term liabilities

Many businesses will also have liabilities that last longer than 12 months (the current liabilities) and we refer to these as long-term liabilities. Examples include mortgages, hire purchase or any type of long term-loan. The portion of such debts that is payable within 12 months will be included in current liabilities; only the portion due after more than 12 months is shown as long-term liabilities.

Net assets

Not to be confused with the net **current** assets, net assets is the difference between **all** assets both fixed and current and **all** liabilities both current and long-term. As mentioned before this may also be called net worth.

Shareholder funds

Share capital

Capital means cash or other assets introduced into a business by an investor. For a company it may be called share capital.

There are many different types of categories of share capital which are explained further in Chapter 9.

Reserves

These are profits (not the same as cash – see Chapter 5) that are retained in the business and not distributed to the owners. There are two types of reserves:

1   Profits that are made but have not been distributed by way of dividend as yet: sometimes called retained earnings

2   Capital reserves which are not to be distributed as they represent an increase in the value of a fixed asset. For instance when a property is revalued and the value is increased this becomes a capital reserve.

Profit and loss account

The second major financial paper which needs language clarification is the profit and loss account. This paper, also known as an income statement, is a statement of the sales (income or turnover) less expenses.

Sales (turnover or income)

Sales are those goods or services sold in a given period or period to date whether or not they are paid for. The figure for sales always excludes VAT as the VAT does not belong to the business, which is merely collecting it on behalf of the government. This can never then be classed as part of its own turnover.

Expenses (costs)

Expenses are divided into cost of sales and overheads.

Cost of sales (cost of goods sold)

Those costs strictly related to the products or services being sold are called cost of sales; they are sometimes called direct costs.

For the non-accountant the key principle is that within the cost of sales you would be unlikely to include items that may sound like a cost of selling, for example marketing, transport or sales rep costs. Nearly always such costs are overheads as technically they do not relate completely to the sale made. As an example, a furniture manufacturer's direct costs would be the nails, wood and fabric that made the chairs and the wages of the man or woman who made the chair. It would not include heat, lights, rent and salesman costs as all these are indirect costs and are called overheads.

Gross profit

The difference between sales and cost of sales (also called costs of goods sold) is called gross profit (nothing to do with a disappointing result … although of course it may be!). This is, for many businesses, an important barometer or key performance indicator (KPI) of their businesses performance. (See Chapter 10 for more information on KPIs.)

Overheads

The next category of costs is overheads, also called indirect costs or fixed costs. An exception is interest, which is always shown in a formal profit and loss account as a separate and discrete cost. Overheads may include advertising, rent, rates, wages, travel costs, utilities and depreciation.

They may also include provisions for doubtful debts: that is an estimate of amounts you consider some customers may have difficulty in paying and therefore, due to taking a prudent approach (an accounting principle) when calculating costs, these are assumed to be an overhead. It may also include bad debts written off, that is amounts owed by customers that have perhaps gone into liquidation. In both these cases the provision or write-off is made after taking credit for any available VAT relief.

Operating profit

The difference between gross profit and the overheads is called operating profit and, as with gross profit, is regarded by most businesses as an important KPI for management performance.

This is due to the fact that, when looking into a manager's ability to run a business as opposed to a director's, a manager may be judged on the operating profit performance (as he or she will have little or no influence on the interest rates agreed, something usually in the remit of a director).

Interest

Interest payable and receivable in formal accounts is shown after the operating profit line.

Net profit

Net profit is the difference between gross profit and all expenses including interest.

Tax

From net profit a business will pay corporation taxes and, after taxes, it may choose to distribute some of its profits left by way of a dividend to its shareholders.

Cash flow statement

The final major financial statement in a formal set of accounts would be the cash flow statement. You can read more about the difference between profit and cash in Chapter 5 and you will discover the two are entirely different.

The cash flow statement is an analysis of cash creation and utilisation. Historically in a set of financial accounts this document was called a source and application of funds statement. This has now been largely superseded by the term cash flow statement but they are, in effect, the same thing.

This is an important document for a non-financial manager to understand. It is important to recognise that this is not the same as a cash flow projection. The former is a statement of funds in and out in a given period; the latter is a projection based on anticipated inputs and outputs of cash in the future and is used by management and funders to manage cash flow requirements in a specific future period.

Accounting language definitions and interpretations

In addition to the language covered above, a full glossary in alphabetical order is available in the glossary of finance and investment terms given in Appendix G. But remember it is appropriate to consider not just definitions but also interpretations.

The accountancy equation

A very basic definition widely learnt and used by the accountancy profession is the accountancy equation. This formula represents the relationship between assets and liabilities and the owner's equity. It can be explained in a number of ways:

$$\text{Assets} = \text{Liabilities} + \text{Owners' Capital}$$

or

$$\text{Liabilities} = \text{Assets} - \text{Owners' Capital}$$

or

$$\text{Owners' Capital} = \text{Assets} - \text{Liabilities}$$

Essentially this means that when preparing accounts there will always be two figures that are the same. We refer to this situation as balancing the balance sheet. This is also sometimes called double entry bookkeeping!

Governance terms

When preparing any formal accounting document there are some standard legal principles. These have been defined in the Companies Act 2006 as follows:

- **Transparency**: this means that information should clearly show the true picture of the situation and nothing should be wilfully omitted.
- **Probity**: that directors should act with honesty and not in their own interests.
- **Accountability**: that directors should be made personally accountable for what they submit into the public domain.

Accountancy principles

Accounts are produced on a historical basis i.e. they are a report on something that has happened up to a given date in the past. Budgets and forecasts are a look into the future to assess potential. In theory each of these is supposed to reflect the other in that, subject to any strategic changes intended, what happened in the past is a good indicator of what may happen in the future. Our current economy makes this a less robust principle but it is the theory.

All financial statements are prepared on a going concern basis. This means that the business is expected to continue to trade for the foreseeable future.

Where an auditor does not agree that the business can continue to trade they would, under UK law, be unable to sign off a set of accounts.

Back to Basics

Ledger

This is a record of all transactions in a particular account or cost centre. The detail in a ledger usually includes the date of the transaction, the amount and whether it was a debit or a credit along with a short memo if needed.

Entry

This is the actual individual item or transaction that is entered into the ledger.

Journal

Where a transaction is first entered it would be called a prime entry but a journal is used to transfer that entry from one location in the ledger to another perhaps because it was incorrectly allocated in the first place; see the example below. VAT has been ignored in this example.

Sales: Consulting services

Debit	Credit	Notes
	6/2 £1,000	Invoice for consulting services
	£1,000	Total

Assets: Debtors

Debit	Credit	Notes
6/2 £1,000		Invoice for consulting services
	6/4 £1,000	Cheque received
	0	Total

Assets: Bank

Debit	Credit	Notes
6/4 £1,000		Cheque received
£1,000		Total

Liabilities: Creditors

Debit	Credit	Notes
	6/3 £200	Invoice received
	£200	Total

Expenses: Subcontractor

Debit	Credit	Notes
6/3 £200		Invoice received
£200		Total

- Sales: Consulting services
- Assets: Debtors
- Assets: Bank
- Liabilities: Creditors
- Expenses: Subcontractors

With these five account ledgers laid out you can trace the transactions related to that one day of work. For example you can see that debtors increased by £1,000 when you sent the invoice, then decreased back to zero when you received the invoice and deposited the cheque.

As a result, the profit and loss account looks like this:

Sale

Consulting services

Revenue (gross income)   £1,000

Expenses

Subcontractor	£200
Net income	£800

The balance sheet will look like this:

Assets

Debtors	0
Bank	£1,000

Liabilities

Creditors	
Subcontractor	£200
Total liabilities	£200
Shareholder funds	£800

Financial language outside the finance department

Once outside the accounting department a whole raft of words appear in yet another language.

The investment world

It's not possible to discuss every technical word used in this field but here are some of the most common and their meanings which are useful for the non-financial manager. I've included these terms as these are the ones that you're most likely to come across.

Anti-embarrassment clause

An anti-embarrassment clause may be found in a sale and purchase agreement (an agreement that transfers a business from one organisation or person to another). It provides protection from a buyer to cover a situation where the buyers sell on the business or asset within a certain period after the original sale for a higher value. The aim is to readjust the original sale price and to ensure the seller is 'not embarrassed' by having lost out on a higher sale price in the original sale.

Amortisation

Amortisation is the equivalent of depreciation but relates to an intangible fixed asset, e.g. goodwill or intellectual property (IP), in that it writes down its value in the balance sheet over its expected lifetime.

Assignment

Similar in meaning to its regular everyday use, assignment generally means to sign a document to authorise transfer of ownership of shares from one person to another.

Balloon maturity

For anyone who has ever bought a car on a lease agreement the term balloon may be familiar. It means that after a number of minor payments for the asset a final much larger payment secures the successful transfer of the asset (e.g the car) from the lessor to the lessee.

In the investment world it has a slightly different meaning in that it is a type of bond maturity schedule where a small number of bonds mature serially (each year) and the large number mature in a later year.

Bear market

This refers to activity on the stock market and is the name used to suggest that in the overall market the current prices will decrease and the general consensus is that most shares are overpriced.

This market can be compounded if there are more sellers than buyers.

To be 'bearish' just means that you think prices will decline.

Bull market

A bull market is the opposite of a bear market, i.e. there is a belief amongst those trading shares that prices will increase.

Call

This is a term used by investors that opens a window of time that provides a buyer with an option to buy shares at a specific price until a specific point in time.

If you are an investor you can actually buy a call option on the basis that you think the price of the underlying security will increase.

If you sell a call option, either you think that the price will not increase or you think the price will decrease.

Capital market

This means the main trading markets like the London Stock Exchange where the general public can buy and sell shares in quoted companies.

Capitalisation

To 'capitalise' is a term used by the finance department when they record a purchase as an asset in the balance sheet instead of as an expense in the profit and loss account. It will then be subject to depreciation and amortisation for tax purposes. For example, if a business uses its own workforce to build some offices within the premises, then the cost of their wages will be 'capitalised' rather than being shown in the profit and loss account as 'wages'.

Do not confuse this with the use of 'capitalisation' to mean the total amount of shares issued by a company.

Convertible

A convertible is a type of share or investment in a business that can be converted into a different type. For example, a bank may make a loan into a business by means of convertible shares, which caries a particular right which may say that if there is a default on a payment they can convert their loan into voting shares.

Covenant

A covenant is a legally drawn up binding agreement to either do or not do something. For example, a bank may say to its customer 'you covenant (promise) not to take a salary increase until our loan is repaid'. Any defaults would cause various penalties as agreed in the contract.

Cumulative preference share

There is a particular type of share which has a dividend agreement attached to it. This effectively allows the owner of this share to roll up unpaid dividends for payment in the future if, for whatever reason, the company is unable to pay such dividends on time.

Debenture

A legally drawn up agreement that allows the owner of the agreement, which is a certificate that acknowledges debt, the right to seize specifically identified assets should certain contractual breaches occur.

Dividend yield

This is an important measurement for an investor as it shows how much a company pays out in dividends each year relative to its share price. It is effectively the way investors measure how much cash flow they are getting back.

For every £1 invested in a business the formula is

$$\frac{\text{Yearly dividends per share}}{\text{Market price of share at time of purchase}}$$

This gives the annual percentage.

Due diligence

This describes the process or activity carried out by either the buyer or their investors when considering whether to acquire a business. In many ways it is a little like an audit but may be wider in scope as it would largely depend on the risk appetite of the acquirers.

Earnings per share (EPS)

This is a formula used by investors to calculate how much each issued share has earned. It is not an absolute scientific formula as if new additional shares are issued this will affect the calculation.

However, the basic formula would be

$$\frac{\text{Profit for the period}}{\text{Average number of issued shares}}$$

Earnings before interest and taxes (EBIT)

The figure for the company's earnings or profit prior to paying interest and tax is very important in the valuation of private companies as it is the base number that is then used against a particular multiple dependent on the industry type.

Escrow

When a business is bought or sold one or both parties may well have to make certain promises about particular activities in the business. For example, a vendor may have to say that he can confirm the business has never been subject to any VAT fines. Very often the acquirer will ask for an indemnity in case the vendor was either negligent or fraudulent in his statement.

In order to protect against the vendor not having funds to cover such a situation the acquirer may insist on funds being set aside for a period of time to cover such an eventuality. These funds are often held in an account which the lawyers of both sides control. This account is called an escrow account.

Face value

As the name suggests, a share's face value is the issued value of a share and is not an indication of market value.

It is also called the par value or principal value.

Fiduciary

A much used word in common law, a fiduciary means any person who is acting for another person and is therefore in a position of trust so must act honestly and in good faith.

Fiscal year

A company's fiscal year is its accounting year.

Gilt-edged

A 'gilt-edged' share issue is a share issue that is considered high grade, i.e. robust and reliable returns are expected in terms of capital growth and dividends. If a business is deemed to have gilt-edged shares it is considered to be an excellent company.

Goodwill

A bit like 'beauty in the eye of the beholder', goodwill resides in many businesses but the quantification of this intangible asset can only really be done when someone acquires it. Essentially goodwill could be the business brand, market position, customer base, intellectual property rights or management skills.

The actual valuation crystallises as the excess an acquirer pays over and above the sum of the business's total assets less its total liabilities (i.e. net assets) at the point of purchase. This figure then becomes goodwill in the acquirer's balance sheet.

Holding company

There are circa 2 million registered companies in the UK, of which approximately one-third are deemed to be subsidiary businesses. To have a subsidiary you must have a holding company; this is sometimes called a parent company or top company. These businesses then hold shares in other businesses, either all or some.

Institutional investor

Institutional investors are corporations, pension funds, investment companies, insurance companies, universities, foundations, banks and the like which bring large pools of funds to invest in another business by taking shares in large numbers.

By and large such investments are fairly benign in terms of influence at board level.

Leveraged buyout

There are a number of ways of buying a business. One of the most common is to borrow the money from someone else, often a bank. When this happens the process is called a leveraged buyout.

The assets of the very company that is being acquired usually secure the borrowed funds.

Letter of credit

Not to be confused with a letter of intent (see below), this is a letter from a bank that **guarantees** that a buyer's payment to a seller will be

1   Received on time

and

2   For the correct amount.

If that does not happen the bank will cover in full any outstanding liability.

Hugely comforting for a vendor, this does not come for free, and is not provided lightly or freely due to the risk the bank is absorbing.

Letter of intent

A letter of intent is simply that: a letter saying the one party intends to do something for another. What is essential to understand is that it is not, in most cases, a binding agreement. Although it would be considered very bad form commercially to renege on this, such documents are nearly always written in a non-binding format.

Last-in, first-out (LIFO) and first-in, first-out (FIFO)

When valuing stock for the balance sheet there are a number of methods. One way is to assume the newest stock purchased is the first to be sold (LIFO); another is to assume that the oldest stock in will be first to be sold (FIFO). LIFO is more usually found in American corporations and FIFO in UK companies. Bear in mind that this will affect a business's profitability if stock costs are moving either up or down.

PE ratio

The formula for this is

$$\frac{\text{Market price}}{\text{Earnings per share}}$$

But of more relevance is what it means. This is one of the oldest and most frequently used methods for business valuations. In simple terms it gives you a start point to use as a multiple for the calculation of the value of a business against its profit.

Pre-emptive right

A pre-emptive right is a right that a shareholder has to retain the same percentage shareholding in an organisation should they so choose.

An example could be: if a business decides to issue some more shares someone with a pre-emption would have the right to buy them first. Alternatively if an individual or institution wishes to sell the person with the pre-emption has the right to buy these first.

Such rights are usually noted either in a business's Articles of Association (that is, its constitutional document) or maybe in a shareholders' agreement.

Prospectus

When floating a business on the Stock Exchange it is necessary to create certain documentation that lays out the opportunity for potential investors. This document is called a prospectus.

The contents of this document are serious and anything negligent or incorrect is deemed to be a personal statement made by the directors of the business whether or not they wrote it.

Not only can directors be liable for content but also for omissions particularly where such errors may result in investors not being fully informed.

Proxy

This is the written authorisation given by a shareholder to someone else authorising them to represent and vote in their place at a shareholders' meeting. It is very commonly used.

Quick asset ratio

Also called the acid test, this is a ratio used by investors and funders to assess a business's liquidity. The formula is

$$\frac{\text{Current assets} - \text{Stock}}{\text{Current liabilities}}$$

The ideal expected result is 1 to 1.

The rationale behind this ratio is that it strips away the stock from the equation, because it is largely regarded as very difficult to convert stock into cash.

On the basis that, where this has been done and the ratio still gives a number of 1 to 1, this would give a financial comfort that, should the funder need to call in a loan which may sit in the current liabilities, the business should be able to pay that loan back without having to sell its fixed assets.

Receivership

A form of bankruptcy where a court-appointed person (the receiver) manages the affairs of the business.

This can also be called administration.

The aim is for the administrator or receiver to run the business until a suitable buyer can be found on the basis that an ongoing business is likely to realise more value than one that is no longer trading.

Working capital

A company's current assets less their current liabilities is called its working capital. The greater the assets in comparison to liabilities the more working capital the business is deemed to have.

Funding terminology is something any astute manager should have a basic understanding of as it touches so many aspects of a business's life, but banking terminology in particular must be understood.

Banking terminology

Bank overdraft

An overdraft is defined as the amount by which withdrawals exceed deposits or the extension of a credit facility by a lending institution to allow such a situation to occur.

Such facilities are granted for a given period, nearly always with the right of the bank to withdraw immediately and without reason. As such, when negotiating such a facility it is always wise to be aware that an overdraft should only be used for working capital peaks and troughs and not for capital expenditure.

Also watch out for the, now commonly used, non-utilisation clause which gives the bank the right to charge you if you **don't** use the facility!

Bank loan

A loan made by a bank to be repaid with interest on or before a fixed date. Nearly always this is for a fixed period and requires the borrower to repay capital and interest until the end of the defined period.

In addition a security of some sort from the company or director is nearly always required.

CID

This stands for Confidential Invoice Discounting. This lending relationship is based on the premise that the lender effectively buys the debtor book from the company and lends a percentage of the invoice value, up to 80% in some circumstances, back to the business in advance of the date for payment by the customer.

This method of funding accelerates cash flow and, because it is confidential (i.e. the customer is not aware of this happening), can be very beneficial for a growing company which cannot afford to extend its working capital beyond a certain point. A traditional bank will not lend at these rates or percentages – typically a bank could only lend up to 50% against a debtor.

Such a facility costs, and the cost is usually based not just on a standard percentage above base rate but also includes an administration fee based on a percentage of the total debtor ledger. As such it can be much more expensive than a bank loan.

Factoring

Factoring is another form of funding. It has nothing to do with producing goods in a factory! Rather it is the sale of the debtor ledger to a third-party funder who then provides an early draw down against invoiced amounts to their client.

Although this looks, on the face of it, like CID it is different in two very important areas.

1 It is not confidential i.e. the customer is aware of the funding route.

2 All the management of credit control resides with the factoring company, which makes direct contact with the end customer to chase debt and manage payment queries.

Because you are effectively outsourcing all your credit control functions, when you factor this it creates an additional cost for the factor but reduced costs for the business (the theory being you don't need a credit controller).

Hire purchase

A well established method of funding, HP is a financial tool that gives customers purchasing power via a fixed cost over a fixed period of instalments. The security for the loan is taken on the purchased asset.

During the repayment period the buyer has the possession and use but not the ownership of the item. Only upon the full payment of the loan does the title pass to the buyer.

Leases

There are two kinds of leases, operating and finance. Correct classification of leases is important as they affect the balance sheet and profit and loss acconts. This in turn affects the solvency and liquidity of the company, debt to equity ratio and its capital structure. A wrong classification would mislead investors into believing that the company's financials are better than they actually are. For example, if a company classified a finance lease as an operating lease, they would understate their liabilities, which is the obligation to pay the lease payments.

A finance lease is a lease that is primarily a method of raising finance to pay for assets, where liability is shown on the balance sheet until paid. With an operating lease the extent of the liability is not shown on the balance sheet (this can sometimes be called off-balance-sheet finance).

Whether a lease is a finance one or an operating one is often a decision directors and auditors must debate.

The key criteria are:

1   If 'substantially all the risks and rewards' of ownership are transferred to the lessee then it is a finance lease.

2   If it is not a finance lease then it is an operating lease.

Speaking finance

So if you now feel you can speak finance all you need to do, like any good linguist, is practise and ask for help if you are unsure.

Only then will you hone your skills and speak with more confidence.

Profit and Loss Business Drivers

The focus of a business, whether it be profit, service or quality, is known as the business driver.

This driver affects business performance in a variety of ways, not least financially. This chapter explores reasons for choosing one route over another and provides templates to help the non-financial manager make a more informed decision for his business and which route to choose to improve success.

Ascertaining the overall business objective

In the early stages of their existence, small businesses will have a different focus than large well-established multinationals. For instance the former may wish to break into a closed market: without reputation and history they may have to offer incentives such as credit terms or discounts to make the opportunity work.

A large business may be unable to offer the service levels a smaller company can offer, perhaps due to more complex management systems. As an example try returning an unwanted or unacceptable product to a local owner-managed retail outlet as opposed to returning the same item to a multinational internet trader.

This doesn't mean one will be ultimately more effective than the other but possibly the former may be swifter in giving you, the customer, a response.

The economic climate has created a fiercely competitive environment. Consumers are more informed and choice is greater than ever. As a result business objectives that were once set in stone need to be revisited on a more regular basis.

At one time price was immoveable and a 'take it or leave it' stance was regularly accepted. This is simply not the case any more, and a discretionary approach is much more suited to businesses in the twenty-first century.

Standard drivers

The following are the generally accepted drivers from which a business may make a choice:

■ Profit

■ Cash

■ Customer service levels

■ Quality

■ Value and ethics.

Profit

Profit as a driver may include decisions on price management: either cutting or increasing them.

The management of overheads could include outsourcing services either to regional or even international providers e.g. call centres being located in Asia is a very typical profit management technique.

Cash

Using cash as a driver may include having low stock holdings, consignment stock (that is, stock you only pay for when you sell it), or just in time (JIT) stock (that is, stock you order to match a specific order). These actions mean non-moving or slow-moving stock does not sit on your shelves waiting for an order and therefore frees up cash.

Reducing debtor days and increasing creditor payment days are further ways of utilising cash as a driver. If you pay your suppliers (creditors) slowly you create cash as you have their goods or services and an opportunity to sell these on although you wouldn't have yet paid the supplier.

Likewise if you insist on speedy or even proforma (in advance of delivery) payments for your sales (debtors) then you create more cash.

Customer service levels

For most organisations their reputations are based on numerous transactions with a multitude of customers.

For some businesses, customer service levels of a consistent and positive nature create additional and loyal business opportunities. This may mean that market share is taken from an alternative supplier or competitor who are not able to provide the standard of service required by the customer. In fact specific levels of customer service may even be mandatory in some industries. Such a service level comes at a cost; the question is who picks up that cost, the buyer or the supplier?

Quality

For some organisations, only the best quality product or service is acceptable. Alternatively some businesses will offer only the cheapest product, in which case quality is much less important.

Consider ladies' high street discount fashion versus couture tailoring.

Value and ethics

Many organisations, including the Co-op Banking Group, The Body Shop and Sainsbury's, have based their business models on ethical trading practices.

Where to start

This chapter is not so much about the strategic merits of any of these drivers but rather the financial impact on a business of choosing one driver over another. By looking at these drivers in this way a non-financial manager should be more informed when debating the merits of one particular strategy over an alternative.

There is an old business saying that it is only possible to have two of the following:

Cheap
Quick
Good

From a financial point of view, if nothing else, this seems entirely sensible. Of course, if you are prepared to accept a less successful business then this may be contestable.

When business is tough a seemingly easy option is to undercut the competition on price. But Tables 4.1 and 4.2 show that both the options of increasing prices and reducing prices have certain ramifications.

Such decisions may be outside your control although ultimately an insight into their impact is certainly of value and may help you to influence the process.

If you increase or cut your prices by the percentage in the left hand column and assume your margin is one of those in bold at the top of each table the resulting figures will show you know how much more or less business you need to stay stable.

Table 4.1   Increase in business needed when cutting price

IF YOU CUT YOUR PRICE BY	WITH YOUR PRESENT GROSS PROFIT BEING						
	10%	15%	20%	25%	30%	35%	40%
5%	100.0%	50.0%	33.3%	25.0%	20.0%	16.7%	14.3%
6%	150.0%	66.7%	42.9%	31.6%	29.0%	20.7%	17.6%
7%	233.3%	87.5%	53.8%	38.9%	30.4%	25.0%	21.2%
8%	400.0%	144.3%	66.7%	47.1%	36.4%	29.6%	25.0%
10%	–	200.0%	111.0%	66.7%	50.0%	40.0%	33.3%
11%	–	275.0%	122.2%	78.6%	57.9%	45.8%	37.9%
12%	–	400.0%	150.0%	92.3%	66.7%	52.2%	42.9%
15%	–	–	300.0%	150.0%	100.0%	75.0%	60.0%
16%	–	–	400.0%	117.8%	144.3%	84.2%	66.7%
18%	–	–	900.0%	257.1%	150.0%	105.9%	81.1%
20%	–	–	–	400.0%	200.0%	133.3%	100.0%

Table 4.2   Decrease in business possible when increasing price

IF YOU INCREASE YOUR PRICE BY	WITH YOUR PRESENT MARGIN BEING								
	20%	25%	30%	35%	40%	45%	50%	55%	60%
2%	9%	7%	6%	5%	5%	4%	4%	4%	3%
4%	17%	14%	12%	10%	9%	8%	7%	7%	6%
6%	23%	19%	17%	15%	13%	12%	11%	10%	9%
8%	29%	24%	21%	19%	17%	15%	14%	13%	12%
10%	33%	29%	25%	22%	20%	18%	17%	15%	14%
12%	38%	32%	29%	26%	23%	21%	19%	18%	17%
14%	41%	36%	32%	29%	26%	24%	22%	20%	19%
16%	44%	39%	35%	31%	29%	26%	24%	23%	21%
18%	47%	42%	38%	34%	31%	29%	26%	25%	23%
20%	50%	44%	40%	36%	33%	31%	29%	27%	25%
25%	56%	50%	45%	42%	38%	36%	33%	31%	29%

So if you cut your price by 10% and your margin is 35% you need to sell 40% more product to stay in the same place.

Similarly, if you increase your price by 10% and your margin is 35% you can sell 22% less and stay in the same place.

Driver impact

Chapter 5 examines the critical differences between profit and cash but in terms of business drivers these two have some correlation.

Profit driver

In theory it is entirely possible to make a lot of profit; buying cheap and selling high is a good start.

Cost of goods	£100
Sale price	£500

Your profit and loss account on this simple equation looks as follows;

Sale	£500
Cost of goods	£100
Gross profit	£400
Gross margin	80%

Not a bad start provided that:

a   You can buy at that price

b   The competition don't undercut your price.

If they do undercut your price you can choose to cut yours again. But if they cut theirs once more then it becomes a price-cutting war (with the customer eventually winning). Someone in the selling chain will reach a point where they cannot decrease their price any more. This decision will possibly be a sales team one but the finance department will need an explanation. They will want to be confident that the price cut will increase sales volume at best and, at worst, retain market share.

The problem with a price war is further exacerbated on two fronts:

1   Stock costs and stock turnover: if you have bought in a certain amount of stock to cover anticipated demand you have to store it. This has a cost attached to it. You also have to pay for it, perhaps in advance of making a sale to a third party. You may also have to write off any obsolete stock if the product you sell has a finite life.

2   Will a reduced gross profit provide enough income to pay the overheads of the business and make a level of acceptable net profit? Look again at Table 4.1.

For example if target net profit is 10% then the business must look like this:

Sale	£500	
Cost of goods	£100	
Gross profit	£400	80%
Overheads	£350	
Net profit	£50	10%

Any reduction in gross profit needs to be handled in the following ways:

1 Increase sales

2 Reduce costs of goods sold i.e. agree a cost reduction with your supplier

3 Cut overheads.

All of these are possible but require specific consideration.

1 Increasing sales will mean increasing stock levels unless you work on JIT or consignment stock: there will therefore be a cost attached to higher stock levels.

2 Reducing prices from your supplier may or may not be negotiable and even if it is there may be a *quid pro quo* requirement such as them wanting regular or proforma payments.

3 Cutting overheads is, of late, a common activity and does enable you to technically maintain a net position but businesses need a minimum level of overheads to operate effectively. In addition some cuts can take time to be effective. For example relocation may cut the fixed cost of rent but the price of relocating may in the first instance create less not more profit.

Such profit-related decisions take time to

1 Maintain

and

2 Implement.

They may also have a knock-on effect on other areas – not least service levels falling or quality not being maintained. Both of these are serious consequences for any business that sits in a highly competitive position.

Cash driver

Sales are vanity, profit is sanity and cash is absolutely essential – this is a well known business saying.

An organisation that chooses cash as a significant strategic financial driver has possibly done so because either its cash reserves are poor or the possibility of raising more money from traditional banking resources is unlikely or difficult.

Businesses by and large do not fail because they are not profitable but because they have run out of cash. Without cash it is simply not possible to trade (see Chapter 5).

Some businesses need less cash than others due to the nature of their trade and, conversely, some businesses need more working capital (the capital that is used in the business on a daily basis to fund stock and debtors).

A service business, for example one selling time or services as opposed to goods, will not have its cash tied up in goods on pallets in its warehouse. That does not mean it doesn't need cash to fund its WIP (unbilled time for work carried out), it's just that it can invoice such time regularly and so free up this cash by billing and, of course, insisting its customers pay to term.

In order for a business to be cash-driven, releasing cash so it can be utilised will require initiatives such as early or prompt payment discounts.

For this to be effective the customer has to see some benefit in paying. Consider the result of the following formula before confirming your offer:

$$\frac{365 \text{ (days of the year)}}{\text{Number of days difference between standard payments and early payments}} \times \text{Discount}$$

If you offer a 2% discount for payment in 10 days, when the norm is 30 days, and payment is made in 30 days, the 2% becomes an interest charge. If money is borrowed at 2% for 20 days, this is equivalent to an annual rate of 36%. Your customer should definitely pay promptly in this case, but the question is, does it achieve your objective of creating cash?

There are a number of other activities to create cash in addition to those mentioned above.

Collecting your debtors quickly and paying your suppliers slowly will create cash, although too much disparity between the two will not help your business's reputation. The concept of paying for goods and services after you have been paid is a well established practice, as indeed is a proforma payment agreement i.e. paying for the goods and services before you even utilise them.

A business that is driven by cash may choose not to tie up any of this precious commodity in fixed assets of any kind so it may rent its buildings and hire its fixtures and fittings.

Companies such as Regus, the office-hire and virtual office business, are based on just that principle: paying for what you want only when you actually need it. Such flexibility is particularly attractive for early stage businesses that tend to be cash poor.

Using CID (confidential invoice discounting) or a factoring agreement (both defined in Chapter 3) also create access to cash, although in themselves these do not create more cash. For a rapidly growing business such a business process can be very beneficial provided the costs are acceptable.

Using associates or subcontractors as opposed to employees can create cash as at the very least the business will save on employer National Insurance contributions (NIC): this is currently as much as 12.8%.

However, you should be careful not to be caught out by HMRC regulations around the utilisation of associates. A particular piece of legislation seeks to eliminate the avoidance of tax and NIC by determining if the associate being treated as such by the company is in fact an employee. The rules are complex and guidance from your accountant or tax advisor is advisable. The following are some of the issues that would be considered in assessing whether or not an associate is, in the eyes of the HMRC, actually an employee:

- Whether the associate personally performs the service
- Whether the services are provided directly with the client or under agreements involving an intermediary
- Whether the circumstances are such that if you had provided the service directly to the client under a contract between you and the client you would have been regarded, for income tax purposes, as an employee of the client and/or for NIC purposes as employed.

Paying staff on commission only (or largely) on **paid-for** transactions is very effective. This way you don't pay your sales person until the opportunity or goods they have sold have been paid for by the customer.

Customer service driven business

For virtually every business the reputation it maintains with its customers is paramount and, for a customer service driven business, consistency is essential.

The customer experience is well established and most buyers are savvy and exacting. This is in particular so because as consumers we are exposed to customer/supplier contact at every stage of our buying experience, from our first meeting with a supplier, be it by phone, email or text, throughout the whole service experience.

The better a business knows and understands its customers, and uses this information sensibly, the more likely it is to be profitable.

Unlike price cutting, detailed knowledge of a customer is hard to replicate. Bearing in mind that obtaining a customer in the first place is much more costly than retention, it is sensible to think about how you will keep your customers.

Consider the following:

1 If you increase customer retention what effect does it have on your profits?

2 What percentage of your customers do you lose each year and how much does it cost you to replace them?

3 Do your long-standing customers buy more of your product or service range than new customers, and if so why?

4 Which is more important to your customers: pre-sales service or after sale service?

5 Do your best (most profitable) customers come from referrals from existing satisfied customers or from marketing?

You may not know the answers to these questions but you should do.

Of course you could find out by asking your customers what they want and what they value. This doesn't have to be a complex process and should concentrate on asking critical questions, then making sure that any necessary changes are implemented.

You may like to try the questions in Exhibit 4.1 **first** with your own staff, then go to your customers to check your position.

Exhibit 4.1

Checklist for identiying customer care business drivers

	Yes	No	Remarks
Have the goals and priorities of the organisation been identified?			
Have these goals been reviewed in the context of the customer care strategy for the organisation?			
Have the means by which customers evaluate your organisation and its services been identified?			
Has the impact of the customer service or call centre organisation on customer evaluations been assessed?			
Has the organisation's own rating of the service provided by its customer care business unit been identified?			
Has the rating of service provided by competitors been assessed?			
Has the rating of service provided by non-competitive service organisations been assessed?			
Have major barriers to improving the current customer service or call centre performance been identified?			
Have major barriers to improving customer satisfaction with the current customer service or call centre treatment they receive been identified?			
Have the strategic business drivers for the customer care organisation been articulated?			

Taken from www.toolbox.com 'Observations from a Tech Architect: Enterprise Implementation Issues & Solutions' by Craig Borysowich, Chief Technology Tactician.

Don't be afraid of lots of negative comments; only on the back of those can you really make changes.

Avoid using a marking system based on 1 = excellent, 4 = poor as inevitably you get 'medium' replies. Enforce a 'free write' system as you can then better implement changes.

Try the following customer service questions:

1   How responsive are we in dealing with your requirements?

2   What was our pre-sale service like?

3   What was our post-sale service like?

4   How did you rate our product or service? Does it meet your expectations and needs? If not how can we improve it?

5   What was our delivery like? Were we on time?

6   How do we compare to our competitors?

7   What do you think of our approach to quality?

8   Tell us, overall, what we can do to retain you as a customer and to make you one of our ambassadors.

Such questions are better completed face to face where possible. Also more important is quality rather than quantity. You need to encourage complete, honest answers or it's a wasted exercise.

Quality as a business driver

For some businesses, quality and accuracy are the only acceptable business drivers. Think nuclear power station builders: anything less than top quality and accuracy could be catastrophic on a monumental scale.

Even for a business for which perhaps safety is not critical, poor quality could at the very least create legal breaches of contracts. To some extent, quality and compliance is a serious consideration that all business owners should consider.

Johnson & Johnson, one of the UK's leading companies, has a strategy called 'beyond compliance' which includes the following goals in relation to its products and services:

1   Meets all Johnson & Johnson standards and regulatory requirements

2   Optimise products, procedures and facilities by understanding the quality, safety, engineering and environmental needs

3 Provide partners with regulations and anticipated changes in regulation and standards

4 Achieve organisational excellence.

Having quality as a critical business driver needs a proactive approach to risk management. This requires an understanding that learning by doing, which has an upfront price, is not always practical for shareholder return.

In order to satisfy this driver **and** the profit targets one idea may be to consider that what appears to be a cost to the business, and therefore a potential reduction in profit, should actually be treated as an investment in future profitability. In other words, look at it as a capital expense rather than an income expense.

For businesses that are able to choose quality as a driver rather than as a mandatory requirement, make sure such a choice is clearly evident to the consumer and that they recognise it is an additional advantage over a competitor product or service.

In other words quality has an appeal that can't be legitimately argued with but actually does not appear to make sound economic sense.

In order to make this driver of real tangible (profitable) value, ultimately you must have a clear definition of what quality means for your products or services and how it is different from anything your competitors do.

Generalisations won't work and no one will believe you. You need tangible evidence to support any quality claims. Only this way can you possibly hope to use this as a competitive advantage and so increase or retain sales volumes or margins.

Don't forget that quality control impacts on virtually every area of a business from compliance and production effectiveness to on-time deliveries and management of product returns or customer complaints.

So that budgets can be controlled, when doing any sort of financial modelling a quality-driven business needs to look at each of these areas as a separate cost centre.

Value and ethics as a business driver

Long held in high regard for their beliefs in ethical trading, the Co-op Banking Group and The Body Shop have proved that such a business driver can have astonishingly positive results on business profitability and sustainability.

Those businesses whose ethics have been challenged find that bad PR can have a devastating effect on business performance. For example, in 2007 it was revealed that child workers (some as young as 10) were employed in near slavery conditions in a Gap textile factory in New Delhi. Of course Gap weren't the first to suffer bad PR and won't be the last but consumers are increasingly aware and vote with their feet. Previously off-piste business principles such as Fairtrade become progressively more mainstream and ethics become a major business advantage.

For consumers in the 'X' and 'Y' generations (those 30-something or younger), 'green business' has recently become not only mainstream but high on the agenda.

Unlike businesses that use some of the previous drivers we've looked at, ethical or value-based businesses look beyond the strict economic objectives and consider the wider business implications of how they conduct their trade.

Consider some of the following benefits when evaluating such a value-based driver: you may

1   Save money (think better waste management and recycling)

2   Attract ethically motivated investors (not least the Co-op Banking Group which have a strict code of investment principles)

3   Increase sales revenues as consumers make a distinctive choice for ethically sourced and produced goods

4   Retain staff and increase their motivation by being seen to treat people fairly.

All of the above can be measured financially against a specific policy introduction.

Help is available to introduce these drivers into your businesses. As an example, Business in the Community (www.bitc.org.uk) has a long history in helping businesses to develop and incorporate their corporate and social reporting policies and to assess their success.

There is a common thread across business drivers, whether you choose one or more of the ones discussed above. That is successful customer engagement, which in turn makes for a more effective and focused business which **should** result in more profit.

5

Cash and Profit – Understand the Difference

One of the most important areas for anyone in business to understand is that profit and cash are not the same. Although both have relative importance, cash, or the availability of it, is by and large the difference between business success and business failure.

This chapter will consider not only the difference between profit and cash but also how the two are linked and how they can be manipulated and managed.

It will also explore some well-proven cash management processes and cash creation techniques that can have both personal and business value.

What is cash?

In business, cash is an asset and in the financial statements it is recorded in the balance sheet as a current asset.

Not all cash on the balance sheet will be liquid cash, i.e. physical money, although some may be sitting as petty cash or, if you are a retailer, in tills. Most will reside in various bank accounts, although the actual figure on the balance sheet is called a reconciled figure, i.e. it assumes all payments made into a bank account and all payments made out of the account, up to the date on which the balance sheet is prepared, are cleared through the banking system.

What is profit?

Profit is the difference between income (sales or turnover) less all its costs (expenses) to a given point in time. There are a number of different kinds of profit.

Gross profit

This is the difference between sales and the direct cost of making the product e.g. direct labour or materials.

Operating profit

This is the difference between gross profit and overheads i.e. all other costs involved in running the business or department. For example, rent, rates, heat, light, administration costs.

Profit after interest and tax – or net profit

This is the operating profit after all interest payable is deducted or interest earned added and less all tax due to the government e.g. corporation tax.

This profit is the profit available for distribution to the shareholders by way of a dividend. How much they take is a business decision recommended by the directors to the shareholders and will be based on a number of considerations including

1 Keeping shareholders happy with their payout in relation to their investment
2 How much profit needs to be retained in the business for future use and to retain value in the balance sheet (see below re: retained profits).

Retained profit

Retained profit is the residual of profits left, after shareholders' dividends have been paid, which remains as profit reserved or retained profits on a cumulative balance in the balance sheet. It is retained for investment in other opportunities or to make future dividend payments.

The relationship between cash and profit

It is important to remember that profitable businesses do fail, as do companies with good cash flow. But companies that are profitable *and* have a good cash flow are almost always successful.

Profit alone is not sufficient to survive. A further complication is that profit can be influenced by accounting policies, which is not something that always affects cash.

For example, ignoring VAT:

Profit and loss account		*Cash flow*	
Sales	40,000	Cash in sales	40,000
Less:		Less:	
Purchases	−10,000	Cash out	−10,000
Rent	−5,000	Rent	−5,000
Depreciation	−10,000	Motor costs	−1,000
Motor costs	−1,000		−16,000
Profit	14,000	**Positive cash**	24,000

Depreciation is a profit adjustment but has no effect on cash flow.

The table assumes that the payment dates of the income and expenses are simultaneous. In reality this rarely happens particularly in a business to business situation, where credit terms are the norm.

For example, if you give your customer 60 days to pay for their goods, but you have to pay for your purchases and overheads within 30 days, your cash flow would evolve as follows:

Cash flow	£
Cash in	
Sales	0
Cash out	
Purchases	10,000
Rent	5,000
Motor Costs	1,000
	16,000
Negative cash	(16,000)

This situation could be made even worse if the business in question also had some capital expenditure requirements or loan repayment to make. All of those items affect cash but make no difference to profit (see the following example). This is equally true of VAT; at the current rate of 20%, cash out would become £19,200, and VAT is becoming a significant item in cash flow assessment.

If a capital item was purchased, ignoring VAT, for £5,000, then the cash position would be as follows:

	£
Cash in	
Sales	0
Cash out	
Purchases	10,000
Rent	5,000
Motor costs	1,000
Loan repayment	4,000
Fixed asset purchase	5,000
	25,000
Negative cash	(25,000)

It is reasonable to conclude that good business practice is to ensure you are paid before you have to make payments. Also bear in mind that accounting policies including depreciation, accruals and prepayments and capital spend will affect the profit and loss and cash flows in different ways (see later).

Changes in working capital also affect the cash flow. Working capital is the movement between creditors, debtors and stock. If you pay your suppliers quickly you will have less cash, likewise if you collect slowly from your customer, you will also have less cash. Finally, if you increase your stock levels you will again have less cash available.

	£
Profit	10,000
add depreciation	<u>2,000</u>
	12,000
Change in working capital	
Add increase in creditors	30,000
Decrease in debtors	<u>20,000</u>
	62,000
Less	
Increase in stock	<u>(15,000)</u>
	<u>47,000</u>

So, cash flow from operations is £47,000.

Which is more important – profit or cash?

This depends on a number of issues and on the role in the business, either internally or externally, of the person making the judgement call. For instance,

- Shareholders, at least in the short term, may be very interested in profits as it is out of profits that dividends are paid. However, even though there may be a profit, if there is no available cash it would not be possible to make the actual payment.
- Funders may have certain covenants in their investment documents such as minimum profit targets, which if not achieved give them the right to withdraw the facilities.
- For aquirers a profitable business is likely to be considered to be more valuable as one method of valuing a company is on a multiple of its profits.
- For employees who may have bonus schemes linked to profit performance, profit is king.
- Credit reference agencies will use profits as part of the assessment process about a company, which may be used by suppliers in their decision to trade with the business or not.

But profit without cash has only short-term value if the business is unable to convert profit into cash. You can trade for some time without profit but running out of cash and/or access to it is something that will only happen once.

Cash flow statements and cash flow projections

Cash flow statement

Formerly known as a source and application of funds report, this documents a company's change in cash and cash equivalents from one balance sheet date to another and classifies these movements against the operating activity or financing activities. An example may look like Exhibit 5.1.

Cash flow projection

This is totally unlike the cash flow statement in that it is about the future cash position of the business or department. Unlike the cash flow statement, this financial paper looks forward not backwards.

Such documents are never 100% accurate but they are one of the most important tools in the business toolbox because they consider the availability of cash.

A cash projection tells the reader the anticipated cash position of the organisation based on a series of scenarios. For instance, what will sales and margins be, and when will customers pay; what are the overheads for the business; when are they due for payment; when will any capital expenditure be made; when are loans due for payment; and when are VAT and PAYE due? These 'assumptions' are critical to the success or failure of a cash flow projection and should always be disclosed as part of the document. This is to enable the reader to judge the reasonableness, or otherwise, of the basis on which the figures have been prepared.

Once this has been modelled the manager should be able to consider if the business or department can work within its banking facility and if not what needs to be done to ensure compliance.

This may take the form of a number of actions, including increasing sales, changing payment terms with suppliers or customers or even cutting overheads.

Only the cash flow projection can give you this information.

The documents are often created annually by the finance department and then updated monthly with actual figures. In times of difficult trading it is not unusual to produce these documents weekly if not daily.

For the non-financial manager, the production of this document may not be in your remit but understanding it and the ramifications of modifications are firmly your responsibility. Knowledge of what is potentially to come can help your business through difficult trading periods. It effectively allows you to negotiate with your funders or supplies in advance of the cash flow problems becoming a crisis.

The Insolvency Act says 'it is an offence to trade your business when you are unable to pay your debts as they become due'. If this is done with knowledge this is a very serious offence – known as fraudulent trading – but even without knowledge it is a civil offence called wrongful trading. The main consideration in deciding which of these categories a business man or woman may fall into is, however, not whether they did know but whether they **should** have known that they were unable to pay their debts as they became due. On this basis alone then the production of a cash flow projection is vital.

The best models allow the user to manipulate data, for example, change payment dates from customers or delay payments to suppliers. This will allow the user to play 'what if' scenarios.

An example of a cash projection is shown in Exhibit 5.2.

There are a number of ways to improve cash flow:

- Reducing stock levels
- Delaying (with their permission preferably) payments to HMRC
- Selling assets or even investments
- Taking 'holidays' on payments such as pension contributions for staff
- Making pay cuts
- Delaying dividends
- Negotiating capital loan repayment holidays.

The most thorough way of looking at the document is to go through each line on the cash flow projections and ask 'what if': what if I increased, delayed, stopped, reduced – all these will jolt your memory and so create a more comprehensive document. Do not forget to change the written assumptions as you do make changes.

Exhibit 5.1

Cash Flow Statement

	Jan	Feb	Mar	Apr	May	Jun	Jul	Aug	Sep	Oct	Nov	Dec
	£k	£k	£k	£k	£k	£k	£k	£k	£k	£k	£k	£k
Retained Earnings before Dividends	42	23	72	60	43	46	59	43	42	88	46	52
Interest paid	2	2	2	2	2	2	2	2	2	2	2	2
Depreciation	8	9	8	(396)	(9)	9	9	9	11	10	9	9
Amortisation	15	15	15	14	15	15	15	14	15	15	15	15
Cash from Operations	67	50	97	(320)	51	72	85	69	70	115	71	78
Accounts Receivable/Debtors	(7)	(31)	(94)	(73)	59	36	(42)	(14)	24	(104)	100	122
Inventory/Stock	(7)	(34)	(36)	113	(37)	(172)	11	(144)	(74)	67	73	(27)
Accounts Payable/Creditors	7	27	32	(44)	(36)	166	(51)	(7)	52	(116)	(78)	(81)
Wages Accruals	1	(3)	6	(2)	1	(1)	(2)	(1)	2	2	(2)	7
Other Creditors	(70)	(51)	14	18	(22)	(8)	27	(34)	268	(72)	(1)	(2)
Prepaid Expenses	(42)	24	(1)	(4)	2	(4)	30	(18)	7	6	9	8
Taxes Payable	19	18	31	28	24	25	32	16	(233)	40	24	26

Cash from Operating Capital	(99)	(50)	(48)	36	(9)	42	5	(202)	46	(177)	125	53
Cash from Operations	(32)	(0)	49	(284)	42	114	90	(133)	116	(62)	196	132
Additions to Plant & Equipment	(10)	(1)	(4)	404	–	(7)	(5)	–	(10)	(7)	(1)	1
Disposals												
Capital & Operating Cash	(42)	(1)	45	120	42	107	85	(133)	106	(69)	195	133
pre Finance & Equity Change												
HP Interest	(0)	(0)	(0)	(0)	(0)	(0)	(0)	(0)	(0)	(0)	–	–
Bank/Loan Interest	(2)	(2)	(2)	(2)	(2)	(2)	(2)	(2)	(2)	(2)	(2)	(2)
Total Interest Payments	(2)	(2)	(2)	(2)	(2)	(2)	(2)	(2)	(2)	(2)	(2)	(2)
Long Term Debt Repayments	(20)	(13)	(12)	(13)	(13)	(13)	(13)	(13)	(13)	(13)	(13)	(13)
Computer Loan Repayments	0	–	–	–	–	–	–	–	–	–	–	–
Comm Mortgage Repayments	3	(4)	(5)	(5)	(4)	(4)	(4)	(4)	(4)	(5)	(4)	(4)
Dividends Paid	(11)	(11)	(11)	(106)	(11)	(13)	(13)	(13)	(13)	(13)	(13)	(113)
Net Financing Decrease	(28)	(28)	(28)	(123)	(28)	(30)	(30)	(30)	(29)	(31)	(30)	(130)
Net Change in Cash	(72)	(31)	15	(6)	12	75	53	(166)	74	(102)	163	1
Cash Beginning of Period	86	14	(17)	(2)	(8)	4	79	132	(33)	41	(61)	102
Cash End of Period	14	(17)	(2)	(8)	4	79	132	(33)	41	(61)	102	103

Exhibit 5.2

Cash Flow Forecast

	Jan	Feb	Mar	Apr	May	Jun	Jul	Aug	Sep	Oct	Nov	Dec	Total
	£k	£k	£k	£k	£k	£k	£k	£k	£k	£k	£k	£k	£k
Retained Earnings before Divi's	43	45	54	33	45	50	52	56	47	50	55	18	548
Interest	2	2	2	1	1	1	1	1	1	1	1	1	15
Depreciation	8	9	8	9	9	9	8	9	8	9	8	9	103
Amortisation	15	15	15	15	15	15	15	15	15	15	15	15	180
Cash from Operations	68	71	79	58	70	75	76	81	71	75	79	43	846
Accounts Receivable/Debtors	19	9	(27)	39	14	(34)	(27)	(26)	0	9	(17)	113	71
Inventory (Stock)	19	19	21	17	19	20	20	21	20	20	21	14	234
Accounts Payable/Creditors	(19)	60	(46)	(18)	(11)	17	7	9	1	(7)	7	(53)	(53)
Wages Accruals	7	–	–	–	–	–	–	–	–	–	–	–	7
Other Creditors	(3)	(42)	30	(1)	(32)	25	19	(23)	24	22	(33)	(7)	(21)
Prepaid Expenses	(12)	2	2	(4)	2	2	(2)	2	2	2	2	2	–
Taxes Payable	21	22	26	16	21	23	24	25	(270)	23	25	10	(33)
Cash from Operating Capital	32	70	6	49	13	53	41	8	(222)	69	6	80	206

Cash From Operations	99	140	85	108	83	128	117	89	(151)	144	85	123	1,052
Additions to Plant & Equipment	(15)	–	–	–	–	(11)	–	(76)	–	–	–	–	(102)
Disposals													
Capital & Operating Cash	84	140	85	108	83	117	117	13	(151)	144	85	123	949
pre Finance & Equity Change													
HP Interest	–	–	–	–	–	–	–	–	–	–	–	–	–
Bank/Loan Interest	(2)	(2)	(2)	(1)	(1)	(1)	(1)	(1)	(1)	(1)	(1)	(1)	(15)
Total Interest Payments	(2)	(2)	(2)	(1)	(1)	(1)	(1)	(1)	(1)	(1)	(1)	(1)	(15)
Long Term Debt Repayments	(13)	(13)	(13)	(13)	(13)	(13)	(13)	(13)	(13)	(13)	(13)	(13)	(155)
Computer Loan Repayments	–	–	–	–	–	–	–	–	–	–	–	–	–
Comm Mortgage Repayments	(4)	(4)	(4)	(4)	(4)	(4)	(4)	(4)	(4)	(4)	(4)	(4)	(48)
Dividends Paid	(11)	(11)	(11)	(11)	(11)	(11)	(11)	(11)	(11)	(11)	(11)	(286)	(408)
Net Financing Decrease	(28)	(28)	(28)	(28)	(28)	(28)	(28)	(28)	(28)	(28)	(28)	(304)	(614)
Net Change in Cash	54	110	55	78	53	87	88	(16)	(180)	115	56	(181)	318
Cash Beginning of Period	87	141	252	307	385	438	525	613	596	416	531	587	
Cash End of Period	141	252	307	385	438	525	613	596	416	531	587	406	

A final litmus test on the accuracy of this document is to compare actual with forecast. If the reading is continually inaccurate, investigation will be paramount, particularly if a funder is monitoring reality versus forecast as major differences will inevitably mean loss of confidence which could come back to loss of the funding.

Make more of what you have, be it profit or cash

I could almost guarantee that every business or department has areas that could be improved upon financially. The problem is that many business people are so busy just trying to make what they have work that they can't see the opportunities and don't have time to do anything about them.

The following is not an exhaustive list and each business or department will have different opportunities.

Don't think just about **savings** that can be made when looking at everyday business wealth – think about **sales** opportunities.

Some of the best ideas will rest with your staff, who in many cases are closer to the opportunities and savings, so ask them! You could make this an incentive-based idea plan and it doesn't have to be a cash reward; lots of people would value an early finish or an extra day's holiday for the best idea generated. Archie Norman, who turned ASDA around in the 1990s, gave his staff his car and chauffeur for the weekend for the best money-making and saving ideas. It worked for ASDA.

Here are a few ideas that may be worth exploring.

Save on overheads

Do a health check of your business or department (see Chapter 10 for further details) – look at every consumable item you purchase and negotiate better rates or even retrospective discounts. Join up with another business or department to negotiate bulk buys on solus supply deals.

Check your credit rating

There are a number of websites that list business credit ratings (and personal ones for that matter). If you haven't checked yours recently the time to do this is not when you or the business is in crisis, but now, when, if it isn't satisfactory, you may have an opportunity to do something about it.

The world is risk-averse at the moment and credit lines are being butchered. A poor credit rating can affect your ability to access supply lines and credit terms so securing the best credit rating possible is important. In the first instance you need to know what your rating is and what that means to anyone outside your business, followed by what actions you need to take to improve your credit score. Late filing of accounts will give you a downgrade on your score but likewise not filing early may also affect you.

First of all check out your rating on one or more of the following www.experian.co.uk and www.equifax.co.uk. There is also an interesting website that helps you repair your credit rating called www.splut.com>money/finance; also, www.lloydstsb.com/advice/you_and_your_credit_rating.asp provides well thought out advice on credit-rating management generally.

Free cash utilisation

If you have cash on deposit, rates are pretty poor at the moment but longer-term rates may be better. Even switching funds into a deposit account overnight is better than leaving them in a no-interest current account.

Whilst rates are low for depositors, pay down as much debt as you can reasonably afford on account as certainly your debt will cost you more than any funds left on deposit.

Grants and free advice

There is a lot of free advice and lots of grants available but the problem is knowing where to look. Try www.grantsnet.co.uk for information on all UK funding. For specific grants on energy saving try www.energysavinggrant.org.uk and for grants to make your business disabled-friendly try www.direct.gov.uk/en/disabledpeople.

Application for grants can be very time-consuming and is by no means guaranteed and although there are not the substantial funds of twenty years ago, there is still funding to be had and there are some organisations who will give you at least some free time to look at what's available. Try www.yourbusinessservice.co.uk.

Sell and lease back assets (or just sell them!)

If you are short of cash it's entirely possible you may be able to release some by selling unwanted assets.

If you actually still need the asset, then there are companies who will buy them and effectively rent them back to you. Ultimately this may cost you more but it is a way of releasing short-term cash.

And as recycling is not only good for the planet, instead of disposing of your old IT kit, mobiles etc., why not sell them on one of the multiple sites set up to recycle this equipment?

The following businesses offer sale and lease back services: www.leasedi rectfinance.co.uk and www.nationwide-asset-finance.co.uk; and try www. weeebuy.co.uk for recycling quotes.

Sell excess stock

Out of date, obsolete or just excessive stock is basically tying up precious cash and in addition may also have storage costs attached to it. De-stocking is something you can do yourself by reducing prices, but that may take time and may taint your business in other ways.

There are numerous excess stock aquirers who will take all your unwanted stock in one go.

The price is usually very low but it's one transaction and so as speed may be the overriding requirement, it's worth checking out. Try these websites: www.globalstockuk.com or www.sgtrading.co.uk.

Make money from excess space

Whether it be parking, office or storage space, if you have this in excess there may be someone willing to rent it from you, particularly on a short-term licence or lease agreement. Adverts in local papers and Post Offices are often the best way to attract these sorts of opportunities.

Although the requirement may be short-term don't cut corners by avoiding legally drawn up agreements. These don't have to be complex but they do have to be binding as resolution of disputes without proper contracts will inevitably cost.

Joint venturing and cost sharing

When I started my first business I had no money but I desperately needed a brochure (long before website days!). I found a small marketing and design agency who agreed to give me a heavily discounted brochure if they could put their details at the bottom. They wouldn't have offered if I didn't ask, but it turned out to be a win-win situation.

I recently did the same when I updated by new website and it worked very well again. You can even look to affiliate your website, which means you get paid every time someone clicks on your page. Try Google's ad service or Amazon's Product Advertising API. They are free to install. Their click rate is low, but the more traffic you get the more the cash will roll in.

Sponsorship is also a great way of reducing costs and attracting cash so why not try it in your business. Don't forget they can only say no so you won't have lost anything by trying.

Check your bank charges

Try www.chargechecker.co.uk, which checks if you are being charged correctly by your bank and then helps you reclaim. Banks do make lots of mistakes both on interest and charges calculations and it's very difficult to check, but it is estimated that 75% of businesses have been overcharged at some point.

This matter has been debated in parliament a number of times and banks are keen to be seen to be doing the right thing now; you just may have to point it out to them in the first instance.

6

The Balance Sheet

For the majority of non-financial people, the balance sheet is one of the more difficult financial statements to understand. Grasping the concept of the profit and loss account, which shows what has happened to a business or department over a given period of time, is one thing. The balance sheet is literally a snapshot of the financial standing of a business at a particular point in time.

This chapter will provide you with an insight into the meaning of a balance sheet, how it is constructed and its variable contents. It will also demonstrate the business value of having a strong or weak balance sheet, and just what that means to anyone who chooses to review and analyse business performance on the back of this particular statement.

The basics

The balance sheet in its simplest form is a statement at a given point in time, usually a month or year end, of a company's assets and liabilities,

- Assets being things a business owns or is owed
- Liabilities being things it owes.

If you like, this is effectively demonstrating where your business finance is coming from and how those funds are being utilised.

The Balance Sheet itself is split into two distinct parts:

1 A statement of fixed assets and current assets less short-term and long-term liabilities, to create net assets (or net worth)

2 A statement showing how these net assets have been financed, for example through profits being retained.

A simple example is given in Exhibit 6.1.

Exhibit 6.1   A simple balance sheet example

A Company Ltd[1]

Year ended 31 December 2012

	2012[2]	2011[3]
FIXED ASSETS[4]		
Tangible assets	9,350	10,840
CURRENT ASSETS[5]		
Stock	800	700
Debtors	5,675	4,722
Prepayments	650	615
Bank account[6]	–	437
Cash in hand	170	142
	7,295	6,616
CURRENT LIABILITIES[7]		
Trade creditors	4,520	3,911
Bank overdraft[6]	325	–
VAT	698	623
Corporation Tax	431	378
Accruals	750	700
	6,724	5,612
NET CURRENT ASSETS[8]	571	1,004
LONG-TERM LIABILITIES[9]		
Bank loan	6,000	8,000
NET ASSETS[10]	3,921	3,844
CAPITAL AND RESERVES[11]		
Called up share capital	100	100
Profit and loss account	3,821	3,744
	3,921	3,844

1   Company name and current year end.

2   Current figures (in this example a balance sheet is produced once a year but it could be more often, e.g. monthly).

3   Figures for previous year (or month etc.) for comparison.

4   **Fixed assets** are those with an expected life of more than two years, bought to help the business operate, not for resale. Examples would be motor vehicles and computers. Can include intangible fixed assets, which are things that you can't see or touch. Examples include the value of patents/trademarks.

5   **Current assets** are those more readily turned into cash. Stock is the hardest to convert (least liquid) so appears first. Next comes debtors (people who owe you money) then cash itself (the most liquid asset). More detail below.

6   Note that bank accounts can be assets (positive bank balance) or liabilities (bank overdraft).

7   **Current liabilities** are expected cash outflows (debts) in up to 12 months. More detail below.

8   **Net current assets**: this figure shows how easily the business can pay immediate debts. A high figure means a safe business. A negative figure means short-term debts payable are larger than the value of assets readily available to turn into cash.

9   **Long-term liabilities**: this shows expected cash outflows after more than 12 months, and often includes bank loans and hire purchase agreements.

10 **Net assets** are total assets less total liabilities. A negative figure indicates that the business is insolvent (cannot repay all its debts).

11 **Capital and reserves**: how the business is funded. Typically an initial cash injection (share capital) plus retained profits to date. More complex companies may have several types of share capital, or share premium (shares sold for more than face value).

Current assets

The main classes of current assets are:

■ **Stock** – can be split down further into raw materials, work in progress and finished goods. Keeping the right level of stock can be difficult. Too much and cash is tied up for ages, plus you risk stock becoming obsolete. Too little and you risk losing sales due to long lead times to get goods to the customer.

- **Trade debtors** – customers you have sold to on credit who have not yet paid.

- **Prepayments** – goods/services that you have been invoiced for but not yet got the benefit of, e.g. insurance paid annually up front.

- **Accrued income** – often combined with prepayments. Work you have (partially) performed but not yet invoiced to the customer, perhaps as the job is not yet complete.

- **Other debtors** – money owed by non-customers. This could be a repayment of tax due from HMRC, or perhaps the business has issued a loan to another business.

- **Bank account** – includes both current and deposit accounts. If you have a positive deposit account balance, but an overdraft on your current account, they should not be combined. The deposit account should appear here, and the overdraft in current liabilities.

- **Cash in hand** – petty cash held.

Current liabilities

The main classes of current liabilities are:

- **Trade creditors** – suppliers you have bought from but not yet paid. Delaying payment to suppliers improves cash flow, but delaying too much may make them reluctant to deal with you again.

- **Accruals** – goods/services used by the business, but not yet invoiced. These can include an estimate of the cost of phone calls recently made, or professional advice received but not yet billed.

- **Deferred income** – often combined with accruals. Work you have invoiced in advance of performance. This can include payments on account and deposits.

- **Bank loan/overdraft** – overdrawn balances on current accounts and loans. For long-term loans, only the amount repayable within 12 months is shown here, the remainder going in long-term liabilities.

- **Taxes** – often current liabilities will include VAT, corporation tax and/or PAYE/National Insurance.

- **Other creditors** – money owed to someone other than the above. In small businesses often this will include things such as director loans to help improve the cash flow.

The Companies Act requires the balance sheet to be included in the published financial accounts of all limited companies. In reality, all other organisations that need to
prepare accounting information for external users (e.g. charities, clubs, partnerships)
will also produce a balance sheet since it is an important statement of the financial
affairs of the organisation.

A balance sheet does not necessarily 'value' a company, since assets and liabilities
are shown at '**historical cost**' and some intangible assets (e.g. brands, quality of
management, market leadership) are not included.

There are several ways you can use a balance sheet:

▨ For reporting purposes as part of a company's annual accounts.

▨ To help assess the creditworthiness of a business at a given
moment.

▨ To help analyse and improve the management of a business.

Analysis of a balance sheet

Financial ratios turn raw financial data from the balance sheet
into information that will help you manage your business and
make knowledgeable decisions. A ratio shows the relationship
between two numbers. It is defined as the relative size of two
quantities expressed as the quotient of one divided by the
other. Financial ratio analysis is important because it is one
method funders use to evaluate the creditworthiness of potential borrowers. Ratio analysis is a tool to uncover trends in a
business as well as allow the comparison between one business
and another.

The following six financial ratios that can be calculated from a
balance sheet are interesting to understand:

▨ Current ratio

▨ Quick ratio

▨ Working capital

▨ Debt/worth ratio (or gearing ratio)

▨ Fixed asset turnover ratio

▨ Return on assets ratio

Current ratio

The *current ratio* (or liquidity ratio) is a measure of financial strength. The number of times current assets exceed current liabilities is a valuable expression of a business's solvency. Here is the formula to calculate the current ratio:

$$\text{Current ratio} = \frac{\text{Total current assets}}{\text{Total current liabilities}}$$

The current ratio answers the question, 'Does my business have enough current assets to meet the payment schedule of current liabilities with a margin of safety?' A rule-of-thumb puts a strong current ratio at two. Of course, the adequacy of a current ratio will depend on the nature of the business and the character of the current assets and current liabilities. While there is usually little doubt about debts that are due, there can be considerable doubt about the quality of debtors or the cash value of stock.

A current ratio can be improved by either increasing current assets or decreasing current liabilities. This can take the form of the following:

- Paying down debt
- Acquiring a loan (payable in more than one year's time)
- Selling a fixed asset
- Putting profits back into the business.

A high current ratio may mean that cash is not being utilised in an optimal way. That is, the cash might better be invested in equipment.

Quick ratio

The *quick ratio* is also called the 'acid test' ratio. It is a measure of a company's liquidity. The quick ratio looks only at a company's most liquid assets and divides them by current liabilities. Here is the formula for the quick ratio:

$$\text{Quick ratio} = \frac{\text{Current assets} - \text{Stock}}{\text{Total current liabilities}}$$

The assets considered to be 'quick' assets are cash, stocks and debtors (all of the current assets on the balance sheet except stock). The quick ratio is an acid test of whether or not a business can meet its obligations if adverse conditions occur. Generally, quick ratios between 0.5 and 1 are considered satisfactory – as long as the collection of debtors is not expected to slow.

Working capital

Working capital should always be a positive number. It is used by lenders to evaluate a company's ability to survive in difficult markets. Often, loan agreements specify a level of working capital that the borrower must maintain. The current ratio, quick ratio and working capital are all measures of a company's liquidity. In general, the higher these ratios are the better for the business and the higher the degree of liquidity.

$$\text{Working capital} = \text{Total current assets} - \text{Total current liabilities}$$

Debt/worth or gearing ratio

The *debt/worth or gearing ratio* (or leverage ratio) is an indicator of a business's solvency. It is a measure of how dependent a company is on debt financing (or borrowings) as compared to owners' equity. It shows how much of a business is owned and how much is owed. The debt/worth or gearing ratio is calculated as follows:

$$\text{Debt/worth or gearing ratio} = \frac{\text{Total liabilities}}{\text{Net worth}}$$

The fixed asset turnover ratio

Fixed assets is another of the 'big' numbers in a company's balance sheet. In fact, it often represents the single largest component of a company's total assets.

A company's investment in fixed assets is dependent, to a large degree, on its line of business. Some businesses are more capital intensive than others. Large capital equipment producers require a large amount of fixed-asset investment. Service companies need a relatively small amount of fixed assets. Mainstream manufacturers generally have around 30% to 40% of their assets in fixed assets. Accordingly, fixed asset turnover ratios will vary among different industries.

The fixed asset turnover ratio is calculated as:

$$\text{Fixed asset turnover ratio} = \frac{\text{Net sales}}{\text{Average fixed assets}}$$

Average fixed assets can be calculated by dividing the year-end fixed assets of two years (e.g. 2012 and 2011 fixed assets divided by 2).

This fixed asset turnover ratio indicator, looked at over time and compared to that of competitors, gives the investor an idea of how effectively a company's management is using this large and important asset. It is a rough measure of the productivity of a company's fixed assets with respect to generating sales. The higher the number of times fixed assets turn over, the better. Obviously, investors look for consistency or increasing fixed asset turnover rates as positive balance sheet investment qualities.

The return on assets ratio (ROA)

Return on assets (ROA) is considered to be a profitability ratio – it shows how much a company is earning on its total assets. It is worthwhile to view the ROA ratio as an indicator of asset performance.

The ROA ratio (percentage) is calculated as:

$$ROA = \frac{Net\ profit}{Average\ total\ assets}$$

Average total assets can be calculated by dividing the year-end total assets of two prior periods (e.g. 2012 and 2011 fixed assets divided by 2).

The ROA ratio is expressed as a percentage return by comparing net profit, the bottom line of the profit and loss account, to average total assets. A high percentage return implies well-managed assets.

The ROA ratio is best used as a comparative analysis of a company's own historical performance and with companies in a similar line of business. From this analysis it is possible that decisions will be taken by shareholders, funders and customers and even employees and potential employees about how and whether they will engage with your organisation.

The information can, however, be skewed, for two principal reasons:

1   It is all presented at a point in time

2   It is always historic in content.

Unlike a budget, a balance sheet does not consider potential purchases or sales of capital, equipment or acquisitions of business or other assets. It simply records what is known at that point. When carrying out your own analysis you must always bear in mind these two points.

The impact of intangible assets

Numerous non-physical assets are considered intangible assets, which can essentially be categorised into three different types:

■   Intellectual property (patents, copyrights, trademarks, brand names, etc.),

■ Deferred charges (capitalised expenses), and

■ Purchased goodwill (the cost of an investment in excess of book value).

Unfortunately, there is little uniformity in balance sheet presentations for intangible assets or the terminology used in the account narrative. Often, intangibles are buried in other assets and only disclosed in notes of the accounts (see later).

Money involved in intellectual property and capitalised expenses is generally not material and, in most cases, doesn't warrant much analytical scrutiny. However, it's wise to look carefully at the amount of purchased goodwill in a company's balance sheet and ask *'is this a reliable value and more importantly if we remove it from the balance sheet what effect does that have on the net worth of the business?'*

Companies acquire other companies, so purchased goodwill happens in financial accounting on frequent occasions so cannot be overlooked but inherent value may need to be questioned.

How assets are valued in a balance sheet

If assets are things that the company owns, they are the resources of the company that have been acquired through transactions, and have future value that can be measured and expressed in sterling. But assets also include costs paid in advance that have not yet expired, such as prepaid advertising, prepaid insurance, prepaid legal fees, and prepaid rent.

So assets that are reported on a company's balance sheet may include:

■ Cash

■ Petty cash

■ Debtors

■ Stock

■ Prepaid insurance

■ Land

■ Land improvements

■ Buildings

■ Equipment

■ Goodwill

Against such assets we must account for certain costs or charges which reduce the net book value of such assets. These charges include:

■ Allowance for doubtful accounts

■ Accumulated depreciation – land improvements

■ Accumulated depreciation – buildings

■ Accumulated depreciation – equipment

■ Accumulated depreciation – motor vehicles.

The effect of cost less charges

The assets reported in the balance sheet reflect actual costs recorded at the time of a transaction. For example, if a business acquired land in the year 1950 at a cost of £20,000, then, in 2011, it paid £400,000 for an adjacent plot, the company's land value will show a balance of £420,000 (£20,000 for the first plot plus £400,000 for the second). This account balance of £420,000 will appear on today's balance sheet even though these parcels of land have appreciated to a current market value of perhaps £3,000,000.

There are two guidelines that oblige the accountant to report £420,000 on the balance sheet rather than the current market value of £3,000,000:

1 The historical cost principle directs the accountant to report the company's assets at their original historical cost

2 Prudence directs the accountant to ignore any possible increase in value unless this asset has been revalued.

These principles mean that some very valuable resources will not be reported on the balance sheet, for example, a company's team of brilliant sales people will not be listed as an asset on the company's balance sheet, because

a The company did not purchase the team in a transaction and

b It's impossible for accountants to know how to put a pound value on the team.

> For many companies, trade names for consumer products are likely to be their most valuable assets. If those names and logos were developed internally, it is reasonable that they will not appear on the company balance sheet. If, however, a company should *purchase* a product name and logo from another company, that cost will appear as an asset on the balance sheet of the acquiring company.

Capital and reserves

This is one of the more difficult sections of the balance sheet to understand as it is a company liability.

This section represents the owners'/shareholders' equity (investment in the business) and can be thought of as a source of the company's assets. Owners' equity is equal to the reported asset amounts *minus* the reported liability amounts.

Owners' equity may also be referred to as the residual of assets minus liabilities.

These references make sense if you think of the basic accounting equation:

Assets = Liabilities + Capital and Reserves

and just rearrange the terms:

Capital and Reserves = Assets − Liabilities

Example:

Capital Reserves		
Share capital[1]	150	150
Share premium[2]	3,275	3,275
Retained profit[3]	2,146	2,928
Total shareholders' funds	5,571	6,353

1 = the share capital i.e. the money invested for the purchase of shares in the business.
2 = the premium paid on the original share issue price when shares are subsequently sold.
3 = also called profit reserves is the accumulation of all profits generated in the business after dividends have been paid and tax due accounted for.

Notes to financial statements

The notes (or footnotes) to the balance sheet and to the other financial statements are considered to be part of the financial statements. The notes inform the readers about such things as significant accounting policies, commitments made by the company, potential liabilities and potential losses. The notes contain information that is critical to proper understanding and analysing a company's financial statements.

It is in these notes that you can find some very interesting facts about a business and particularly about the balance sheet. As such, notes should always be read as part of any financial analysis.

The following are some typical relevant notes in relation to the balance sheet.

NOTES TO THE ACCOUNTS FOR 20X2

1. Tangible Fixed Assets

Depreciation is provided at rates calculated to write off the cost of each asset evenly over its expected useful life as follows:

Land and Buildings	2%
Plant and Equipment	15%
Motor Vehicles	25%

In prior year, depreciation on motor vehicles was charged at 15%.

2. Stocks

Manufactured goods include the costs of production. Stock and work in progress are valued at the lower of cost and net realisable value. Bought in goods are valued at purchase cost on a first in first out basis. In prior year, stock was valued at average purchase price.

3. Tangible Fixed Assets

	Land & Buildings	Plant & Equipment	Motor Vehicles	Total
	£'000	£'000	£'000	£'000
Cost				
1 January 20X2	4,401	4,503	1,588	10,492
Additions	570	656	265	1,491
Disposals	–	(35)	–	(35)
31 December 20X2	4,971	5,124	1,853	11,948

Depreciation

1 January 20X2	269	1,430	348	2,047
On disposals	–	(20)	–	(20)
Charge for the year	46	345	104	495
31 December 20X2	4,971	5,124	1,853	11,948

Net Book Value

1 January 20X2	4,132	3,073	1,240	8,445
31 December 20X2	4,656	3,369	1,401	9,426

4. Stocks and Work in Progress

	£'000	£'000
	20X2	**20X1**
Raw Materials	1,362	87
Work in Progress	27	42
Finished Goods	62	754
Total	**1,451**	**883**

5. Debtors

	£'000	£'000
	20X2	**20X1**
Trade debtors less provision for doubtful debts	1,837	1,007
Prepayments	28	26
Other debtors	46	28
Total	**1,911**	**1,061**

6. Current Liabilities

	£'000	£'000
	20X2	20X1
Trade creditors	750	801
HMRC	240	125
Accruals	413	193
Cash in advance	120	10
	1,523	1,129
Bank overdraft	1,894	613
Taxation	206	193
Proposed dividend	184	131
Total	3,807	2,066

7. Long-Term Liabilities

	£'000	£'000
	20X2	20X1
Director loan	7,000	6,000
Bank loans	8,000	6,000
	15,000	12,000

The loans are secured by a charge over the Company's assets.

8. Post Balance Sheet Events

Since the year end the Company acquired 10% of the issued share capital of B Ltd., a company importing high quality Italian sanitaryware. The cost of the investment was £1,500,000.

9. Transactions with Directors

The Company buys, on normal commercial terms, a substantial proportion of its materials from 2 Ltd., a company which Miss A. Parr is a substantial Shareholder and Director.

The value of such purchases during the year ended 31 December 20X2 was £1,478,000, and the balance outstanding at the end of the year was £157,000.

These notes demonstrate a number of key issues to understand in relation to a balance sheet.

Notes:

1. Explains the differing depreciation policies utilised by the business and highlights in this case that the business has changed percentage policy on its motor vehicles from 15% to 25%. This would reduce the business profits but make no difference of course to its cash.

2. Tells the reader how the business values its stock and in this case this company has changed its method to a 'first in first out' basis i.e. all stock will be valued at the cost of the oldest stock from a position in the previous year when all stock was valued at an average purchase price.

3. Provides the reader with the breakdown of assets into their various categories of

Land and buildings
Plant and equipment and
Motor vehicles

and gives further information on depreciation and prior year net book value.

4. Provides the reader with the breakdown of stock and work in progress. Interesting in this case are the large increase in raw materials from the previous year and the reduction in finished goods.

5. Breaks down the generic debtor numbers on a balance sheet including trade debtors (people who owe the business), prepayments and other debtors.

6. Is the full analysis of current liabilities showing important changes in a number of assets in accruals and cash in advance both of which have substantially increased year on year.

7. Provides the reader with the breakdown of long-term liabilities, in this case between directors' loans and bank loans.

8. Explains to the reader that after the production of these figures a significant investment was made by the business into another company and because this was done after the year end this investment is noted but will not be part of the financial statement itself.

9. Explains that the company trades with another business which has a director and shareholder who also sits on its own Board; it also quantifies and explains that transaction value.

Notes 8 and 9 are legal requirements in financial reporting statements and are part of the procedures the accounting professional must adhere to in relation to transparency of data.

To summarise

Although a balance sheet may be available on one piece of paper in a set of accounts, to understand it fully, a reader must examine numerous other elements of the accounts and especially the notes and policies, as it is only by reading these as a whole that a true understanding of a balance sheet can be gained.

7

Budgets and Forecasts

This chapter considers what budgets are comprised of, how they are created and who uses them. It will also look at how a budget differs from a forecast and why both are important in running an effective business or department.

For some people a budget is something they are given to work with or within, or even to spend up to, but for those managers wanting to have greater control of their company or division it is essential to understand the value of a budget and forecast, how they differ and, of most importance, how to create them.

Only by having this insight can a manager hope to run a more effective business.

What is a budget?

My old manager would say the only thing you can say with any degree of certainty about a budget is that it is wrong.

A more technical definition would state that a budget is a financial statement that is created to project the future sales and profit, cash flow and balance sheet of a business or a specific department for a given period in the future.

It could be a very simple one page synopsis or a multidimensional, sophisticated spreadsheet. But the whole point of the document is to give consideration to what the future may hold. It sets goals and targets for the business or department and looks at individual components within the business such as sales margins and staff numbers.

A budget is usually either created for a specific event or activity, for example an acquisition, or is created on an annual basis as part of an overall business planning process.

One way to consider a budget is as a route map to an intended destination. This assumes you have a final destination in mind and indeed this may be part of a whole budgeting exercise. If you don't have a budget it's a little like getting into a car and having no idea where you are aiming for or how you are going to get there.

Budgeting basics

For some, particularly those who believe they have a good, well performing business or department, creating a budget can seem rather a boring process. But it is in fact vital in keeping your financial house in good order.

It isn't all about reducing and cutting money spent, although that certainly may be part of its requirements. It is more about understanding better what you have and how best to allocate these resources.

The word budget actually comes from the Old French word *bougette* meaning little bag or purse and a good housekeeper, aka business person, should know how much they have in that purse and how much they need to keep it at optimum levels.

Budgeting rationale and types

There are a number of reasons for creating a budget in addition to the annual budgeting exercise.

New enterprise

When looking at starting a new business or department the creation of a budget is necessary to examine, amongst other things, working capital and capital expenditure requirements.

Anyone looking to support a new opportunity, either from an investment (share ownership) or funds point of view, would be very unlikely to consider this sort of activity seriously unless they were provided with a budget.

Spend or expenses budget

Government bodies and academic departments will habitually be given a budget that provides the management with a breakdown of agreed spend limits on everything including travel allowance, entertaining, training and marketing. This allocation of spend allowance was historically tagged with the 'spend it or lose it' mantra. In other words if you do not use the allowance allocated to you it will be lost and may not be carried forward into a future period. In fact an underspend was likely to indicate that future budgets allocated would assume a lack of requirement, the position being that, if the funds had not been spent historically, they wouldn't be needed in the future.

Nevertheless the budget principle is still the same in that a budget figure is agreed and the plan is that no more or less will be spent.

What is a forecast?

In pictorial definition a forecast looks very like a budget but, unlike a budget which is usually a one-off or annual exercise, a forecast is a much more active document. A forecast is changed to reflect what actually happened, usually on a monthly basis. In this case then a forecast becomes a mix of actuals and estimates (budgets) to the end of the year. We would say this gives you the forecast outcome for the year, the budget in total remaining unchanged.

Differences between budgets and forecasts

A forecast is not a goal. It is just a sophisticated financial tool that allows you to look a little more accurately into the future based on what is actually happening.

A forecast is more up-to-date than a budget in respect of actual performance and because it is current it becomes a better barometer of business performance.

It shows where you are going with the business or department as opposed to a budget which says where you would like to go. Hopefully they will be the same, but this may not always be the case.

If, as a result of your forecast, you understand you are not going to achieve budgeted expectations the idea of the forecast is it allows you to take pre-emptive, remedial action. Because it also continues to look into the future it should allow the manager to spot future problems before they become insurmountable.

A sample budget is given in Appendix E.

How to create a budget

For first-timers this exercise can seem very daunting when they are provided with a blank piece of paper. So it is an exercise that is probably best broken down into categories.

There are various schools of thought on whether it is more appropriate to start with the desired end result (whether that be a cash or profit target) and work backwards, or to go through the transaction headings on the main financial papers of a profit and loss account, cash flow and balance sheet. Both have various merits for the person producing the document to feel more or less comfortable with the process.

Whichever you choose there will be some circular activity as either the first results will be unacceptable to one or more parties or they will simply require you to play some 'what if' scenarios. This could be the question that if we don't hit those sales targets what will happen to our cash flow?

Suggested budget headings to consider

Income or sales

To get the most accurate projection I advise you break this down as follows:

- Existing customer sales
- Existing customer new product/service sales
- New customer sales
- New customer new product/service sales.

It allows you to consider how new business from new customers and new business from existing customers can impact on the business.

Other income

Does your business receive any other income, for example grants, subscriptions, donations, unearned income e.g. rent from properties? If not, does it plan to and, if so, from what source?

Gross profit (GP)

As we've seen before, you are likely to be more accurate in your budgeting if you break this down into customer groups and products in the same way as I have suggested with sales.

Are you planning a price increase? Are your suppliers? Gross profit is made up of the difference between sales and cost of sales so by understanding what you are aiming for you will be able to calculate the difference between GP and sales that will give you your budgeted cost of sales.

If you are a manufacturer you will need to break this down into cost of labour and material costs of sales. Then you need to consider pay rises, efficiencies and material price changes.

For an established business it is sensible to compare your budgeted gross profit with that achieved in the previous year/period.

A critical figure is the GP% (the gross profit $\times$ 100 and divided by the turnover). Your budgeted GP% should be reconcilable with what was actually achieved in the previous year/period. Although your indirect costs may change, they are likely to fluctuate; it is critical that the gross profit is achieved at a level to absorb the indirect costs.

Indirect costs

A standard list for a typical business may include:

- Rent
- Rates
- Heat, light
- Post and print
- Stationery
- Travel
- Motor expenses
- Entertaining
- Telephone and communications
- Bank charges
- Advertising
- Training
- Repairs and renewals
- Cleaning
- Insurance
- Salaries and National Insurance
- Sundries
- Depreciation
- Professional fees

This is far from being an exhaustive list but it is a good start.

In a number of businesses the indirect costs are grouped under headings such as Establishment, Administration, Selling Costs, Financial Expenses. Others list them, particularly in overseas companies, in alphabetical order. For a mature, established business there will be a list of cost headings to follow.

It is always best to overestimate costs in the first instance and to have a contingency for the inevitable overspend.

If you are developing a budget for a mature business with known costs start with an inflationary rise and add known extras, for example if you are planning on re-branding or have extensive training courses planned.

You can always revisit these later if the final objectives of profits are not being met. This way you have worst case scenarios as a starting point.

Interest

Dependent on your role you may be required to estimate borrowing requirements for the period and this is the place in the budget that we provide for the interest related to those borrowings, whether it be over-drafts, loans, hire purchase or leases. Largely these should be known but do remember that many lends are based on a percentage above bank base rate and as such this will be subject to change.

Profit before tax (PBT)

The sum of the overheads when taken from the gross profit will give you the PBT figure.

As this point it may be necessary to revisit your assumptions if the results you get are not the desired ones. If that is the case you have a number of choices:

1   Increase sales

2   Increase gross profit

3   Reduce overheads.

Some or all of these will have the desired effect but a word of caution: stick to reality, or as near as possible; there is no one really to deceive but yourself.

The balance sheet

When looking at the balance sheet budget for an established business, you need to start the process from the closing balance sheet (i.e. the last balance sheet of the previous period). The idea is to project forward what you antici-pate is required. Some of these decisions will impact on cash flow.

Sophisticated tools that are used in budgeting include Sage products (see www.sage.co.uk) or Microsoft's spreadsheet program Excel (see www.microsoft.com). These will normally have some integration links built into them so that when you enter a decision on capital expenditure into the balance sheet it will also link automatically to the cash out requirements on the cash flow.

Technology aside the practical process of building a balance sheet is as follows.

Fixed assets – tangible

These are the infrastructure of your business so you need to be considering what you have versus what you need. For example:

Buildings

Do you have sufficient capacity where you are? Do you need extra space? If you do, the next question is will you be buying this or renting? If the former this is a fixed asset purchase and the latter an expense to the profit and loss account.

How you will buy this is another matter but the question for the balance sheet forecast is when and how much that will be.

When you have decided that, the cost of the asset purchase needs to go into your balance sheet (that is the actual cost not the net cost i.e. the full cost of the building regardless of mortgages).

Plant and equipment

The assumption around the balance sheet assets is that these are purchased items (if they were hired or rented, that would be an expense cost to the profit and loss account).

For the balance sheet you need to consider what you need and estimate the cost of the investment and, if you are providing a month by month balance sheet forecast as opposed to an annual year end one, in what month you will acquire the asset.

Fixtures, fittings and motor vehicles

Follow the same thought and action process as with plant and equipment.

Fixed assets – intangible

Goodwill

As you will have already learnt from Chapter 3, intangible fixed assets include purchased goodwill, which is the net difference between the net asset value of a business you buy and the actual sum you pay.

If you are going to introduce this into a balance sheet then it is because you must be considering investing in another business and paying more than the sum of the net assets. Such budgeting is unlikely to be in the remit of a non-financial manager but it's worth understanding where such a number could come from.

Other intangible items

This may include the purchasing of patents or investment in research and development; it is possible to treat the latter as an expense (i.e. a cost to the profit and loss account). The decision to capitalise this, i.e. include it as a fixed asset in the balance sheet, would certainly be one to debate, not only with the finance professional within your business but also with the auditors, who will have a view on the legitimacy of such a process and on the various tax implications attached to this.

Current assets

Stock and WIP

From Chapter 5 you will understand that holding optimum levels of stock provides cash and enables efficiencies. As a business increases its sale volumes actual stock value must increase in order to fulfil orders. However, stock days should, unless the supply chain alters, stay stable.

Stock management is an ongoing challenge for businesses. As you can't sell fresh air you have to have stock available for customers but equally too much stock costs money to hold and to store.

In order to budget you should begin by looking at historical stock days (see Chapter 4) and then consider:

1   How efficient was that to meet customer requirements?

2   How realistic is it practically to either increase or decrease these levels?

A budgeting tool such as Sage will allow you to play with 'what if' assumptions such as: what if we hold more stock, how much cash will that absorb and can we afford that investment?

If you decide to de-stock, i.e. release your stock holding to release cash, bear in mind when you are budgeting that things rarely, if ever, happen at the speed you expect so build that into your projections.

Debtors

Your debtors figure is the outstanding amounts owing from your customers for goods or services paid for. These amounts also include VAT.

As with stock calculations one of the most effective budgeting tools is to consider what your optimum debtor days should be – in other words how long, on average, your customers are taking to pay. This needs to take into account your terms of payment. So if you habitually give 60 days' credit to your customers it is not reasonable from a budgeting point of view to assume you collect in 45 days. The quicker you collect your debtors the more cash you free up.

Integrated budgeting tools such as Sage will allow you to look at 'what if we collect in 60 days as opposed to our current collection rate of 75 days' and it will show you the results, in the cash flow budget, of altering your collection.

Cash and bank

This is your reconciled positive cash balances available at a given point in time and, alongside its counterpart of overdrawn cash positions, is often the final balancing figure on a budget as it is this element that affects one of the other calculations.

Current liabilities

These are those debts or obligations that are due for settlement within one year and they include:

Trade creditors (supplier unpaid invoice)

When budgeting think how many days' credit you intend to take before you pay your suppliers (trade creditors are those suppliers of the material cost of sale and do not include overheads e.g. rent, heat, rates, light). Only outstanding liabilities at that point in time will be shown as relevant.

Overdrafts

As with cash at banks, this is the reconciled figure that would fall out of the calculations and will be the anticipated amount by which the business is overdrawn at that point in time.

PAYE and NI

Pay As You Earn and National Insurance – these are the outstanding payments due to HMRC (Her Majesty's Revenue and Customs) for tax and National Insurance you have collected from your employees, and the National Insurance you must pay on their behalf but haven't, at that point in time, paid to HMRC.

Accruals

These are provisions for invoices that are outstanding for goods and services you have utilised but not been charged for. Usually when budgeting these are ignored.

VAT

Value Added Tax is the tax we collect on our sales on behalf of HMRC. When calculating a budget it is important to reconcile the figure on VAT payments which is the difference between VAT collections on sales invoices and VAT paid on purchase invoices.

Other liabilities payable in next 12 months

This will be entirely dependent on your business but consider such things as hire purchase, outstanding balance, short-term loan balance.

Long-term liabilities

Long term is anything due after the 12 month period. Remember it is the outstanding balance we record in the balance sheet, not the payment, which is for the cash flow.

Long-term liabilities may include HP balances longer than 12 months, mortgages and long-term loans.

Share capital

If yours is a start-up business this represents the amount of money invested initially by the shareholders. If it is an established business this will only change if there is an intention to issue (sell) more shares, in which case it will increase by that amount.

Retained earnings (profit reserves)

The profits that are not distributed to shareholders (via dividends) or paid in tax to HMRC are kept back by the company on behalf of the shareholders and represent the accumulation of all their undistributed profits from the date of incorporation i.e. from when the business started.

Cash flow

For many businesses this is the most important budgeting paper as without knowing what cash you require to run either your business or department, it is almost impossible to survive without cash.

Put simply this is a summary of all monies expected to enter a business's bank account less the total of all the money expected to be paid out. The important thing to remember is that not everything that affects the profit and loss account will affect cash flow and not everything that affects the cash flow will affect the profit and loss account (see Chapter 5).

Simple cash flow budgeting steps

1   Start with your current cash position i.e. what you have in the bank (don't forget this must be the reconciled figure). If yours is a new business or department this may be zero.

2   Look at the cash using your sales projections. Consider when you are likely to collect the monies from your customers. Don't forget if you give 30 days' credit to a customer you need to consider that month one sales, at best, will not turn into cash until month two. Also you need to include the VAT element of that sale value as, although this technically is not your cash as it will ultimately be paid to HMRC, it will come into your bank account in the first instance.

A word of advice: cash collection is rarely done to term. In other words just because you allow someone to pay 30 days after the invoice is raised does not mean they will do. They may pay quicker but they are more likely to pay slower, so build this carefully into your cash flow; you can always look to adjust this later if it makes your cash position untenable, but stick to reality. The only person you are kidding if you don't is yourself.

Other cash in

What other revenue streams does your business or department have? For example:

■   Has it loaned monies to a third party, and if so are any sums due for repayment?

■   Does it rent space to another department or business and takes a payment for their use?

■   Do you take deposits from customers?

■   Are shares being sold?

All these represent additional funds into the business. You must now consider in what month or period you will receive these.

Cash out – monthly outgoings

Monthly costs payable in the month of use need to be considered first. These direct costs will almost certainly be wages and salaries, but you must carefully examine every item on your profit and loss account and identify those costs that will need actual payment in the same month.

Don't forget that if any of these costs attract VAT you will need to include that cost in the cash flow even though it won't be in the profit and loss account.

Costs payable in arrears

Most businesses pay in arrears for a large proportion of their costs, especially for supplies of direct materials. After confirming your agreed terms of credit with a given supplier you need to anticipate at what point in the future that cost will have to be paid and of course don't forget to include the VAT.

Costs payable in advance

Some costs require payment in advance of use. For example, rent is usually chargeable three months in advance, and insurance premiums often payable 12 months in advance. So although these costs will be allocated on a monthly basis to your profit and loss account they will come out of your cash flow in lumps at agreed points in time. As always consider if these are variable items and include as relevant.

Periodic payments

These are some costs that a business accrues and then pays for out of cash periodically. These will vary from business to business but many companies pay their VAT payments to HMRC quarterly in arrears. Likewise corporation tax is paid annually. These will therefore appear in the cash flow forecast at the relevant payment date.

Capital sums out

Although the date when you purchase an asset such as a car or a piece of equipment has nothing to do with the profitability of a business, this will affect your cash flow. So consider what you have included in your balance sheet in terms of additions to your assets and when you will need to pay for them (don't forget VAT!).

What NOT to include

Do not include in the cash flow non-cash expenses such as depreciation which, although it reduces profit and reduces asset value, has nothing at all to do with cash.

Net position

This is based on a calculation of all the inputs (cash in) and all the outputs (cash out) and gives you your budgeted cash position, positive or negative, at the end of each period.

Review and change

So you now have your anticipated cash position; the question is, is it satisfactory? That is, do you have access to funding if your cash position is negative and if it is positive is it at the level you require?

Whatever the answers to these questions go back and revisit every line in the budget and play a game I call 'what if'.

- What if I don't make the sales I anticipate?
- What if customers pay later than I expected?
- What if I don't get the credit terms I anticipate from my suppliers and have to pay quicker?
- What if I have to reduce my prices or prices to me are increased?

These 'what if' scenarios are more technically called sensitivities and are an essential part of budgeting as what you first anticipate rarely happens. It makes sense commercially to run various options if for no other reason than to test your own assumptions.

Back to forecasting

Now you have set and agreed your budget, it is possible there may be a sign-off process (i.e. agreement) internally and externally. If you are seeking to borrow money, your funders will have to be happy with these numbers and how robust they are.

Essentially the budget is now a fixed target and the forecast is the financial tool that is used to ensure that the management team can see information that is as up-to-date as possible as the forecast now provides the user with an anticipated outcome on performance. This allows future decisions on any changes needed on strategy to be based on actual results.

Ultimately these are all just plans and plans have a way of going wrong. As

Burns put it, 'the best laid plans of mice and men gang aft aglae'. In business there is another saying, 'failing to plan is planning to fail', and in a fragile economy it is very important to have a budget, keep it updated with a forecast and use this plan to set targets for the important departments in your business.

Only this way can you hope to steer your business through to success.

8

The Management Accounts Pack

The management accounts pack tells the story of the business performance. For all but the smallest of businesses it is an essential business tool for the board of directors and senior management team. These documents allow those not involved in the daily minutiae of the business to see what has happened in the organisation from a financial point of view over the period that the pack covers.

This chapter examines what a great management accounts pack should contain and what it shouldn't. It will examine distribution protocol and layout principles and how to interpret the data it includes. It will also look at what answers it should provide and what questions it should seek to address. It will examine whether it is possible to provide too much information and a note about the importance of timeliness in its production.

What is a management accounts pack?

Packs are extremely varied so it's not possible to describe a typical accounts pack. But there are some common factors and an example of a good quality pack is given in Appendix A.

The most important requirement is that the pack should relate to the needs of the business and be tailored for those who need to see it. It should not follow a formula on the basis of 'we have always done it like this' unless it's been very, very successful. If you keep doing what you have always done you will keep getting what you have always got!

The basis of a pack

From the premise that the pack should relate to the needs of the particular business and not anyone else's, you could argue that every pack will be unique.

When we talk about 'pack' this does suggest a certain volume of information but the size of the 'pack' will be more or less dependent on the complexity of the business and its intended audience. Too much information can be as useless as too little and knowing when enough is enough is not an easy concept to grasp.

I have known a number of finance professionals spend two weeks of every month compiling this data and then for much of it to be given a cursory glance or not even looked at. On the other hand, and especially for non-executive directors who have little if any day-to-day knowledge of the business, a one-page synopsis may be wholly inadequate.

The minimum content should ideally include the critical financial papers:

■ Balance sheet
■ Profit and loss accounts for the month and for the YTD (year to date)
■ Funds flow.

These should be compared to budget, prior year and forecast and should include a written summary of the key issues in the month.

It's entirely possible to include much, much more and I will explore the relevance of additional information in this chapter. This will help you understand better the financial issues of your business.

What is the real point of a management accounts pack?

These packs are not something that can be produced in a few minutes and possibly not even in a few hours. As such it will inevitably take up a considerable amount of precious management time in their creation, reading and absorbing. It's important to make these worthwhile for the reader and in particular to understand why you are creating them.

Internal users

The management accounts pack is of principal use and value to

■ The board of directors
■ The executive management team.

The board of directors

Directors have a legal duty to understand the financial mechanics of their business sufficiently to allow them to discharge their duties fully. Some directors will have a more comprehensive understanding of the finances of the business than others but this does not in any way excuse ignorance from those less financially adept.

With this in mind, the person producing the document must appreciate that the level of understanding amongst a board will be diverse. There are a number of ways this can be addressed but there is an underlying principle in the production of all management information called KISS – 'keep it simple stupid'.

It doesn't mean that the value of the pack should be diluted in any way, rather it should achieve the exact opposite if it is constructed correctly. If the person both presenting and preparing the pack speaks in a language the audience can relate to and understand, it's more likely that the information will be useful.

Very often board directors are reluctant to admit a lack of understanding for fear of looking ignorant. They may even feel embarrassed by what seems to them like a stupid question. If you can relate to this, remember there is rarely a stupid question. It is likely to be the very question someone else wishes to ask but was afraid of voicing.

Some finance directors who prepare and present the document will understand their audience. Sadly only a few finance directors speak in financial language that their fellow directors understand. Asking for clarification is the most sensible route to take and, if you are a director, it is in line with your legal obligations.

The executive management team

In some businesses these groups of people may be one and the same as the directors. However, when the management team are acting in a functional role they will be running a department. This may be, for example, sales, operations, HR or marketing. In other businesses, the directors and the executive management will be an entirely different group of people. As with a board of directors, it is usual that the financial understanding of the executives will be diverse.

Whilst a board is looking at the information in relation to the company's total performance, a particular executive may be interested in certain elements of the pack. For instance:

- The sales executive may be interested in gross margin, sales, or new customers won and lost
- The HR manager may be interested in head count, leavers and new starters
- The operations manager may want to look at efficiency ratios in the warehouse.

However, all executives need at least a basic understanding of how their own department is affected by other departments. For example, sales activity, which increases sales volume, could create staffing issues and operational concerns. Although they may initially be seen as isolated activity, all areas of a report will have a correlation to another department.

It is likely that the management accounts pack for these executives may be more comprehensive than for the Board.

For the head of sales exemplary content should include the following:

- **Aged debtors listing** – that is the list of customers, what they owe and how old or overdue this is for payment
- **Gross margin – or gross profit**, i.e. the difference between sales and cost of sales by customer, product, product categories or region.

If the head of sales has responsibility for a number of sales staff it is also important to have a breakdown of performance by individuals either against targets or prior year or both.

For the head of operations detailed clarification in this pack may include the following:

- Fleet or individual vehicle efficiency
- Analysis of delivery times
- Product returns
- Stock days and stock turn.

For the head of HR some of the following would undoubtedly help them advise the board on staffing issues:

- Sick days taken
- Absence ratios
- New starters and leavers
- Recruitment costs v. budgeted costs

■ Staff to sales ratios.

For the head of finance (who may have additional duties in terms of preparing reports for third parties such as funders etc.) it is likely he or she will be interested in:

■ Margin percentages, for instance gross margin and net profit

■ Covenants that have to be maintained such as interest cover or dividend cover.

This person may also be responsible for funding efficiencies such as

■ Debtor collection and creditor payment monitoring

■ Cash collection

■ Financial targets generally being met.

This sort of management data is unlikely to be closely reviewed by the directors but is vital for the management team because it keeps them focused on specific areas that may need their attention.

External users

Bank or stakeholder covenants

As part of their formal engagement with your business, a covenant (a binding promise) may require that your bank or another influential stakeholder has the right to be provided with such financial information. It is also possible that failure to comply will result in penalties including, for example, the removal of a bank facility.

In all likelihood the only external user of a management accounts pack is someone who has the right to request this as part of an investment agreement. Generally a management accounts pack is only for the management and board.

The right of an external person to see such information may be absolute but is more likely to be related to only certain parts of the pack. It would be unusual for an external party to want to see the amount of detail that we've discussed. Whatever the situation I recommend that you provide the external user with **exactly** what they have asked for and no more and **certainly no less**.

Although this may seem obvious, my experience is that there is a tendency to do one of the following:

- Produce far too much detail to someone who is only interested in specifics

- Produce too little detail either because results are not as planned or the preparation isn't as thorough as it should be. *This may be because it is not seen by those preparing it as important.*

Both of these scenarios could prove to be a serious problem.

Too much information doesn't allow the user to focus on what's important and so distracts them from what is required – it can also be very annoying personally, if with limited time you are faced with an overwhelming amount of data so cannot get quickly to the salient point.

Too little information is also annoying for the user, who may have to analyse this and report to yet another party and finds the actual facts are inaccurate or insufficient. You should also be aware that where there is limited data to make a clear decision and therefore assumptions have to be made, it is more likely that a negative at worst or a cautious view will be taken.

Provide exactly what is required and in a timely manner. If this is not possible then above all explain yourself **before** you are asked to do so.

How the packs change

Evolution

Good management accounts packs should evolve and develop over years in relation to the changing needs of the business and the economic climate.

Some of the details discussed may be less necessary in a small start-up than in a highly developed international businesses. Having said that, there is an argument for establishing good business reporting sooner rather than later. In the early days of a new business the problem encountered with producing comprehensive packs is one of time, as an owner-manager in a start-up is preoccupied almost entirely with establishing a foothold in his or her market.

But these days, accounting technology means that even a relatively modest business can electronically produce reasonably accurate management accounts, which even if they are not wholly accurate at least give a good indicator of performance each month.

Revolution

Having sat on multiple boards during my career, I have seen the good, the bad and the indifferent management accounts pack. During that time what has become clear is that periodically it is necessary to simply scrap the whole lot and start again. Knowing when this is necessary should be instinctive but often is not so. Substance seems to outweigh form as all parties struggle on with what is not an acceptable management tool.

My role is often one of non-executive director and so perhaps as the person with a fresh pair of eyes I can take a more objective view of the information and make suggestions for improvement based on best practice seen elsewhere.

If you have no such third-party objective advisor, it is a useful activity to see what other companies practice. This can be via friends or business contacts, who may be willing to share their own information on a corporate basis. The point is, try to be honest about what works and what doesn't and then go about making it work for you and the other parties who need to use the pack. A management accounts pack will never be quite right but it can definitely be all wrong and admitting this is the first step to getting into shape.

Who prepares the management accounts pack?

The size of the business will dictate who prepares the pack, but by and large the production of this rests in the hands of the finance department, be that one or 21 people.

Although it may be this team that co-ordinates the data they are reliant on multiple departments for its content and therefore the whole management team is best recognising this and must be sensitive to deadlines that the finance department may need to be adhered to so that all the information that needs to be fully integrated and presented in the agreed format is available.

The finance department do not operate in isolation, however much this may seem to be the case. In order to produce a credible and useful accounts pack all functional departments must be willing and able to assist with delivery of information.

Outside the finance department, deadlines for data sharing may seem tiresome or unimportant but it's a fact that all financial analysis cannot be completed without this other management information being available. For example, new starters and leavers information and sales representatives performance returns must be given to the finance department or they simply cannot do their job and then the whole management accounts pack is delayed and so everyone is affected. Very often the management accounts pack is produced to meet a deadline, for instance a board meeting date.

When the production of information is date sensitive:

a   The finance department should communicate this to the other departments that they rely on for certain data

b   The other departments should give some priority to the production of such information.

It is only with this relatively obvious co-operation that deadlines can be met.

Current and future use and value of management accounts packs

Current value

A good quality management accounts pack which has critical emphasis on requirements for the business, has salient sections created in a manner that can be monitored, is in a readable and understandable format and is as up-to-date as possible is invaluable. It allows the user to make decisions about the business and take action as necessary, be that remedial or maximising a particular position. A really good management accounts pack has value in helping to run a better business or department but it does require focus:

1   **On the cultural business factors.** These will vary from business to business but, for instance, for a business that is a heavy borrower, there should be a focus on operating profit and whether the business in question is generally doing enough to cover its interest payments.

2   **On its construction.** In other words consider the audience. How financially astute are they? Are they more comfortable looking at graphs, for instance, than pages of numbers?

3   **On its timeliness.** Largely information that is over a month old becomes less and less relevant as the chance to action anything or to build on an opportunity has lapsed.

Of course, it's pointless producing management accounts if they don't lead to actions. However good and focused the pack is, if it's not used as a management tool then it's been a less than worthwhile exercise.

Future value

Management accounts are very useful in the budgeting process discussed in Chapter 7. They provide an excellent historical and detailed summary of the business, which allows the individual preparing the budgets to be more accurate in estimating what worked and what worked less well.

For businesses which must legally or which choose to have an audit, good quality management account packs:

1 Make the auditor's job much easier, as problems should have been identified and dealt with throughout the year instead of at the year end.

2 May allow you to negotiate lower audit fees as your auditor should be more comfortable with the information.

And (3) for anyone who wishes to ultimately sell their business, good quality management accounts packs assist with the due diligence activity and keep negotiations on business value as tight as possible. This is because price chipping is less likely if the integrity of the financial data is intact and of appropriate substance.

In summary

Although there is no perfect management accounts pack there are some sound good practice principles:

1 Fit the pack to the user

2 Make it timely

3 Keep it well presented and easy to follow and use

4 Keep asking how it can be improved.

And never lose sight of its inherent short-term and long-term value.

9

Capital Investment (Capex) and Investment Appraisal

Although it is unlikely that a non-financial person will be involved directly in the mathematical process of compiling a Capex evaluation, their input may be required in the data-gathering exercise and also in the articulation of the business case as opposed to the purely financial case that is part of any presentation to an investment committee or financier.

Understanding the arithmetical process then should both help the non-financial person prepare appropriate documentation for submission and assist with their commercial presentation.

Appraising an investment opportunity before committing to investment spend is commercially sensible. Capital is scarce for many businesses and spending it needs to be carefully considered. In terms of returns required, coupled with the multiple calls on capital available, appraising each option thoroughly is the most reliable approach to capital allocation.

This chapter will consider

- Why you should appraise an investment
- How this should be undertaken and the various methods
- Risk management and identification.

Why is the appraisal process necessary?

- Capital expenditure often involves investment of substantial funds, which could be used elsewhere.

■ Funds can be tied up for many years and be incapable of being liquidated.

■ Risk management minimises risk and the cost of maintaining company performance.

Some examples of potential investment issues may include:

1 International currencies. An investment appraisal committee may have to consider whether borrowing for a particular project should be segregated from the normal borrowings. Thus an acquisition in Europe may be funded by euro borrowing long-term, rather than through sterling overdraft funds. In such a case it is not just the total but the nature of funds available which should be considered.

2 Should projects be considered in isolation and reviewed as to whether they can stand alone on their own borrowings (for example in relation to leasing equipment), or should they be looked at in totality along with all the business investment needs?

To some extent, all business decisions have within them an intuitive element. This may be considered the same as taking a bet and as with all gambling, sometimes the wins are spectacular but very often the losses are phenomenal. Research shows that most mergers are unsuccessful in producing business benefits, that in the first few months post deal production may be reduced by up to half, and that many companies formed by merger perform well below industry average.

This means that all appraisals should consider the following:

1 If an investment is to be made, the expectation certainly from shareholders and funders would be that the future return outweighs the original investment at a return on that investment (ROI) that is at an acceptable rate for the business and

2 That the appropriate amount of funds are invested in the right projects and in a timely manner.

Bear in mind that too little investment or investment made at the wrong time can be just as damaging to a business as too much investment.

Easy win and across the board capital expenditure (Capex) cuts are unlikely to work in the long term. This is because shareholders tend to be attracted to businesses that invest in Capex provided such investments increase profits: out of those profits dividends are paid. So we can see that well thought out investments improve businesses. The critical factor is the robustness of the investment appraisal process.

Later we will be exploring the ways in which an investment can be appraised financially but in the first place you should consider the actual project itself and then its impact on the company.

Project appraisal

As with any sort of appraisal process, it's important to start with having clearly defined objectives of what exactly this investment is meant to achieve as well as the process required to achieve this desired end result.

It is very easy to overspend on a project as we all know to our cost. Anyone capable of selling is more than capable of selling the benefits and spending less time than needed on the pitfalls.

It is also common to move from simple discrete requirements to a fully fledged overspend. For example, a new piece of equipment for a factory line becomes a complete fit-out. So remember not to let the best become the enemy of the good.

The critical process

Focus on the essentials and bear in mind the following:

1   Have a well defined project that identifies the required outcome
2   If any additional requirements are later identified revert back to (1) and ask if it adds anything to the brief and whether it is essential or just desirable
3   Do not be tempted to change your initial objectives unless there have been significant changes in direction.

Corporate needs versus project needs

Just because an investment appears pertinent and relevant at a project level does not necessarily mean it is appropriate at corporate level. As there are multiple calls on limited funding any investment must be considered alongside the overall business objectives and the strategic direction of the company. This will at least allow some sort of prioritisation.

In a large and diverse business, it is entirely possible that multiple investment projects may be considered, some of which may have similar objectives. On the basis that not all will be taken up for corporate review before the final decision, in the worst case scenario this could create an overspend as the improvements required were already being dealt with by another project.

In order to minimise this capital mismanagement, you need to note the following.

Optimising capital investment decisions

There are a number of reasons why investment appraisal doesn't achieve desired results. One reason may be lack of financial detail (we will explore later what is optimum data), though in fact it's possible that too much financial detail can mask analytical rigour because the analyst has insufficient understanding of possible technical or even strategic alternatives.

But the following points are critical.

Major obstacles in making capital investment work

1 **Business objectives not understood by the management.**

   You can minimise this obstruction if you ask a very simple question: *'Will this investment improve our chances of achieving our business objective and if so how and when?'*

2 **Alternative strategies to attain the desired result have not been fully explored.**

   A very simple question is *'Does a repair achieve the same results as buying new?'*

3 **Inappropriate methodologies have been used to evaluate the investment.**

   As you will see later in this chapter, there are a number of ways to analyse a project. Some are more appropriate to a particular scenario than others. For the manager who wants to ensure that their investment requirement is prioritised, it may be tempting to resort to an appraisal process that delivers the more compelling positive rationale even if it's based on a less than appropriate process. In other words, make the results fit the desired outcome.

4 **Project delivery.**

   What works on paper for a project appraisal doesn't always translate in reality. Largely this is due to communication with those who have to deliver the project but who may possibly have had little or no involvement in the appraisal and development process. Overruns on time and contingency costs should always be part of the investment appraisal analysis. However, far too often there is too much optimism on fulfilment capacity to accurately account for the inevitable delays.

To help prevent unnecessary failure on Capex projects, consider the following:

1 Have clear, well defined objectives that are transparent and well documented.

2 Understand and confirm whether the investment philosophy is short-term or long-term: does the business have a policy of expecting high returns on its investments in a minimum period (anything from a few months to a few years dependent on investment type) or is it actually investing for the long-term (five years plus)?

3 Ask what would happen if we did not do this investment at all, or if we did it at a later stage.

4 Question and evaluate other possibilities.

5 Ask if you have used the most appropriate methodology (see later in this chapter) to evaluate the investment and whether the assumptions you have used are valid.

6 Have clearly defined benchmarks and key performance indicators so that project evaluation is determinate. In other words the benefit of the investment can be checked against agreed criteria.

7 Ensure you have risk-checked the whole process and are aware of risks and have a methodology to mitigate them.

The nature of investment decisions and the appraisal process

Different investment types have different considerations – *consider first* what are the benefits from investing.

Benefits from investing

▪ Savings
  ▪ In staff costs
  ▪ In other operating costs
▪ Income benefits because of improvement/enhancements
  ▪ More sales income
  ▪ More efficient systems

- Savings in staff time
- Cash from sale of currently in use assets
- Intangible benefits
  - Customer satisfaction
  - Better decision making.

Then consider the category of the investment type.

Categories

- Capital expenditure
- Revenue expenditure
- Working capital expenditure.

Capital expenditure is expenditure which results in the acquisition of fixed assets or an improvement in the earning capacity of fixed assets. The benefits from capital expenditure are likely to be seen over the long term rather than immediately.

Revenue expenditure is expenditure which results in maintaining the existing earning capacity of fixed assets, i.e. the repair rather than the initial cost. It also includes expenditure related to selling and distribution expenses, administration expenses and finance charges.

Investments in **working capital** involve funds invested in resources such as stock before it can be recovered from sales of the finished product or service. Such funds are only committed for a short period of time.

Risk

Risk is a matter of interpretation in part and there are proven methods to analyse this but first consider acceptable risk.

It is feasible for a profitable project to be rejected on the grounds that the risk is so overwhelming that it would be unacceptable to the organisation. This does not mean that the project is rejected for ever, it merely means that it is beyond the scope of the existing organisation. A fresh analysis will be required to consider whether the project can be partially undertaken or whether it is sensible to bring in joint venture partners etc.

Approved methodology

Cash

Only one thing really matters ultimately in an investment appraisal: CASH.

It comes in three forms:

Cash in
Cash out
Cash not in or not out.

Project appraisal must be ruthless about cash identification.

Cash in

From sales (normal or exceptional)
Disposals – from fixed or other assets.

Cash out

Real cash costs – not apportionments or allocations.

Cash not in or cash not out

These are cash flows avoided or opportunity costs. They need to be the next best alternative in terms of cost, not unrealistic savings or incomes. Thus if a process is used to make a product with a profit of £10 and this prevents another product with a profit of £8 being produced, then the opportunity cost of using the process is £8 more than the cost of the process itself. There is a cost of the opportunity forgone. In the same way efficiency savings can only generate cash if the costs are truly avoided.

For instance, saving space costs at head office only reduces the rent if the head office is sold. Merely emptying the space achieves very little.

All methodologies must utilise sensitivities to test and re-test the outcome. This helps manage risk.

In any project proposal all numbers are mercurial. For example, sales figures will inevitably vary. Professional fees may be unknown and variable in time.

To manage these unknowns consider the following:

■ Identify **all possible risks**

■ Quantify their impact on the project.

For example, exposure to foreign exchange rate movements can be reduced by taking out forward contracts (i.e. buying at an agreed fixed rate for a given period). This increases the cost of the project but reduces the risk.

Sales in the future are always subject to risk but this can be mitigated by agreeing volume and prices with known large customers in advance of starting the project. Again, this will impact on the project's profitability but may reduce risks to an acceptable level.

Catalogue all assumptions

A good investment appraisal document will not only include the key assumptions and the sensitivity of the project to those assumptions but also include a brief outline of the best and the worst case as well as a note of the total cost should the project fail to achieve its objectives and need to be cancelled. Always, always carry out a 'what if' scenario to ensure you have covered every angle.

Arithmetical appraisal techniques

Before examining specific appraisal methodology consider first the type of investment, as it may be relevant and necessary to apply a different type of methodology to a specific expenditure type. The four types are broadly:

- Maintenance – replacing old or obsolete assets for example
- Profitability – quality, productivity or location improvement for example
- Expansion – new products, markets and so on
- Indirect – social and welfare facilities.

You should also consider that projects that are not necessarily meant to generate profits should still undergo an investment appraisal. This is principally to identify the best way of achieving the project goods.

The typical methods used for investment appraisal are

- Payback period
- Accounting rate of return (ARR)
- Net present value
- Internal rate of return (IRR).

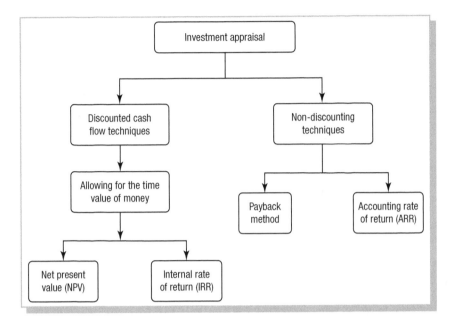

The first two are called non-discounted cash flow techniques; the second two are called discounted cash flow techniques.

Non-discounted cash flow techniques

The non-discounted cash techniques are

■ Payback, and

■ Accounting rate of return (ARR).

First of all it is necessary to consider what costs are to be 'paid back'.

■ **Relevant costs** are costs that are incurred as a result of a decision, and include

  ■ Opportunity costs

  ■ Variable costs, e.g. working capital cost

  ■ Assorted costs, e.g. training.

■ **Non-relevant costs** include

  ■ Sunk costs

  ■ Committed costs

  ■ Overhead absorbed arbitrarily

  ■ Non-cash-flow-related costs.

The payback method

The payback method is the method that calculates the time it takes for cash in from a capital investment project to equal the cash out or cost out per year.

A business might work to a target payback period of a particular length, set internally as a target, and so it may decline a capital project if a project is unable to deliver within that timescale.

But indirectly payback should be a *first* screening process. Other methods should always be used.

As it is cash that matters in these particular calculations, payback is calculated using **profits before depreciation** as depreciation has no effect on cash.

Payback is not a fool-proof process. Look at the example in Exhibit 9.1.

Exhibit 9.1

	Project A	Project B
	£	£
Capital cost of asset	60,000	60,000
Profits before depreciation		
Year 1	20,000	50,000
Year 2	30,000	20,000
Year 3	40,000	5,000
Year 4	50,000	5,000
Year 5	60,000	5,000

Project A pays back in Year 3 (one quarter of the way through Year 3). Project B pays back halfway through Year 2. Using payback alone to judge projects, project B would be preferred. But the returns from project A total £200,000 over its life and are much higher than the returns from project B, which totals just £85,000.

Payback period is the simplest of all the tools available. You just ask how long the project takes to pay back. It is an easy concept to explain to non-financial people. The disadvantages are that the tool ignores the profit of the whole life of the project and the time value of money. But in summary, from a ranking perspective, the best project is the one with the shortest payback period.

The advantages of payback

■ It is easy to calculate and understand

■ It is a measure of risk since rapid payback minimises the risk

■ It is useful approach for ranking projects where a company faces liquidity constraints

■ It is useful for where future cash flows are difficult to predict

■ It uses objective cash flows rather than subjective accounting profits.

The disadvantages of payback

■ It ignores the time value of money

■ It does not measure the return on investment

■ It ignores cash flows that occur after the payback date

■ It is unable to distinguish between projects with the same payback period

■ It has to be used with other methods to give a fuller picture

■ The choice of any cut-off payback period is done arbitrarily.

Use of the method

The payback period technique is the single most widely used technique of all the techniques currently reported to be in use virtually anywhere in the world! It is so widely used for two major reasons:

■ It is the simplest method available

■ It acts as a proxy for risk.

The first reason should be self-explanatory. The second reason means that most people would appear to be risk-averse – they do not like taking risks – and thus they prefer to minimise or offset risk altogether.

Accounting rate of return (ARR)

Accounting rate of return (ARR) expresses the average accounting profit as a percentage of the capital outlay.

The capital outlay (the denominator in the ARR calculation) may be expressed as the initial investment or as the average investment in the project.

The decision rule is that projects with an ARR above a defined minimum are acceptable; the greater the ARR, the more desirable the project.

Formula

ARR means estimating the accounting rate of return that a project or capital spend should yield. If it exceeds a target rate of return then the project is acceptable.

There are two different ways of calculating the ARR.

$$ARR = \frac{\text{Average annual accounting profit}}{\text{Initial investment}} \times 100\%$$

$$ARR = \frac{\text{Average annual accounting profit}}{\text{Average investment}} \times 100\%$$

The average investment is calculated as ½ (initial investment + final or scrap value).

Note that this method ignores cash flow and is concerned with profit only.

An example using initial investment

Capital expenditure is £110,000. Plans are for this to generate annual profits before depreciation of £24,000 for five years. Scrap value is calculated at £10,000 at the end of the fifth year.

$$\text{Average profit} = \frac{\text{Profits before depreciation} - \text{depreciation}}{5}$$

$$= \frac{(£24,000 \times 5) - (£110,000 - £10,000)}{5}$$

$$= £4,000 \text{ p.a.}$$

$$ARR = \frac{£4,000}{£110,000} \times 100\% = 3.6\%$$

The advantages of ARR

- It is easy to use, calculate and understand
- It is widely accepted as a reliable measure
- It can be calculated from available accounting data
- It shows the impact an investment will have on a company's profit.

The disadvantages of ARR

- It fails to take into account the project life

■ It fails to take into account the timing of cash flow

■ It uses subjective accounting profit as opposed to objective cash flow.

Discounting

Discounting starts with the future value (a sum of money receivable or payable at a future date) and converts the future value to a present value, which is the cash equivalent now of the future value.

For example, if a company expects to earn a (compound) rate of return of 10% on its investments, how much would it need to invest now to have the following investments?

a   £11,000 after 1 year

b   £12,100 after 2 years

c   £13,310 after 3 years

The answer is £10,000 in each case and we can calculate it by discounting.

The discounting formula to calculate the present value (X) of a future sum of money (V) at the end of n time periods is $X = V/(1 + r)^n$

a   after 1 year, $£11,000/1.10 = £10,000$

b   after 2 years, $£12,100/1.10^2 = £10,000$

c   after 3 years, $£13,310/1.10^3 = £10,000$

The timing of cash flows is taken into account by discounting them. The effect of discounting is to give a bigger value per £1 for cash flows that occur earlier. £1 earned after one year will be worth more than £1 earned after two years, which in turn will be worth more than £1 earned after five years and so on.

The discount rate (r) used when calculating the present value is the relevant interest rate (or cost of capital) to the entity in question.

Discount factors

In the calculations above, we were converting each cash flow into its present value by effectively multiplying by a discount factor. This discount factor is calculated as $1/(1 + r)$.

The calculations could be presented as follows:

	Multiply by 10% discount factor	Present value £
After 1 year £11,000	× 1/1.l0	10,000
After 2 years £12,100	× $1/(1.l0)^2$	10,000
After 3 years £13,310	× $1/(1.l0)^3$	10,000

Timing of cash flows: conventions used in discounted cash flow techniques

Discounting reduces the value of future cash flows to a present value equivalent and so is clearly concerned with the timing of the cash flows. As a general rule, the following guidelines may be applied.

- A cash outlay to be incurred at the beginning of an investment project ('now') occurs in time 0. The present value of £1 now, in time 0, is £1 regardless of the value of the discount rate r.

- A cash flow which occurs during the course of a time period is assumed to occur all at once at the end of the time period (at the end of the year). Receipts of £10,000 during time period 1 are therefore taken to occur at the end of time period 1.

- A cash flow which occurs at the beginning of a time period is taken to occur at the end of the previous time period. Therefore a cash outlay of £5,000 at the beginning of time period 2 is taken to occur at the end of time period 1.

Discounted cash flow techniques

There are two methods which use discounted cash flow:

- Net present value (NPV), and
- Internal rate of return (IRR).

Net present value method

The net present value (NPV) method is a key appraisal technique. It accepts projects with a positive NPV. It is the value obtained by discounting all cash flows and inflows of a capital investment project by a chosen target of return or cost of capital.

Discounted cash flow (DCF) techniques are used in calculating the net present value of a series of cash flows. This measures the change in shareholder wealth now as a result of accepting a project.

NPV = present value of cash inflows **less** present value of cash outflows.

▪ If the **NPV is positive** it means that the cash inflows from a project will yield a return in excess of the cost of capital, and so the project should be undertaken if the cost of capital is the organisation's target rate of return.

▪ If the **NPV is negative**, it means that the cash inflows from a project will yield a return below the cost of capital and so the project should not be undertaken if the cost of the capital is the organisation's target rate of return.

▪ If the **NPV is exactly zero**, the cash inflows from a project will yield a return which is exactly the same as the cost of capital and so if the cost of capital is the organisation's target rate of return, the project will have a neutral impact on shareholder wealth and therefore would not be worth undertaking because of the inherent risks in any project.

The cost of capital is the cost of funds that a company raises or the return that investors expect to be paid for putting funds into the company. It is therefore the minimum return that a company should make from its own investments.

The idea behind the NPV technique is that it DISCOUNTS the cash flows generated by an asset back to the present day: thus the NPV technique is concerned with the time value of money. An example is shown in Exhibit 9.2.

Exhibit 9.2   Net present value calculation

Year	Cash flows (£)	Discount factors (15%)	Present values (£)
0	−25,000	1.0000	−25,000.00
1	20,000	0.8696	17,392.00
2	25,000	0.7561	18,902.50
3	12,500	0.6575	8,218.75
4	9,000	0.5718	5,146.20
Net present value			24,659.45

The residual value is taken to be zero.

Advantages of NPV

▨ It is directly linked to the objective of maximising shareholder value as it measures, in absolute (£) terms, the effect of taking on the project now, i.e. year 0.

▨ It considers the time value of money, i.e. the further away the cash flow the less it is worth in present terms.

▨ It considers all relevant cash flows, so that it is unaffected by the accounting policies which confuse profit-based investment appraisal techniques such as ARR.

▨ Risk can be incorporated into decision making by adjusting the company's discount rate.

▨ It provides clear, unambiguous decisions, i.e. if the NPV is positive, accept; if it is negative, reject.

Internal rate of return (IRR)

▨ The internal rate of return (IRR) is the DCF rate of return that a project is expected to achieve. It is the discount rate at which the NPV is zero.

▨ If the IRR exceeds a target rate of return, the project would be worth undertaking.

The internal rate of return (IRR) is the rate of return promised by an investment project over its useful life. The internal rate of return is calculated by finding the discount rate that equates the present value of a project's cash outflow with the present value of its cash inflow. In other words, the internal rate of return is the discount rate that will cause the net present value of a project to be equal to zero.

An example

A business is considering the purchase of a piece of equipment. This will cost £16,950 and will have a useful life of ten years. It will only have a negligible scrap value at its end of life, which can be ignored. The equipment will do the job much more quickly than the old equipment and would result in a labour saving of £3,000 per year.

To compute the internal rate of return promised by the piece of equipment you must find the discount rate that will cause the net present value of the project to be zero.

The simplest and most direct approach when the net cash inflow is the same every year is to divide the investment in the project by the expected net annual cash inflow. This computation will yield a factor from which the internal rate of return can be determined.

The formula or equation is as follows:

$$\text{Factor of internal rate of return} = \frac{\text{Investment required}}{\text{Net annual cash inflow}}$$

$$= £16,950/£3,000$$

$$= 5.65$$

This is the discount factor that will equate a series of £3,000 cash inflows with a present investment of £16,950.

Initial cost	£16,500
Life of the project (years)	10
Annual cost savings	£3,000
Salvage value	0

Item	Years	Amount of cash flow	12% (annual discount rate) factor	Present value of cash flows
Annual cost savings	1–10	£3,000	5.65	£16,950
Initial investment	Now	(£16,950)	1,000	(£16,950)
Net present value				£0

Notice that using a 12% discount rate equates the present value of the annual cash inflows with the present value of the investment required in the project, leaving a zero net present value. The 12% rate therefore represents the internal rate of return promised by the project.

The advantages of IRR

- ▪ It recognises the time value of money
- ▪ It is based on objective cash flows as opposed to subjective profits
- ▪ It allows for the timing of cash flows
- ▪ It is a universally accepted method
- ▪ It is easily understood as a percentage return on investment.

The disadvantages of IRR

- ▪ It does not indicate the size of investment

- It can give conflicting signals with mutually exclusive projects
- It assumes that earnings throughout the period of the investment are re-invested at the same rate of return
- NPV is easier to calculate than the IRR.

But the major disadvantage is that the IRR calculations are relatively complex and the concept is a difficult one to present to other managers, unless they have had sufficient financial training.

Other considerations

Before finalising your appraisal consider the following.

Inflation

Should you allow for inflation?

- **Real cash flows** are cash flows which have had the effects of inflation removed.
- **Monetary cash flows** are cash flows that have not had the effect of inflation removed. They are the cash flows that actually occur – the cash that is actually received or paid out.

When should you use the real rate and when should you use the monetary rate? If the real cash flows are being used, then the rate of return must be the real rate of return, i.e. the rate that excludes inflation. If the money cash flows are being used then the rate of return must be the money rate of return, i.e. the rate that includes inflation.

The money rate of return is sometimes called the nominal rate.

Advantages and disadvantages of using inflation

The advantage of allowing for inflation is that it is realistic to anticipate that prices will increase.

The disadvantage is that it is extremely difficult to forecast the rate of inflation.

Taxation

Organisations must pay tax and the effect of undertaking a project will be to increase or decrease tax payments each year. These incremental tax cash flows should be included in the cash flows of the project for discounting to arrive at the project's NPV.

Taxes can affect the calculations of DCF. You have to calculate the writing down allowance (WDA) but the timing of tax relief can be complicated.

Risk and uncertainty

The appraisal processes we discussed at the outset of this chapter are largely to do with risk management. So consider the difference between risk and uncertainty.

- **Risk** can be applied to a situation where there are several possible outcomes and, on the basis of past relevant experience, probabilities can be assigned to the various outcomes that could prevail.
- **Uncertainty** can be applied to a situation where there are several possible outcomes, but there is little past relevant experience to enable the probability of the possible outcomes to be predicted.

In order to take these issues into account, all projects should contain a sensitivity analysis.

Sensitivity analysis

Sensitivity analysis assesses how responsive the project is to changes in the variables used to do the calculations. They work on the process of asking 'what if' questions – for example what if:

- Selling price increased/decreased
- Sales volume increased/decreased
- Cost of capital becomes onerous or even unavailable
- Initial set-up costs are more than originally anticipated.

All these should be considered as part of a review.

Ultimately decisions have to be made and although this chapter has given you sufficient data to consider an investment the final decision is a human one and in most cases it is usually hindsight that tells us if the right choice was made.

10

Health Checks and KPIs

Business health checks

Carrying out a health check may have been forced upon you and your organisation or may be a choice.

Whatever the circumstances, checking out the performance of a business or department against agreed milestones on a regular basis (probably annually) is good business practice. This is true for many practical reasons which are discussed in this chapter, but there's one great reason and that's because it allows you to focus on the business rather than be preoccupied working inside it.

Business health checks and key performance indicators have been essential business tools for many years. The real essence of any business health check is to make an assessment of the company against predetermined ideal criteria.

Once such a diagnosis or assessment has been carried out, a series of measures to improve or remedy the given conditions can be considered. These 'health checks' can take place randomly or even better on an ongoing systematic basis and will ensure that the business is monitored and any health problems identified before they become severe or even terminal.

This chapter will examine the various different ways to carry out a business health check and the benefits and potential pitfalls from such an exercise. It will also provide the reader with an insight into the critical success factors and key performance indicators that need monitoring. With the use of appropriate diagnostic tools you should be able to ensure that a potential business problem is resolved entirely satisfactorily.

Although a business health check may include what on the face of it appears non-financial matters, for instance staff turnover or morale, often there will be a less obvious financial implication. In this instance its the cost of recruitment and the downtime lost if morale is low, so do not dismiss such measures as not relevant to finance without considering the broader issue.

Business health check definition

A business health check is an intense, short-duration review of the critical processes involved in a business or within an identified area of the business. Its aim is to identify opportunities to improve the efficiency and effectiveness of the business.

Why bother with a health check?

When you're busy working in your business, it can be difficult to step back and see what's really happening.

- You become blind to inefficiences and missed opportunities.

- You continue to do things not because it's the right thing to do but because 'that's how we've always done it'.

- You can become emotinally tied up in the daily goings-on and unable to make objective, effective business decisions.

- You can end up surrounded by 'yes' men and women who don't give you any ideas, suggestions or feedback about the business (or on the way you're running it).

- You can start to feel bogged-down, overwhelmed and under pressure – even when things are going well.

The important elements within a health check include the scope (the area for report), assessment (of the issues), report (on actions), and feedback (on results).

What a business health check includes

A business health check generally includes:

- Business strategy and competitive positioning – how you compete, differentiate and win in today's highly competitive market place

- Sales activity including current, new markets and routes to market

- Operations and people – how efficient and robust are your processes? Do you have the capability, structure and processes to deliver your plans?

- Business development – how do you acquire and retain customers? Are you targeting the right organisations?
- Marketing plans – how do you create awareness of your company amongst your target market? Do you have an effective revenue growth plan?
- Company finances – is your company being financed effectively and do you have the funding and the cash to deliver your plan?
- Process efficiency
- Use of resources, cost and waste
- Supply chain and purchasing review
- Systems, policies and procedures
- Income, expenditure, profit and loss, balance sheet and cash flow
- Staff skills, training and development
- Legal – is your business compliant with the law and regulations?
- Culture – what is your culture – is it correct for growth?

The report would then identify what needs to be done and how to do it. Provide a plan of agreed goals and the most cost-effective solutions.

The report will vary from company to company but could include some of the following:

- Customer/supplier satisfaction audits
- Staff surveys
- Reviewing board effectiveness
- Annual staff appraisals
- Service user surveys
- Benchmarking.

Report and feedback

A report should cover the key themes within a business. What is the current situation? What are the opportunities for improvement? What is the potential recommended improvement approach? It should then provide a presentation of the findings of the assessments, a priority plan to allow targets to be set and to prioritise and create an outline implementation plan. Think of it as a continuous process, as shown in Figure 10.1.

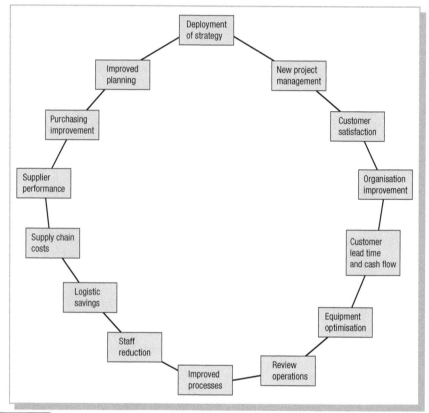

Figure 10.1

The external environment

Good business reviews don't just look internally. To do so is to lose sight of the wider issues that affect business performance. It is just as important to examine the aspects, characteristics, trends and issues that are based outside the business.

Thinking about the following external forces will be an important aspect of a health check:

- Competition (direct and indirect)
- Industry advances
- Technology changes
- The general business environment nationally and, if applicable, internationally.

For each single one of these areas, you should discuss its current state, trends and the impact it will have on the business. Having done this, discuss each issue and determine if it is an opportunity or a threat and determine its importance.

A simple health check example process

Stage 1 – Assessment

A health check measures performance in a supportive and non-judgemental way and people taking part in the assessment may be asked to complete a questionnaire, which forms the basis of the health check. Ideally this should be anonymous.

Stage 2 – Consolidation and data interpretation

Once the questionnaires have been completed the data should be evaluated and a report completed; reports are much better received and understood when they contain an illustrative graphical presentation which will identify areas of strength and those requiring improvement.

Stage 3 – Planning meeting

The report and graphic illustration of the assessment results should be reviewed by the board or management team, and an action plan for improvement agreed.

It's useful to break down a report into operational areas particularly if this is to be cascaded down to different departments for action.

Specific elements that may be included in the report

Finance

Business issues

- Business performance
- Cash position and availability of credit
- Stock levels and trade debtors
- Gross margins
- Staffing arrangements
- Capital expenditure

Cash flow management

- Business projections
- Trade debt
- Banking facilities
- Current overdraft
- Profit improvement
- Capital expenditure
- Raising cash

Tax matters

- Ways of reducing tax
- Dividend payments and remuneration strategy
- Tax compliance and risk
- Protecting assets
- Tax deferral arrangements

The future

- Strategic planning
- A 'plan B'
- Acquisition opportunities
- Sustaining growth

People

Absence

- How many days' absence have there been during the last 12 months?
- Do you have an absence management policy and procedure?
- Do you know how much persistent and unauthorised absence is costing your business?

Poor performance

- Do all of your staff perform at or above an acceptable standard, all of the time?
- Do you provide thorough business and job role induction training for your new recruits?

Redundancy/dismissal

▪ Have you had to make any staff reductions in the last two years?

▪ Do you know whether you meet the minimum statutory dismissal requirements?

Grievance and staff continuity

▪ Have any of your staff resigned in the last six months?

▪ Have your managers been trained to interview?

▪ Are you confident with interview questions you are using, i.e. do you have a matrix to measure interview performance?

▪ How many employees have left your business in the last six months, approximately?

▪ How many employees have you recruited?

Health and safety

▪ Do you have an up-to-date health and safety policy statement?

▪ Do you have an up-to-date health and safety manual?

▪ Are you carrying out any risk assessments?

▪ Do you provide basic health and safety awareness training for your staff?

For a more detailed approach and process see the checklist of health check questions on pages 168–172; and the sample health check report form in Appendix F.

When to do a health check

Health checks should be done at least annually. However, it is possible that a particular sign or signs suggest a more proactive approach.

Although businesses can fail ovenight it's a rare event. Usually there are plenty of warning signs to follow and some to look out for.

Typically, the origin of a crisis can be traced back two or three years before its onset, when the initial problems began to surface. In many situations, top management is in a state of denial and relies on rationalisations and quick fix answers to issues that are fundamental to the success of the business.

While this list can be applied rather broadly to most businesses, every company and industry will have early warning signs which are unique.

Early warning signs

1. Selling

- A significant sales forecast shortfall for three or more months and is it down over prior years?

- Are you growing slower than the industry?

- Did you increase your sales forecast to cover your overhead expenses?

- Are there negative trends in industry pricing practices?

- Has your business experienced a decline in market share during the past two years?

- Are sales concentrated with customers who are experiencing problems?

2. Cost

- Have gross margin percentages declined for three consecutive months?

- Are salaries greater than industry norms?

- Have actual costs exceeded budgeted costs for three consecutive months?

- Does the company need better cash flow monitoring?

- Does the company need better capital expenditure controls?

- Have capital projects fallen short of the expected revenue growth or cost savings projected?

3. Financial

- Have debtors over 60 days (or other period, dependent on your credit terms) increased over the past three months?

- Is the current ratio below standard industry norms?

- Are non-critical cash expenditures being made when cash conservation is called for?

- If business improves, will it be difficult to generate or borrow working capital to support the growth?

- Has your business experienced stock shrinkage problems over the past year?

- Has the company had trouble reducing stock levels on sales declines?

4. Industry

- Is your market or industry shrinking or consolidating?

■ Is your market or industry impacted significantly by economic cycles or seasonal shifts?

■ Are there a large number of competitors in your market?

■ Has foreign competition increased?

5. *Management*

■ Have the top managers expressed a need to improve teamwork?

■ Have there been any significant changes in the company 'culture' in the past year?

■ Has morale or turnover in top or middle management become a growing concern?

■ Is there a need for better communications throughout the company?

■ Are plans, programmes, budgets and accountability for their results made clear to managers?

■ Has absenteeism increased?

■ Has there been a formal redundancy programme initiated within the company in the past year?

■ Is the company's infrastructure adequate to handle the present and near-term business levels?

■ Has top management not visited all key locations at least once in the last year?

Some of the most serious warning signs

1 The company does not have documented pricing processes
2 The only hard data the company uses for pricing is the cost
3 The company does not know its customers' true willingness to pay
4 The company's sales people are not trained to defend prices
5 The company's sales people are allowed too much leeway in discounting
6 The company has not segmented the customers based on their decision behaviour
7 The company benchmarks its prices on 'the market place'.

Output

Measure performance and set targets

Once you have carried out a diagnostic on the business or department, setting objectives and putting into place an action plan is the next step. One way to do this is to use KPIs.

Choosing and using key performance indicators

About KPIs

KPIs are a central way of presenting business intelligence for an organisation. Also known as status indicators or scorecards, KPIs evaluate business data against business goals and display current status by using easy-to-understand graphical indicators.

KPIs increase the speed and efficiency of evaluating progress against key business goals. Without KPIs, employees and business managers would have to painstakingly extract performance data and evaluate that data against goals, and then spend time to present that data in a separate report for business decision makers.

Selecting the right KPIs and using them effectively will help improve your business's performance.

Selecting KPIs

- Link them to the top-level goals for your business.
- Relate them to aspects of the business environment over which you have some control.

When properly developed a KPI should provide all staff with clear goals and objectives, coupled with an understanding of how they relate to the overall success of the organisation. Published internally and continually referred to, they will also strengthen shared values and create common goals.

KPIs connect business data from various sources.

The key components of a KPI

A great KPI should be of fundamental importance in gaining a competitive advantage and is a make or break component in the success or failure of the enterprise. Like turning the gas up or down on a hob you are either cooking or you are not!

KPIs relate only to performance when it can be clearly measured, quantified and easily influenced by the organisation. If you can't take action it is not key.

Some KPIs provide leading information on future performance. Some KPIs only have value for historical purposes – for example debtor and creditor days – however, this data provides a guide for future plans.

KPIs cannot operate in isolation. You cannot establish a KPI without a clear understanding of what is possible – so we have to be able to set upper and lower limits of the KPI in reference to the market and how the competition is performing (or in the absence of competition, a comparable measurement from a number of similar organisations or indeed your own budgets and targets). This means that an understanding of benchmarks is essential to make KPIs useful and specific to your organisation, as they put the level of current performance in context – both for start-ups and for established enterprises.

What you need to measure and monitor: some examples

Administration

- Time keeping
- Health and safety incidents
- Time management
- Cost cutting
- Stress levels
- Environmental controls
- Employee suggestions
- Training

Finance

- Cash flow
- Profit and loss
- Balance sheet movements
- Invoicing amounts
- Credit management and debtor days

Marketing

- Market research activities
- Market size gains v. losses
- Customer transition gains v. losses
- Customer satisfaction/complaints

Production/logistics/service delivery

- Suppliers' delivery times
- Supply chain charges
- Obsolescent stock levels
- Vendor ranking
- Service satisfaction

Personnel

- Overtime
- Bonus levels
- Training needs analysis
- Employee record keeping

Product/service development

- Supplier charges

Contingency planning

- Success and failures
- Lessons learnt

The whole process could effectively be summed up as:

establish current performance, benchmark and target levels

i.e. for each monitoring module, establish what the current level is in a measurable and understandable way. Then benchmark the level to be introduced due to industry knowledge etc., then target your desired level.

An example is shown in Table 10.1.

Table 10.1 Financial KPI

	Current	Benchmark	Target
Gross profit %	68	52	60
ROCE %	13	10	11
EBITDA%	0.2	n/a	6
Interest cover multiple	2.3	3.7	3
Debtor days	102	95	80
Creditor days	60	63	55
Stock turn multiple	5	4	4

Be careful not to try to measure everything – this defeats the object and stops you concentrating on core criteria.

KPI project control elements

For KPIs to be effective, it's important to not only have target amounts and values but also to time-frame these requirements. An example is shown in Table 10.2.

Table 10.2 Time frame

Project	Due date
Debtor days	August 2012
Interest cover	September 2012
Gross profit	August 2013
Stock turn	September 2013

How to format, develop and understand what is key

Different individuals and organisations will put a different emphasis on what is important information. There is no definitive list of what is, and what is not, a KPI. It will depend on what decisions are required and will vary considerably according to the stage of a company's development. Start-up enterprises need to place their emphasis on different factors than companies that are well established.

But whatever the stage of your business, KPIs are valuable as they can answer the following crucial planning questions:

- Where are we?
- Where do we want to be?
- When do we want to be there?
- How are we going to get there cost-effectively?

Diagnosis leads to action

It's no use having a health check if on the back of the results you don't take action. The action needed will be determined by the diagnosis but there are a few sound ways to improve your business whatever the results.

- **Start the year in a positive manner**
  Is it time to get excited at the prospects of a new year/month/season/ whatever? List down ideas on new product lines, or new projects that you want to take on. Write down your ideas on how to expand and energise your business.

- **Dust off your business plans**
  Review, review and review your business plans. Go find your business plans and update them.

- **Rekindle your relationship with your customers**
  Marketing and advertising are important to get more customers. Quality, service and customer satisfaction are what keep a business successful in the long run.

- **Evaluate your pricing**
  Think about raising your prices.

- **Find ways to cut your costs**

- **Resolve to improve your weak spots**

- **Institute measures to assess the performance of your business**
  Set some benchmarks and periodically assess how your business is doing. You need to know what you consider an improvement before you can start to improve on it.

- **Explore new markets or improve marketing**

- **Ask the right questions**
  - Why has the problem occurred?
  - What is the purpose of our business?

- What will it take to accomplish the results we wish for?
- What are the data sources and do we know how to access them?
- Who is accountable for making these plans happen and are they aware of what needs doing?

- **Commit to the right methods**

  A good management system should include an optimum balance of 'result metrics' and 'process metrics'. The result metrics measure the output quality while the process metrics help in predicting the process output. The former act as lead indicators while the latter act as lag indicators.

- **Communicate 'why we are doing what we are doing'**

  It is the duty of management to relentlessly communicate to all concerned the purpose of the improvement.

- **Promote growth of capabilities**

  There are no off-the-shelf approaches to improvements. Don't set unrealistic timelines as it may lead to bogus improvements without creating the desired capabilities to carry the initiative on an ongoing basis.

How to improve quality at your business

- **Learn to listen to your customers** – ask what you can do to help them.
- **Look at all complaints about your service as an opportunity to improve.**
- **Establish an environment where great service is recognised and rewarded and poor service is challenged and rectified.**
- **Have a weekly fun staff meeting where good service elements are discussed.**
- **Ensure that your staff feel that they are an important part of your success.**
- **Lead by example** – show respect for every person at every level in your company.
- **Do things regularly to improve the workplace** – little things get noticed and mean a lot. Happy staff = happy customers.
- **Give your staff a reason to come to work with a big smile on their face and a great attitude** – be sure you show your employees you care by giving them a decent wage.

Seven smart moves to improve your business

1 **Get good help.**

2 **Know when to throw in the towel** – if you're working too much for free and don't really have a passion to work on the project, then get out as quickly as you can.

3 **Standardise your processes.**

4 **Measure your process** – if you don't measure what you're doing, there will be no way for you to know if you're making improvements.

5 **Money** – how much money does this process make you? How much money does the process cost you?

6 **Time** – how much time does it take you to complete?

7 **Widgets** – how many widgets do you create? How many phone calls do you make? How many blog posts do you write?

Finally,

■ **Compare your actual results** with the **desired results.**

Basically, '**what you measure you manage**', so this must be a reliable business improvement process.

The changing face of business is relentless. Understanding where you and your business are at any one time is the only way you can hope to keep up with the changing horizon and as such a business health check and its resulting actions is your best possible method to manage a better business.

Checklist of health check questions

Organisational and personnel

1 Organisation chart including current and projected operating management

2 Discuss any managerial positions that remain to be filled or eliminated

3 Detailed list of current and projected personnel by function and location showing:

   ■ Compensation (base, bonus, shares or similar)

   ■ Key employees' biographies

   ■ Bonus/compensation plan

   ■ Copy of standard contracts and any variations

4 Non-compete agreements with senior management

5 Copies of benefit plans

6 Holiday/sick leave policies

7 Manual of personnel policies and procedures

8 Severance agreements

9 Discuss labour/employee relations and union issues (if any)

10 Discuss use of consultants and part-time employees

11 Management team – are they capable of running and growing the business? If they are leaving, what is the structure of non-compete agreements?

Corporate ownership

1 Share ownership details

2 List of all offices

3 Minutes of meetings of board of directors – last six months

4 Joint venture and partnership agreements

5 Distribution and licensing agreements

6 Other material contracts

Insurance

1 Current and expected insurance policies (property and combined, D&O, etc.)

Property

1 Schedule of all property and values, leased or otherwise occupied

2 Charges, personal and corporate

Intellectual property

1 Copyrights, trademarks, service marks, patents

Material litigation

1 Documentation as to litigation involving any executive officers or directors (bankruptcy, crimes, securities, taxation)

2   Documentation regarding any material litigation or disputes (pending and within last five years)

Taxation

1   Copies of tax returns (last three years)

2   Discuss any acquisitions, goodwill or amortisation

3   Have you any annual or outstanding payments with HMRC?

Profit and loss/cash flow data

1   Annual profit and loss accounts (three years historical, three years projected)

2   Quarterly profit and loss accounts (two years historical)

3   Review by customer, products and services and geography

4   Expenses and margin analysis by customer, products, services and geography

5   Capital expenditure schedules (current and projected)

6   R&D cost breakdown

7   At least two years' quarterly projected cash flows

8   Discuss margin trends

9   Discuss policy regarding software capitalisation/amortisation

10 Discuss sale lead management systems and detailed pipeline analysis

11 Discuss backlog, unbilled revenues, general revenue visibility and percentage of each future quarter's revenue that is already known v. what remains to be sold

12 Show revenue flows for a typical customer over a two year period

13 Show revenue flows for a typical P&L product for a two year period

14 What is customer concentration? Who are 10 top customers, with percentage of revenues for last two years?

15 Discuss revenue recognition policies

16 Discuss invoicing and terms of credit

Balance sheet

1   Balance sheets (last five years and quarterly for last two years)

2   At least two years' projected balance sheets

3 Discuss banking relationships – communications with creditors for borrowed money relating to any defaults, waivers of covenants or termination of credit relationships

4 Discuss and provide documentation regarding any personal obligations or other long-term or short-term debt

Sales

1 Current and projected market share data by markets served or product group

2 What is the current and projected market size for your products/ services?

3 What is the role of product/service customisation in your market?

4 How many sales people? What is their quota? What percentage achieve quota? What is the sales compensation structure?

5 Extent to which telemarketing and direct mail efforts have been utilised

6 What is the company's pricing strategy for each of its product groups? Describe pricing elasticity

7 Channel strategy – past, present and future. How will you build your sales and marketing organisation? What is the budgeted percentage of revenues for sales and marketing? Describe new hires to date

8 Describe the typical sales cycle

9 Describe typical sales agreement

10 What geographic markets are expected to be most important over the next three years and why?

11 Customer references (existing accounts, recent wins, recent losses)

12 Distribution channels – how is the product sold? How good and loyal is the sales force?

13 Promotion – how is the product promoted? i.e. advertising, trade shows, websites etc.

Competition

1 How the company compares versus the competition in terms of price, positioning, margins, distribution channels and other relevant financial and qualitative comparisons

2   What is the company doing to meet the competition?

3   Who are the company's competitors? What is the company's relative market share?

4   What are potential competitive threats in the future? Substitute products?

5   Have any of the company's competitors recently changed their tactics with regards to how they market their products (e.g. offering new services, teaming with other vendors, shifting distribution channels)?

6   What deals has the company lost recently? To whom did the company lose in those cases?

Products and services

1   What are unique features of the company's products – how differentiated from competition?

2   What are the potential competitive threats in the future? Substitute products?

3   Information regarding new products/service introductions

4   Describe product development process/plans

5   What is the typical product life cycle, if any?

6   What is the average development lead-time needed to introduce new services and upgraded features?

7   What is the long-term new product plan/vision?

8   What is the typical product development cycle? How extensive is testing?

9   Have you missed product development deadlines in the past?

Research and development agreements

1   Are you dependent on the development cycle of other organisations?

2   Are you dependent on the intellectual property (IP) of other organisations?

Inherent liability

1   It is important to understand the risk of any major financial 'surprises' in the future. Often this also requires representation letters from lawyers or environmental study firms. Topics include:

a   Warranty issues

b   Environmental (superfund)

c   Patent infringements

d   Liens/lawsuits

e   Pending regulatory issues

f   Unfair dismissals.

Failing to plan is planning to fail: a checklist of 50 important items for surviving and prospering during tough times

1 Do not overreact – take action based only on data.

2 Get key employees' input in planning strategies.

3 Do a revised business/strategic plan for the next six months.

4 Revise cash flow for the next six month period.

5 Revise a proforma statement for the next six months based on a revised business plan.

6 Explain your plan to the entire staff and ask for their input.

7 Evaluate personnel needs across the board.

8 Hold off replacing personnel that have resigned, retired or been terminated.

9 Make cuts in personnel (quickly if necessary), starting at the top of the organisation.

10 Maintain larger cash position to take advantage of sale prices.

11 Do a monthly ageing of debtors.

12 Enforce collection terms.

13 Be flexible in looking for new solutions.

14 Review stock for slow-moving items – turn into cash.

15 Do an analysis of stock. Only re-order those items that sell, but don't overorder stock.

16 Do a monthly ageing of creditors.

17 Make sure your customers acknowledge your company's excellent customer service.

18 Owner should sign all cheques for 60 days to a get feel of cost areas of company.

19 Establish a temporary line of credit through your bank.

20 Re-evaluate timing of capital expenditures.

21 When capital expenditures are necessary, cost-justify and shop for prices.

22 Use bartering to reduce cash needs.

23 Maintain close contact with existing customers.

24 Review all former clients to see who you can sell to again.

25 Look at related type products or services that you could sell to your same market niche.

26 Don't decrease advertising or marketing budget. Instead, increase budget to take advantage of competition cutbacks.

27 Don't cut off training for employees.

28 When it becomes necessary to replace personnel, look for the most experienced candidates.

29 Analyse your mailing costs, i.e. post office v. others.

30 Be very careful to not cut back on your marketing, as this will create a double problem in your sales.

31 Look at independent sales representatives to increase sales effort.

32 Review postage expense and look for ways to cut down.

33 Review and justify travel expenses. Replace unnecessary travel with video conferencing, webinars, and teleconferencing.

34 Review and justify any entertainment expenses.

35 Review and justify any office supply expenses.

36 Refigure your break-even analysis based on new business plan.

37 Review recent monthly P & L statements for percentage trends.

38 Reuse office supplies, folders, paper clips, etc. when possible.

39 Save poor quality or misprinted copies and outdated stationery and use them for scrap paper.

40 Tighten up credit checks for new customers.

41 Do a monthly check of P & L statement against revised proforma statement.

42 Do a monthly current ratio and take steps to strengthen the ratio.

43 Keep your bank informed of your company's progress. Bankers hate surprises!!!

44 Do a monthly KPI summary.

45 Offer settlement on debtors before turning it over to collection agency or lawyer.

46 Use a small claims court to collect a certain amount of debtors.

47 Join a monthly meeting group of other companies to exchange ideas and learn new techniques.

48 Review your insurance and consider increasing deductibles.

49 Don't manage for the moment. Consider long-term goals of the company before taking any action that could affect the future of the company.

50 Take time to plan and review operations against plans.

Appendix A

Sample Management Accounts Pack

Management Accounts
Pack to June 20X2
A Company Ltd

A Co. Ltd
Balance Sheet as at 30 June 20X2

	Cost	Accum Depn	NBV
Tangible Fixed Assets			
Freehold Property	623,640.00	96,085.01	527,554.99
Computer Equipment	96,581.31	84,941.47	11,639.84
Plant & Machinery	825,167.64	610,095.06	215,072.58
Fixtures, Fittings, Equipment	130,633.19	87,988.85	42,644.34
Motor Vehicles	9,800.00	544.44	9,225.56
	1,685,822.14	879,654.83	806,167.31
Intangible Fixed Assets			
Goodwill	3,445,628.32	1,941,909.68	1,503,718.64
Patent Costs	–	–	–
Shares in Subsidiary Company			1.00
Long-Term Assets			**2,309,886.95**
A/C Receivable			807,224.49
Inter Company Trading			(1.00)
Other Debtors / Prepayments			60,387.04
Inventory			943,244.07
Bank/Cash in Hand			356,196.72
			2,167,051.32
Creditors: Amounts falling			
due within one year			
A/C Payable			(504,088.56)
Bank Loans & Overdrafts			(482,402.09)
Payroll Accruals			(16,353.59)
Accruals			(42,284.78)
HP Creditor			(3,021.04)
VAT Creditor			(13,743.10)
Tax Payable			(403,418.51)
			(1,465,311.67)
Net Current Assets			**701,739.65**
Total Assets – Current Liabilities			**3,011,626.60**
Long-Term Loans			(454,125.00)
Deferred Taxation			(40,011.00)
Net Assets			**2,517,490.60**
FINANCED BY:			
Ordinary Shares			(230,000.00)
Retained Earnings – Prior Years			(2,143,510.63)
Retained Earnings – Current Year			(123,979.97)
Total Shareholders' Equity			**(2,517,490.60)**

Profit & Loss Account for June 20X2	Period			Year to Date		
Sales		367,454.90			2,195,722.11	
Cost of Sales						
Opening Stock	770,700.00			770,003.11		
Material Purchases	326,284.00			1,100,083.11		
Transport / Carriage	16,834.19			95,084.48		
Wages & NI	38,606.50			225,742.79		
	1,152,421.69			2,190,913.49		
Closing Stock	(943,244.07)			(943,244.07)		
Total Cost of Sales		209,177.62			1,247,669.42	
Gross Margin		158,277.28	43.1%		948,052.69	43.2%
Overheads						
Selling & Distribution						
Motor	1,087.24			6,492.55		
Travel / Entertaining	575.13			9,376.61		
Advertising	3,215.73			25,965.25		
Bad Debts	1,000.00			5,786.71		
Commissions	-			596.55		
Discounts Allowed/(Received)	148.90			160.32		
		6,027.00			49,368.99	
Administrative Expenses						
Rates	1,444.86			5,383.13		
Insurance	1,907.32			11,766.96		
Repairs & Renewals	2,854.00			18,021.54		
Light & Heat	2,024.05			13,365.51		
Health Insurance	488.77			3,278.05		
Staff Salaries	25,563.82			150,793.72		
Bonus Payments	1,661.00			10,550.58		
Employers' NIC	2,751.99			16,442.28		
Staff Pension	4,885.41			26,920.61		
Postage Costs	203.72			3,239.85		
Stationery	817.82			4,775.58		
Telephone, Fax, etc	375.65			2,732.21		
Audit / Accountancy	1,000.00			6,178.54		
Legal & Prof Fees	217.14			1,634.88		
IT Support	2,492.99			12,297.47		
QA Costs	843.03			2,038.56		
Recruitment Exps	1,710.00			2,410.00		
Staff Training	221.11			1,612.26		
Exchange Differences	51.17			(449.98)		
Profit on Disposals	-			(1,500.00)		
Bank Charges	2,190.65			10,617.99		
Sundries / Incidentals	899.07			8,570.19		
		54,603.57			310,679.93	
Depreciation						
Freehold Buildings	1,299.25			7,795.50		
Patent Costs	-			-		
Computer Equipment	1,150.88			6,773.04		
Plant & Machinery	5,750.01			34,004.21		
Fixtures & Fittings	661.97			3,558.02		
Motor Vehicles	272.22			544.44		
		9,134.33			52,675.21	
Total Overheads		69,764.90			412,724.13	
		88,512.38			535,328.56	
Other Operating Income		-			-	
Operating Profit		88,512.38	24.1%		535,328.56	24.4%
Interest						
Bank Interest	2,043.68			12,634.47		
HP Interest	96.77			580.62		
	2,140.45			13,215.09		
Less Interest Received	-			-		
		2,140.45			13,215.09	
Exceptional Items - Share Buy Back		-			-	
Goodwill Amortisation		14,743.04			88,458.24	
Profit Before Taxation		71,628.89	19.5%		433,655.23	19.8%
Taxation Charge for Period (30%)		(25,695.65)			(148,766.26)	
Profit After Taxation		45,933.24	12.5%		284,888.97	13.0%
Dividends Paid		(112,651.50)			(160,909.00)	
Retained Earnings for Period		(33,281.74)			123,979.97	
EBITDA		97,646.71	26.6%		588,003.77	26.8%

A Co. Ltd

Profit & Loss Account 20X2
Summary Analysis by Month

	Jan	Feb	Mar	Apr	May	Jun	Jul	Aug	Sep	Oct	Nov	Dec	YTD	Budget Dec	Variance	Budget YTD	Variance
Sales																	
A	92,904	80,708	129,039	107,420	100,725	113,699	94,306	77,797	108,651	103,216	90,069	77,493	1,176,025	64,242	13,251	1,045,000	131,025
B	24,140	20,576	27,756	20,821	17,435	25,467	21,151	25,813	26,970	19,337	28,042	14,725	272,231	16,414	(1,689)	267,000	5,231
C	87,334	77,515	136,907	122,541	109,554	87,970	131,783	130,121	150,388	182,665	124,172	146,435	1,486,549	84,529	61,906	1,375,000	111,549
D	6,058	2,935	8,910	1,662	9,596	5,970	1,733	3,023	3,222	1,107	1,082	1,107	23,076	1,107	(1,249)	18,000	5,076
E	9,818	2,915	15,186	15,669	4,879	5,443	5,466	9,241	3,023	11,011	2,505	2,889	85,534	2,889	2,783	47,000	38,534
F	27,990	12,811	21,670	36,804	23,946	23,461	37,029	30,789	16,507	20,991	19,251	12,619	265,696	9,836	(5,224)	160,000	105,696
G	28,318	32,627	30,903	41,475	16,448	37,794	22,823	13,216	25,834	48,868	32,001	9,285	339,264	14,508	(5,224)	236,000	103,264
H	23,318	25,919	37,389	17,068	22,360	14,105	23,374	11,648	44,475	55,959	36,855	82,689	400,158	17,213	65,476	280,000	120,158
I	1,508	2,845	2,057	2,172	2,665	823	1,008	647	3,207	1,763	2,781	247	21,723	2,336	(2,089)	38,000	(16,277)
J	1,570	2,457	2,096	2,720	1,265	1,921	597	3,482	3,316	3,418	1,669	4,376	25,847	2,459	1,917	40,000	(14,153)
K	78	687	442	300		205	998	675	279	888	213	81	4,846	307	(226)	5,000	1,570
L	581	4,305	3,580	(242)	3,227	4,321	1,421	1,576	5,767	9,857	2,457	276	38,387	1,721	1,917	28,000	10,387
M	18,876	7,917	7,599	12,557	16,840	11,289	16,226	13,518	6,501	7,883	10,865	8,464	138,536	9,898	(1,434)	161,000	(22,464)
N	76	4,254		840	91	1,412			4,756	540	226	1,552	13,077	1,352	199	22,000	(8,923)
O		712		825		2,143	45	199	199				2,915		(246)	4,000	(1,085)
P	185	713	768	319		650	1,330	352	566	615	133	1,931	7,423	246	1,885	4,000	3,423
Q	2,620	3,025	1,617	342	5,681	527	566	1,009	7,888	4,425	553	2,866	30,823	246	2,866		30,823
R	439	933	1,354	1,011	1,240		1,187	797	1,690	1,425	462	462	11,616	615	(153)	10,000	1,616
S	6,476	7,511	19,976	17,516	7,844	22,514	37,554	18,406	21,385	21,389	9,690	22,589	212,847	4,918	17,671	80,000	132,848
T	11,139	10,393	15,710	11,511	10,946	11,508	13,032	11,298	14,175	15,401	12,862	9,033	147,006	8,299	734	135,000	12,006
Sales	319,525	298,857	454,479	410,146	345,261	367,455	412,406	348,956	446,963	510,621	375,624	399,917	4,690,208	243,135	156,781	3,955,000	735,208
Cost of Sales																	
Opening Stock	770,003	777,076	811,330	847,085	734,322	770,700	943,244	931,530	1,075,892	1,149,792	1,083,080	1,010,525	770,003	772,000	(278,525)	732,000	(38,003)
Material Purchases	130,181	149,904	249,968	68,462	175,284	326,284	171,256	287,353	306,872	156,418	91,217	14,224	2,330,298	94,215	(122,884)	1,532,563	(797,736)
Transport / Carriage	14,789	12,603	19,101	13,058	18,698	16,834	15,642	13,548	19,362	20,073	14,771	14,224	192,704	11,770	(2,454)	166,465	(26,239)
Wages / NI	36,244	34,626	39,498	38,630	38,544	38,606	35,635	38,299	38,591	38,594	34,454	31,552	445,442	27,944	(3,608)	454,562	10,133
Closing Stock	(777,076)	(811,330)	(847,085)	(734,322)	(770,700)	(943,244)	(931,530)	(1,075,892)	(1,149,792)	(1,083,080)	(1,010,525)	(1,037,188)	(1,037,188)	(732,000)	(407,471)	(732,000)	(852,857)
Total Cost of Sales	174,141	162,880	272,813	232,514	196,144	209,178	234,247	197,708	290,632	281,794	212,997	236,212	2,701,259	133,929	(102,282)	2,153,589	(547,669)
Gross Margin	145,384	135,977	181,666	177,631	149,117	158,277	178,159	151,249	156,330	228,827	162,627	163,705	1,988,950	109,206	54,499	1,801,411	187,539
	45.5%	45.5%	40.0%	43.3%	43.2%	43.1%	43.2%	43.3%	35.0%	44.8%	43.3%	40.9%	42.4%	44.9%		45.5%	
Overheads																	
Selling & Distribution																	
Motor	976	1,017	1,157	976	1,278	1,087	1,344	1,076	1,639	1,037	1,388	1,387	14,363	978	(408)	13,726	(638)
Travel / Entertaining	1,887	1,987	833	4,069	1,435	575	30	293	4,767	1,590	1,180	2,191	19,428	310	(1,881)	16,720	(2,708)
Advertising	3,105	16,028	8,310	928	1,810	3,216	10,375	4,349	3,322	1,629	1,867	2,160	48,899	855	(1,325)	43,087	(5,812)
Bad Debts	1,000	1,000	1,000	787	1,000	1,000	1,000	1,000	1,000	1,000	1,000	(8,920)	1,867	1,000	9,920	17,000	10,133
Commissions					597							597	597	50	50		302
Discounts Allowed/Rebate Gv	121	272	252	(0)	367	149	316	130	337	2,282	116	(414)	3,926	1,000	1,414	13,000	9,074
	7,089	20,305	4,112	6,760	5,077	6,027	13,266	6,848	11,065	7,538	4,571	(3,577)	89,080	4,193	7,770	99,033	9,953
Administrative Expenses																	
Rent & Rates	1,128	565	107	1,070	1,068	1,445	1,230	1,575	1,135	1,068	1,068	1,359	12,818	1,860	501	14,493	1,675
Insurance	1,919	2,238	1,887	1,907	1,907	1,907	2,157	1,907	1,907	1,907	1,818	2,088	23,552	2,211	122	26,174	2,622
Repairs & Renewals	2,422	2,793	2,803	4,225	2,924	2,854	3,886	4,264	4,775	5,611	4,049	1,165	41,772	1,838	673	24,000	(17,772)
Light & Heat	2,018	1,633	4,011	2,174	1,507	2,024	2,292	2,157	184	2,710	(461)	2,569	22,816	2,000	(569)	25,050	2,234
Health Insurance	532	532	532	597	597	489	528	528	628	246	427	427	6,060	585	158	6,807	747
Staff Salaries	23,739	23,674	27,412	25,531	24,873	25,564	26,377	27,573	28,502	30,163	30,228	34,467	328,105	24,558	(9,910)	294,692	(33,413)
Bonus Payments	2,701	1,661	1,661	2,246	1,661	1,661	2,315	994	2,817	1,269	11,673	2,107	31,726	1,661	(446)	19,935	(11,791)
Employers' NIC	4,402	3,232	2,710	2,823	2,175	2,752	2,324	2,238	3,017	3,031	4,827	4,195	36,074	2,650	(1,545)	31,805	(4,270)
Staff Pension	489	4,402	4,408	4,409	4,415	4,885	4,416	4,417	4,059	4,069	4,065	4,077	52,057	4,338	261	52,057	1,424
Postage Costs	348	(3)	1,068	994	488	204	500	1,188	671	16	475	730	6,148	4,738	7	7,573	1,424
Stationery	493	1,008	882	853	867	818	136	578	501	647	826	1,068	9,043	513	(555)	8,066	(977)
Telephone, Fax, etc	1,000	405	585	442	432	376	312	578	501	1,057	286	823	6,288	512	(311)	5,998	(290)
Legal & Accountancy	1,663	2,517	1,179	1,000	1,000	1,000	1,000	919	1,000	1,000	1,000		11,179	1,000	1,000	12,000	821
Legal & Prof Fees	2,115	2,164	1,897	1,603	2,013	2,493	1,449	3,648	4,172	8,252	2,185	6,288	20,971	550	(1,635)	6,600	(14,371)
IT Support	185	96	386	286	243	843	171	1,658	1,645	2,670	1,157	157	3,588	1,675	(265)	19,814	(2,765)
H&S / QA Costs				350	350	1,710	350	239	6,350	181	389	342	13,490	195	(147)	3,890	(9,890)
Recruitment Expenses	232		444	233	482	221	221	350	291	281	350	1,710	4,204	300	(1,410)	3,600	(1,204)
Training	1,792	1,174	(4,375)	(406)	1,313	51	(3,900)	1,997	(3,316)	(2,568)	(2,270)	1,356	(10,562)	250	(1,106)	3,000	22,562
Exchange Differences																(1,500)	1,500
Profit on Disposals																12,000	1,500
Bank Charges	1,499	1,433	1,822	1,479	2,193	2,191	886	1,584	1,761	2,130	1,699	1,515	20,193	1,788	273	21,212	1,019
Sundries / Incidentals	1,254	2,096	1,481	875	1,965	899	1,680	860	1,883	1,376	374	167	14,910	1,335	1,168	16,864	1,954
	50,393	50,320	50,616	53,006	51,741	54,604	48,748	58,245	63,409	67,585	63,357	63,453	675,477	51,555	(11,897)	615,630	(59,847)

	Jan	Feb	Mar	Apr	May	Jun	Jul	Aug	Sep	Oct	Nov	Dec	YTD	Budget Dec	Variance	Budget YTD	Variance
Depreciation																	
Freehold Buildings	1,299	1,299	1,299	1,299	1,299	1,299	1,299	1,299	1,299	1,299	1,299	1,299	15,591	1,299	-	15,591	-
Patent Costs	-	-	-	-	-	-	-	-	-	-	-	-	-	-	-	-	-
Computer Equipment	1,118	1,118	1,118	1,118	1,151	1,151	1,151	1,151	(824)	1,165	1,165	1,165	11,745	1,150	(15)	13,550	1,805
Plant & Machinery	5,596	5,596	5,596	5,717	5,750	5,750	5,793	5,792	1,802	5,868	5,868	5,868	64,996	6,742	874	73,672	8,676
Fixtures & Fittings	565	565	565	577	623	662	661	661	(1,151)	660	660	660	5,710	565	(95)	6,785	1,075
Motor Vehicles	-	-	-	-	272	272	272	272	272	272	272	272	2,178	-	(272)	-	(2,178)
	8,578	8,578	8,578	8,711	9,095	9,134	9,176	9,175	1,398	9,265	9,265	9,264.86	100,219	9,756	492	109,597	9,378
Total Overheads	66,061	79,203	63,306	68,476	65,913	69,765	71,190	74,268	75,873	84,387	77,192	65,505	864,776	69,141	(3,636)	824,260	(40,516)
Other Operating Income																	
Operating Profit	79,323	56,774	118,360	109,155	83,204	88,512	106,969	76,981	80,458	144,440	85,435	94,564	1,124,174	43,701	50,863	977,151	147,023
Operating Profit %	24.8%	19.0%	26.0%	26.6%	24.1%	24.1%	25.9%	22.1%	18.0%	28.3%	22.7%	23.6%	24.0%	18.0%		24.7%	
Interest																	
Bank/Loan Interest	1,951	2,198	2,011	2,252	2,179	2,044	1,903	2,185	1,961	1,850	1,810	1,782	24,126	2,429	648	27,705	3,579
HP Interest	97	97	97	97	97	97	97	97	97	97	(7)	-	968	357	357	2,064	1,096
	2,048	2,294	2,108	2,349	2,276	2,140	2,000	2,282	2,058	1,947	1,803	1,782	25,093	2,786	1,005	29,769	4,676
Less Interest Received	2,048	2,294	2,108	2,349	2,276	2,140	2,000	2,282	2,058	1,947	1,803	1,782	25,086	2,786	1,005	29,769	4,682
Exc'l Item – Co. Reorganisation																	
Goodwill Amortisation	14,743	14,743	14,743	14,743	14,743	14,743	14,743	14,743	14,743	14,743	14,743	14,743	176,916	14,743	-	176,916	-
Profit Before Taxation	62,532	39,737	101,509	92,063	66,185	71,629	90,226	59,956	63,657	127,750	68,888	78,039	922,171	26,171	51,868	770,465	151,706
Taxation	(21,637)	(15,373)	(30,210)	(31,775)	(24,076)	(25,696)	(31,228)	(16,504)	(21,952)	(39,898)	(23,385)	(26,011)	(307,745)	(10,172)	(15,839)	(270,399)	(37,345)
Profit After Taxation	40,895	24,364	71,299	60,288	42,109	45,933	58,998	43,451	41,705	87,852	45,504	52,028	614,427	15,999	36,029	500,066	114,360
Dividends Paid	(10,666)	(10,666)	(10,622)	(105,652)	(10,652)	(12,652)	(12,652)	(12,652)	(12,652)	(12,652)	(12,652)	(112,652)	(336,818)	(145,652)	33,000	(357,818)	21,000
Retained Earnings for Period	30,229	13,698	60,677	(45,363)	31,458	33,282	46,346	30,800	29,053	75,200	32,852	(60,623)	277,609	(129,652)	69,029	142,248	135,360
EBITDA	87,901	65,353	126,938	117,866	92,299	97,647	116,145	86,156	81,856	153,704	94,699	103,829	1,224,393	53,457	50,371	1,086,748	137,645
EBITDA %	27.5%	21.9%	27.9%	28.7%	26.7%	26.6%	28.2%	24.7%	18.3%	30.1%	25.2%	26.0%	26.1%	22.0%		27.5%	

112.7%

Finance - Mr Joe Brown

Financial Results – June 20X2

Sales

Sales for the fourth month in a row exceeded expectations, returning a total of £367.5k; some 8% above budgeted levels. Export sales performed well to aid this performance. Sales in the month were £27.1k higher than budgeted figures when adjusted for the SP Group rebate (£367.5k vs. £340.4k). In addition, sales were £43.1k higher than previous year levels for the same month (June previous year was a very poor £324.4k). Export sales were at £104.6k, up £36.0k higher than June previous figures. This equated to 28.5% of the month's total sales and 28.9% YTD against a monthly average of 26.5% for previous year.

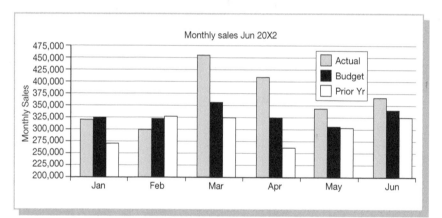

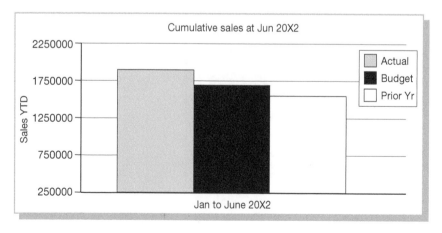

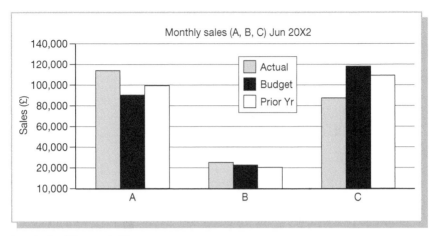

Product A, B and C

A and B performed very well against budget and vs. the corresponding period in previous year; A was £23.8k ahead of budget and £13.9k above June previous year levels. Year to date, A has maintained its position ahead of budget and 20.. levels, given the excellent sales levels in the first quarter; the category is £102.0k ahead vs. budget and £116.8k ahead of the previous year position. C sales were poor in the month and were £30.4k short of budget and £21.5k below June previous year levels. Year to date, C is £66.2k lower than budget, but is now £19.1k ahead of previous year levels. B sales performed reasonably well in the month; they were £2.5k higher than budget in the month and £6.2k higher than previous year levels. Year to date, B is £2.7k ahead of budget, but short of previous year levels by £2.7k.

Margins

Following the stocktake at the end of the quarter, margin was validated at 43.2%, this being the same level as March quarter end. Labour costs in the month were at 10.5% (lower than the budget for the month of 11.5%). Transport/carriage costs in the month were lower at 4.6% (higher than the budgeted level of 4.4%).

Overheads

Selling and distribution costs were more or less on budget in the month and were underspent by £12.4k year to date due to accrued rebates being below expected levels and the timing of advertising expenditure.

Costs were £2.3k higher vs. the same period last year, which was entirely due to Fespa costs which did not take place in 20X1.

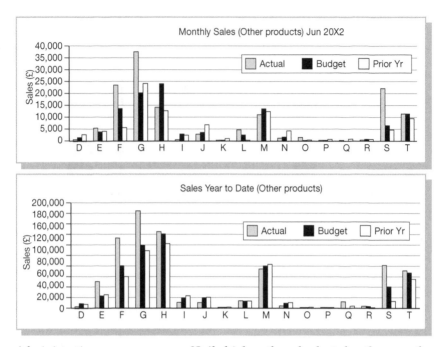

Administrative expenses were £3.4k higher than budget for the month and £5.5k higher year to date. The overspend vs. budget in the month of any consequence were Repairs & Renewals equating to £1.0k which was a general overspend. Salaries were also over budget by £1.0k due to the recruitment of Mrs A on the special project. Recruitment expenses were also overspent by £1.4k in the month; again as a consequence of the engagement of Mrs A. In the opposite direction, a positive variance of £0.9k crystallised on a marginal exchange gain over the month. Overspends vs. June 20X1 were in the following areas:

- Light & Heat £1.8k – due to bill timings in previous year

- Recruitment Expenses £1.7k – as specified above

There were no other individual overspends of any substance in the month.

There were also no major underspends in the month.

Total expenditure was £3.6k worse than budget (YTD lower by £7.0k) and in line with June previous year levels (YTD, higher by £54.6k).

This left operating profit on budget for the month at £88.5k (YTD higher by £58.0k) and £8.8k higher than June previous year (YTD up £58.2k).

EBITDA/Retained Earnings

Retained earnings for the month were below budget by £2.7k (YTD up £40.2k) and EBITDA was on budget in the month at £97.6k. Year to date EBITDA was up £57.9k vs. budget and £55.0k above 20X1 levels.

Cash Flow Management

£422k was available for draw down at the end of June 20X2, £86k lower than last month.

Collections were £8.0k higher than May, yet cash availability generated in the month was lower by £15.0k.

	Jan	Feb	Mar	Apr	May	Jun
Cash Collections (£k)	334	303	423	373	442	450
Balance – BoSCF A/C (£k)	177	317	243	361	176	269
Availability at Mth End (£k)	388	289	363	383	508	422
Availability Generated (£k)	346	330	493	438	393	378

Exchange Rates

The £:US$ exchange movement during the month was slightly upwards; equating to about 1.2% of its value during the month. The month started at US$1.4710 and finished at US$1.4889, with a high of US$1.5052 just before month end and a low of US$1.4421 on 04/06/20X2. Rates have improved substantially since month end. As I write £ vs. US$ is trading at around US$1.5950.

The profile of activity for sterling vs. the euro was very similar to that of the US$; rates have risen marginally over the month by 1.2%, although the profile was more volatile. The euro started the month at €1.2030 and finished at €1.2173. The high in the month was €1.2310 just before month end and the low was at €1.1964 on 18 June. Rates have fallen slightly since month end and are currently trading at around €1.2050.

Sterling has fallen further in the month against the Japanese yen, by 2.2%. Yen started the month at around JPY134.7, moving to JPY131.7. JPY is currently trading at JPY136.7.

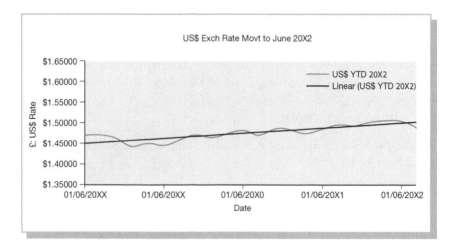

Interest Rates

The Bank of England's Monetary Policy Committee held interest rates at 0.5% in the month. As I write, a decision was made early May 20X2 to leave rates on hold at 0.5%. There are still no indications that rates are likely to rise during 20X2; forecasters are suggesting there may be rises from Q4 20X3.

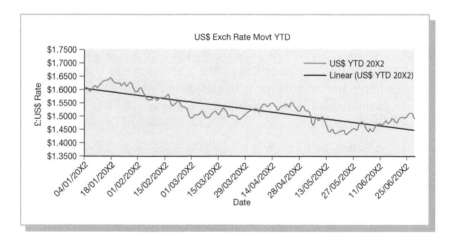

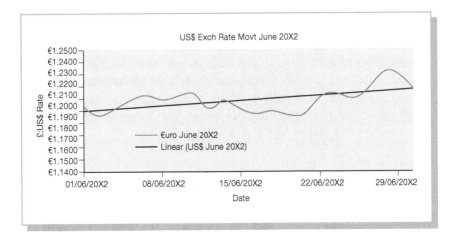

Liquidity/Debtor Days

Debtor days reduced by a further four days to 63 days on a rolling 12 month basis predominantly as a consequence of the movement on both the UK and the export ledger. UK accounts fell by three days to 67 days and the export ledger fell by six days in the month to 52 days. Creditor days improved by 24 days to 74 days as a consequence of the increased purchases spend in the month. Stock turn worsened further to 2.70 (from 3.00 last month) reflecting the higher level of stocks at month end. The current ratio moved from 1.88 to 1.71 and quick ratio moved from 1.10 to 0.96.

Absence

Absence levels were improved in the month. These were at 1.2%, equating to about 10 man days; 8 days being due to Mr Jones's absence.

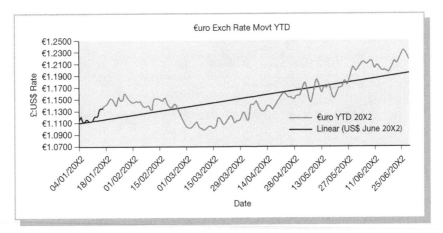

Overtime

Overtime in the month was back down to 0.9% of sales, up on the 20X1 average of 0.7%. Costs were also back below budgeted levels by £614 (£3,267 vs. £3,881). Actual equivalent hours were higher than budget by 75 hours (4,581 hrs vs. 4,506 hrs). Despite this, average pay for weekly paid employees came down slightly to £6.54 per hour (from £6.65 in May) for the month (£7.11 including CTL's).

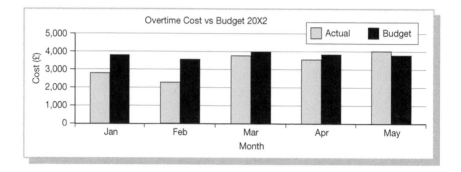

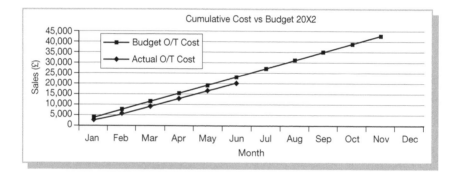

Overtime costs by month 20X2

	Jan	Feb	Mar	Apr	May	Jun	Jul	Aug	Sep	Oct	Nov	Dec
Actual O/T Cost	2,862	2,353	3,848	3,566	4,040							
Budget O/T Cost	3,881	3,582	4,030	3,881	3,881	3,881	3,956	3,956	3,881	3,881	3,881	4,030

Employee information

Headcount is at 43.

Percentage absence 20X2

	Jan	Feb	Mar	Apr	May	Jun	Jul	Aug	Sep	Oct	Nov	Dec
Actual	0.5%	0.6%	0.8%	0.4%	1.9%	1.2%						
Target	2.0%	2.0%	2.0%	2.0%	2.0%	2.0%	2.0%	2.0%	2.0%	2.0%	2.0%	2.0%

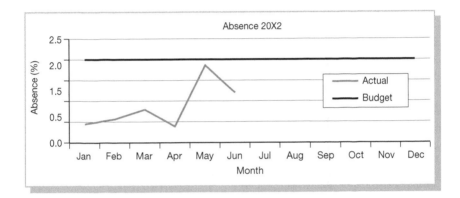

A Company Ltd

Key Performance Indicators – Previous year

Metric	Prior year	Prior year	Jan	Feb	Mar	Apr	May	Jun	Jul	Aug	Sep	Oct	Nov	YTD/AVG
Sales Based														
Total Turnover	£312,073	£3,744,878	£319,525	£298,857	£454,479	£410,146	£345,261	£367,457	£412,406	£348,956	£446,963	£510,621	£375,624	£4,690,211
UK Turnover	£229,214	£2,750,563	£233,873	£204,178	£318,693	£297,584	£244,275	£262,845	£310,769	£294,337	£326,488	£384,990	£274,516	£3,446,944
Export Turnover	£82,729	£992,750	£85,652	£94,679	£135,786	£112,561	£100,986	£104,612	£101,637	£54,619	£120,475	£125,631	£101,108	£1,243,268
Export Turnover %	26.5%	26.5%	26.8%	31.7%	29.9%	27.4%	29.2%	28.5%	24.6%	15.7%	27.0%	24.6%	26.9%	26.5%
No. of Invoices Raised (Total)	48	576	561	634	762	686	651	668	664	600	759	665	686	667
No. of Invoices Raised (UK)	43	515	485	545	640	598	562	589	582	550	664	569	604	581
No. of Invoices Raised (Export)	5	62	76	89	122	88	89	79	82	50	96	96	82	86
Average Invoice Value (Total)	£542	£6,502	£570	£471	£596	£598	£530	£550	£621	£582	£589	£768	£548	£639
Average Invoice Value (UK)	£445	£5,343	£482	£375	£498	£498	£435	£446	£534	£535	£492	£677	£454	£540
Average Invoice Value (Export)	£1,042	£16,099	£1,127	£1,064	£1,113	£1,279	£1,135	£1,324	£1,239	£1,092	£1,268	£1,309	£1,233	£1,311
Sales Value per Employee	£8,002	£96,023	£7,988	£7,471	£11,362	£10,254	£8,421	£8,546	£9,591	£8,308	£10,902	£12,454	£9,162	£114,142
Carriage recharged in Sales	£9,314	£111,774	£11,139	£10,393	£15,710	£11,511	£10,946	£11,508	£13,032	£11,298	£14,175	£15,401	£12,682	£137,793
Carriage recharged in Sales %	4.1%	4.1%	4.8%	5.1%	4.9%	3.9%	4.5%	4.4%	4.2%	3.8%	4.3%	4.0%	4.6%	4.0%
No.of Credit Notes Issued	18	219	15	19	16	12	19	18	14	10	17	18	22	180
Value of Credit Notes Issued	£13,901	£166,811	£5,717	£10,636	£5,807	£1,829	£7,760	£22,534	£4,012	£2,835	£14,593	£2,551	£16,084	£74,358
Order Based														
Value of Orders on Hand	N/A	£170,413	£188,409	£287,101	£270,697	£205,725	£265,234	£276,442	£527,834	£498,435	£440,575	£314,559	£334,829	N/A
Average Number of Orders	N/A	263	331	609	553	503	350	353	850	857	655	857	716	N/A
Number of Days Orders on Hand	N/A	11.0	11.8	19.2	13.1	10.0	14.6	15.8	28.2	30.0	20.7	12.9	19.6	N/A
Order Intake in Month - Total	£76,686	£320,232	£330,597	£405,214	£443,072	£345,452	£398,400	£393,303	£669,671	£321,556	£403,333	£391,171	£402,727	£409,518
Order Intake in Month - UK	£19,397	£232,764	£203,797	£293,190	£310,640	£245,455	£289,951	£279,181	£577,570	£248,681	£300,939	£273,145	£244,180	£297,884
Order Intake in Month - Export	£7,289	£87,468	£126,800	£112,024	£132,432	£99,997	£98,449	£114,322	£92,101	£72,875	£102,394	£118,027	£158,547	£111,633
Export %	27.3%	27.3%	38.4%	27.6%	29.9%	28.9%	24.7%	29.1%	13.8%	22.7%	25.4%	30.2%	39.4%	27.3%
Average Daily Order Intake in Month- Total	N/A	£15,416	£16,530	£20,261	£19,264	£17,273	£20,968	£17,887	£30,440	£15,312	£18,333	£18,540	£18,306	£19,374
Average Daily Order Intake in Month - UK	N/A	£11,200	£10,190	£14,659	£13,506	£12,273	£13,187	£12,690	£26,253	£11,842	£17,279	£17,920	£17,099	£14,082
Average Daily Order Intake in Month - Export	N/A	£4,216	£6,340	£5,601	£5,758	£5,000	£5,182	£5,196	£4,186	£3,470	£4,654	£5,620	£7,207	£5,292
On Time Delivery	N/A	97.0%	93.3%	96.2%	97.5%	94.8%	95.0%	96.40%	98.70%	95.70%	94.00%	96.90%	98.00%	96.0%
Profit Based - Actual/Budget														
Gross Margin to Sales %	N/A	46.0%/43.1%	45.5%/45.3%	45.5%/45.3%	40.0%/45.7%	43.3%/45.2%	43.2%/45.2%	43.1%/45.5%	43.2%/46.0%	43.1%/46.1%	35.0%/45.8%	44.8%/45.6%	43.3%/45.8%	42.5%/45.6%
Operating Profit to Sales %	N/A	25.30%/22.0%	22.7%/22.7%	16.8%/19.0%	26.0%/26.3%	26.0%/24.1%	24.1%/22.9%	24.1%/26.0%	25.9%/25.5%	22.1%/26.9%	18.0%/25.5%	28.5%/25.5%	22.7%/26.9%	24.0%/25.1%
EBITDA to Sales %	N/A	28.4%/24.7%	25.4%/25.3%	19.6%/21.6%	27.9%/28.8%	28.7%/26.9%	24.1%/25.8%	26.6%/28.7%	28.2%/28.8%	24.7%/29.6%	18.3%/28.7%	30.1%/28.4%	25.2%/29.6%	26.1%/27.8%
Gross Margin Value per Employee	£3,664	£43,963	£3,635	£3,399	£4,542	£4,441	£3,637	£3,601	£4,143	£3,601	£3,813	£3,964	£3,964	£44,417
Operating Profit Value per Employee	£2,016	£24,198	£1,816	£1,252	£2,959	£2,729	£2,029	£2,058	£2,488	£1,833	£1,962	£352	£2,081	£25,054
EBITDA Value per Employee	£2,261	£27,130	£2,030	£1,466	£3,173	£2,947	£2,251	£2,271	£2,701	£2,028	£1,996	£3,749	£2,307	£27,268
Return on Capital Employed (ROCE)	N/A	30.1%	30.0%	29.0%	29.0%	31.3%	31.5%	31.0%	32.3%	32.5%	31.8%	33.0%	33.3%	33.3%
Working Capital Based														
Current Ratio	N/A	1.85	1.54	1.49	1.50	1.46	1.56	1.47	1.52	1.52	1.55	1.62	1.65	1.92
Quick Ratio	N/A	1.02	0.85	0.86	0.88	0.94	0.92	0.82	0.87	0.81	0.77	0.86	0.94	0.86
Stock Turnover	N/A	2.63	2.64	2.62	3.79	3.85	3.00	2.70	2.96	2.16	2.67	2.43	2.15	1.99
Total Debtors	N/A		£703,677	£745,394	£827,716	£904,427	£847,178	£809,477	£849,040	£862,979	£839,797	£943,099	£843,222	
Export Debtors	N/A		£140,048	£171,377	£203,542	£211,769	£179,269	£167,653	£161,289	£108,308	£147,501	£216,949	£186,136	
Total Sales - Last 12 Months	N/A		£3,793,963	£3,764,917	£3,893,921	£4,039,898	£4,081,269	£4,175,245	£4,196,914	£4,241,691	£4,347,355	£4,532,012	£4,568,056	
Export Sales - Last 12 Months	N/A		£1,004,791	£990,766	£1,034,998	£1,088,846	£1,129,618	£1,165,660	£1,158,448	£1,145,996	£1,174,138	£1,223,642	£1,207,979	
Debtor Days - Total	N/A	60	63	64	69	72	70	67	65	65	67	67	60	60
UK Only	N/A	63	63	64	68	73	70	67	70	76	68	68	61	61
- Export Only	N/A	52	51	63	72	71	58	52	51	34	46	65	56	56
Sales Value per Calendar Day (Cum. YTD)	N/A	£10,260	£10,307	£10,673	£14,661	£13,672	£11,137	£12,249	£13,303	£11,257	£14,899	£16,472	£12,521	£12,521
Interest Impact per Calendar Day	N/A	£23.62	£23.62	£24.46	£33.60	£31.33	£25.52	£28.00	£25.80	£25.80	£34.14	£37.75	£28.69	£28.69
Debtor Improvement/Decline on Previous Mth	N/A	N/A	£3,781.77	-£46,353.66	-£71,789.81	-£48,131.69	£61,556.84	£45,344.12	-£23,510.13	£3,867.94	£40,766.00	-£88,840.18	£96,274.28	
Additional Interest Saving/Cost	N/A	N/A	£8.67	-£106.23	-£165.37	-£110.30	£141.07	£103.91	-£53.88	£8.86	£93.42	-£203.59	£220.63	
Cash Collections	£350,083	£4,200,996	£333,500	£302,833	£422,868	£373,098	£441,882	£449,689	£425,985	£373,903	£793,555	£355,140	£499,863	£5,222,745
Availability Generated	£346,555	£4,158,665	£346,425	£329,621	£492,841	£438,302	£393,221	£377,865	£459,614	£385,752	£447,186	£443,357	£427,876	£4,542,059
Total Creditors	N/A		£358,666	£386,364	£416,202	£374,001	£337,931	£504,089	£453,556	£446,845	£498,186	£381,751	£304,188	
Import Creditors			£178,588	£178,418	£185,761	£134,066	£127,106	£247,821	£167,922	£181,746	£153,415	£90,091	£73,749	
Total COGS - Last 12 Months			£2,048,404	£2,030,937	£2,138,779	£2,225,447	£2,256,368	£2,290,382	£2,332,765	£2,364,242	£2,330,669	£2,376,035	£2,376,035	
Creditor Days	N/A	59	59	64	65	55	50	74	64	63	71	52	45	45

			Jan	Feb	Mar	Apr	May	Jun	Jul	Aug	Sep	Oct	Nov	YTD
Staff Based														
Hrs Sickness - Works	49	586	22	0	16	8	52	70	0	28	124	16	119	455
Hrs Sickness - Staff	24	293	7	37	41	16	62	13	0	32	79	82	8	376
Hrs Sickness - Total	73	879	29	37	57	24	113	83	0	60	203	98	127	830
Hrs Sickness as % of basic working hrs	N/A	1.1%	0.5%	0.6%	0.8%	0.4%	1.9%	1.2%	0.0%	0.9%	3.0%	1.5%	1.9%	1.1%
Hrs Sick as % of basic work hrs (excl. long term)	N/A	1.1%	0.5%	0.6%	0.8%	0.4%	1.9%	1.2%	0.0%	0.9%	3.0%	1.5%	0.5%	1.0%
Headcount	39		40	40	40	40	41	43	43	42	41	41	41	41
Actual Equivalent Production Hrs	49,947	4,162	4,275	3,915	4,575	4,329	4,518	4,581	4,685	4,841	4,739	4,531	3,974	48,963
Budget Equivalent Production Hrs	54,817	4,568	4,506	4,159	4,679	4,506	4,419	4,506	4,593	4,593	4,505	4,505	4,505	49,475
Variance	4,870	406	231	244	104	177	-99	-75	-92	-248	-234	-26	531	513
Average Weekly Paid Hourly Rate (Ex NIC)	N/A	£6.31	£6.68	£6.64	£6.75	£6.69	£6.65	£6.54	£6.40	£6.52	£6.58	£6.56	£6.43	£6.54
(With CTL's) (Ex NIC)	N/A	£6.95	£7.29	£7.28	£7.30	£7.27	£7.22	£7.11	£6.97	£7.07	£7.13	£7.15	£7.09	£7.12
Overtime Hours														
x 1.25 (Actual vs Budget)	127.18 vs 249.97	1,526.20 vs 2,999.61	147.75 vs 185.47	92.25 vs 171.20	201.25 vs 192.60	284.92 v 185.47	333.75 vs 181.94	171.79 vs 185.47	257.33 vs 189.03	264.13 vs 189.03	269.50 vs 185.47	134.67 v 185.47	117.83 v 185.47	2057.34 vs 1851.11
x 1.50 (Actual vs Budget)	54.96 vs 182.58	659.54 vs 2,191.00	126.67 vs 182.00	84.00 vs 168.00	94.00 vs 189.00	25.00 vs 182.00	14.88 vs 178.51	106.63 vs 182.00	5.50 vs 185.50	83.00 vs 185.50	206.33 vs 182.0	536.67 v 182.00	95.42 v 182.0	3047.32 vs 1816.00
x 1.33 (Actual vs Budget)	73.57 vs 104.33	882.81 vs 1,252.00	68.75 vs 85.54	103.00 vs 78.96	174.25 vs 88.83	137.04 vs 85.54	142.02 vs 83.90	125.00 vs 85.54	60.00 vs 87.19	172.42 vs 87.19	120.50 vs 85.54	156.83 v 85.54	99.83 v 85.54	1259.89 vs 853.77
Nights	11.98	143.75	0.00	0.00	0.00	0.00	0.00	0.00	0.00	0.00	0.00	0.00	0.00	0.00
Overtime as a % of Sales	0.7%	0.7%	0.9%	0.8%	0.8%	0.9%	1.2%	0.9%	0.6%	1.2%	1.1%	1.4%	0.7%	0.9%
Adjusted Overtime as a % of Sales	0.7%	0.7%	0.9%	0.8%	0.8%	0.9%	1.2%	0.9%	0.6%	1.2%	1.1%	1.4%	0.7%	0.9%
Actual Overtime Cost	£2,057.48	£24,689.76	£2,862	£2,353	£3,848	£3,566	£4,040	£3,267	£2,391	£4,172	£4,882	£7,060	£2,651	£41,092
Nights Premium Time Cost	£105.54	£1,266.47	£0	£0	£0	£0	£0	£0	£0	£0	£0	£0	£0	£0
Adjusted Overtime Cost	£2,163.02	£25,956.23	£2,862	£2,353	£3,848	£3,566	£4,040	£3,267	£2,391	£4,172	£4,882	£7,060	£2,651	£41,092
Budget Overtime Cost	£4,317.65	£51,811.76	£3,881	£3,582	£4,030	£3,881	£3,806	£3,881	£3,956	£3,956	£3,881	£3,881	£3,881	£42,617
Variance	£2,154.63	£25,855.53	£1,019	£1,230	£182	£315	-£234	£614	£1,565	-£216	-£1,001	-£3,179	£1,230	£1,524

Footnotes: *W Tochel 31 hrs   *K Simpson 41 hrs   *T Williams 28 hr   *T Williams 62 hrs   *D Goude 23 hrs   *M Brookes 39 hrs   *R Duthie 24hrs   *R Duthie 32 hrs   78 Hrs C Matthews   24 Hrs G Latham   D Goude 26 hrs   R Duthie 32 hrs   C Price 94 hrs

Formulae for Ratios

$$\text{Current Ratio} = \frac{\text{Current Assets}}{\text{Current Liabilities}}$$

Shows company's ability to service its current liabilities.
Ratio should be above 1 and the higher the better.

$$\text{Quick Ratio} = \frac{(\text{Current Assets} - \text{Stocks})}{\text{Current Liabilities}} \quad \text{(Also known as Acid Test ratio)}$$

Shows company's ability to service its current liabilities using assets that can be readily turned into cash, i.e. without having to liquidate stock.
Should ideally be above 1 and the higher the better.

$$\text{ROCE} = \frac{\text{Operating profit in period}}{\text{Total Reserves} + \text{Debt}}$$

Gives a measure of how well the company's reserves are working for it, i.e. what operating profit is generated from the company's investments and assets. Reserves defined as total P&L plus share capital (also known as net worth).

$$\text{Debtor Days} = \frac{\text{Debtors Balance (ex VAT)}}{\text{Sales in period}} \times \text{No. of days in period}$$

Shows how many days on average, customers are taking to pay us. Obviously, the lower the better.

$$\text{Creditor Days} = \frac{\text{Creditors Balance (ex VAT)}}{\text{Cost of goods in period}} \times \text{No. of days in period}$$

Shows how many days on average, we are taking to pay suppliers. The higher the better.

$$\text{Stock Turnover} = \frac{365}{\text{Stocks}} \times \frac{\text{Cost of goods sold in period}}{\text{No. of days in period}}$$

Shows an annualised measure of how many times the value of stock is turned over. The higher the better. The higher the value the more times stock is used and replenished, thus avoiding obsolescence.

Carriage Recharge Info

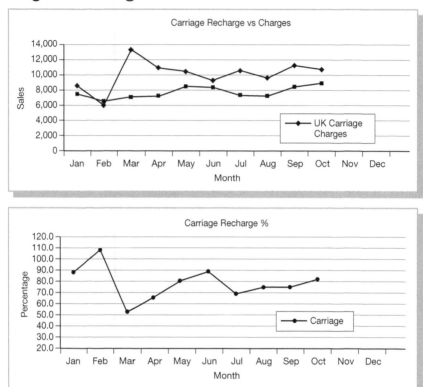

Sample Full Published Accounts

Registered Number: 9765432

A Good Deal Limited
Directors' Report and Financial Statements
for the Year Ended 31 March 20X2

A Finance LLP

The Works

Grangemouth Road

Birmingham

BM4 5LJ

A Good Deal Limited

Company Information

DIRECTORS:	A Ryan
	P Ryan
SECRETARY:	A Dent
REGISTERED OFFICE:	Unit 34A
	Oakley Road
	Salford
	Manchester
	M4 2LP
BANK:	Bank of Good Deals
	39 Wishful Thinking Road
	Edinburgh
	EH10 2GJ
AUDITORS:	Brown & Company LLP
	Oakham Way
	Huddersfield
	West Yorkshire
	HD7 2MR

A Good Deal Limited

Directors' Report for the Year Ended 31 March 20X2

The directors present their report and the audited financial statements for the year ended 31 March 20X2.

Directors' responsibilities

The directors are responsible for preparing the Directors' Report and the financial statements in accordance with applicable law and regulations.

Company law requires the directors to prepare financial statements for each financial year. Under that law the directors have elected to prepare financial statements in accordance with United Kingdom Generally Accepted Accounting Practice (United Kingdom Accounting Standards and applicable law). Under company law, the directors must not approve the financial statements unless they are satisfied that they give a true and fair view of the state of affairs of the company and of the profit or loss of the company for that period. In preparing these financial statements, the directors are required to:

- select suitable accounting policies and apply them consistently,
- make judgements and accounting estimates that are reasonable and prudent,
- state whether applicable UK Accounting Standards have been followed, subject to any material departures disclosed and explained in the financial statements,
- prepare the financial statements on the going-concern basis unless it is inappropriate to presume that the company will continue in business.

The directors are responsible for keeping adequate accounting records that are sufficient to show and explain the company's transactions and disclose with reasonable accuracy at any time the financial position of the company and enable them to ensure the financial statements comply with the Companies Act 2006. They are also responsible for safeguarding the assets of the company and hence for taking reasonable steps for the prevention and detection of fraud and other irregularities.

Each director has taken steps that they ought to have taken as a director, in order to make themselves aware of any relevant audit information and to establish that the company's auditors are aware of that information. The directors confirm that there is no relevant information that they know of which they know the auditors are unaware of.

The directors are responsible for the maintenance and integrity of the corporate financial information included on the company's website. Legislation in the United Kingdom governing the preparation and dissemination of financial statements may differ from the legislation in other jurisdictions.

Principal activity

The principal activity of the company is that of retailing.

Business review

Fair review of the business

The directors are pleased with the results of the 20X2 financial year, which has seen an increase in turnover of 39.8%. The company benefited significantly from the reduction in VAT rate. Gross profit margin has dropped slightly, due to the increase in supply chain costs.

Profit before tax has decreased slightly due to a payment made to the Employer Financed Retirement Benefit Scheme of £1,000,200.

The company opened an additional 24 stores during the year. Post year-end, the company is continuing to open further stores, with a year-end target of over 40 new store openings.

The directors are confident that they will continue the organic growth and profitability in the year to 31 March 20X3 This will be achieved by improved profit margins and turnover in existing stores and the opening of new stores. The company has had a very promising start to the year.

Development and performance of the business

	20X2	20X1
Turnover	£93,646,014	£67,010,504
Turnover growth	40%	34%
Gross profit margin	38%	40%
Profit before tax	£1,182,497	£1,361,338

Position of the business

At the end of the year the net assets totalled £4,093,322.

Financial risk

Price risk, credit risk, liquidity risk and cash flow risk

The business's principal financial instruments comprise bank balances, bank overdrafts, trade debtors, trade creditors and loans to the business. The main purpose of these instruments is to finance the business's operations.

In respect of bank balances, the liquidity risk is managed by maintaining a balance between the continuity of funding and flexibility through the use of overdraft at floating rates of interest. All of the business's cash balances are held in such a way as to achieve a competitive rate of interest. The business makes use of money market facilities where funds are available.

Trade debtors are managed in respect of credit and cash flow risk by policies concerning the credit offered to customers and the regular monitoring of amounts outstanding for both time and credit limits. The amounts presented in the balance sheet are net of allowances for doubtful debtors.

Trade creditors' liquidity risk is managed by ensuring sufficient funds are available to meet amounts due.

Loans comprise loans from the directors. The business manages the liquidity risk by ensuring that there are sufficient funds to meet the payments.

The company buys from suppliers based overseas and transactions with these suppliers may be in foreign currencies, which are subject to exchange rate fluctuations. The company, when it considers it prudent, uses foreign currency forward contracts to mitigate these risks.

Results and dividend

The results for the company are set out in the financial statements.

An interim dividend of £153,000 was paid during the year.

Employment policies

The company's policy is to give full and fair consideration to applications for employment made by disabled persons, having regard to their particular aptitudes and abilities.

Disabled employees receive appropriate training to promote their career development within the company. Employees who become disabled are retained in their existing posts where possible or retrained for suitable alternative posts.

Regular meetings are held between senior management and employee representatives to discuss matters of concern. Employees are kept well-informed about the progress and position of the company.

Directors

The directors who held office during the year were as follows:

– A Ryan

– P Ryan

Auditors

The auditors, Brown & Co. LLP, will be proposed for re-appointment in accordance with Section 487 of the Companies Act 2006.

Approved by the Board and signed on its behalf by

A Ryan

Director

Date: 13 August 20X2

Independent Auditors' Report to the Members of A Good Deal Limited

We have audited the financial statements of A Good Deal Limited for the year ended 31 March 20X2, set out on pages 202 to 204. The financial reporting framework that has been applied in their preparation is applicable law and United Kingdom Accounting Standards (United Kingdom Generally Accepted Accounting Practice).

This report is made solely to the company's members, as a body, in accordance with Sections 495 and 496 of the Companies Act 2006. Our work has been undertaken so that we might state to the company's members those matters we are required to state to them in an auditors' report and for no other purpose. To the fullest extent permitted by law, we do not accept or assume responsibility to anyone other than the company and the company's members as a body, for our audit work, for this report, or for the opinions we have formed.

Respective responsibilities of directors and auditors

As explained more fully in the Directors' Responsibilities Statement set out on pages 196–197, the directors are responsible for the preparation of the financial statements and for being satisfied that they give a true and fair view. Our responsibility is to audit the financial statements in accordance with applicable law and International Standards on Auditing (UK and Ireland). Those standards require us to comply with the Auditing Practices Board's (APB's) Ethical Standards for Auditors.

Scope of the audit of the financial statements

An audit involves obtaining evidence about the amounts and disclosures in the financial statements sufficient to give reasonable assurance that the financial statements are free from material misstatement, whether caused by fraud or error. This includes an assessment of whether the accounting policies are appropriate to the company's circumstances and have been consistently applied and adequately disclosed, the reasonableness of significant accounting estimates made by the directors, and the overall presentation of the financial statements.

Opinion on financial statements

In our opinion the financial statements

- give a true and fair view of the state of the company's affairs as at 31 March 20X2 and of its profit for the year then ended,

- have been properly prepared in accordance with United Kingdom Generally Accepted Accounting Practice, and

- have been prepared in accordance with the requirements of the Companies Act 2006.

Opinion on other matter prescribed by the Companies Act 2006

In our opinion the information given in the Directors' Report for the financial year for which the financial statements are prepared is consistent with the financial statements.

Matters on which we are required to report by exception

We have nothing to report in respect of the following matters where the Companies Act 2006 requires us to report to you if, in our opinion

- adequate accounting records have not been kept, or returns adequate for our audit have not been received from branches not visited by us, or

- the financial statements are not in agreement with the accounting records and returns, or

- certain disclosures of directors' remuneration specified by law are not made, or

- we have not received all the information and explanations we require for our audit.

Peter Jones FCA CF
Senior Statutory Auditor

For and on behalf of
Brown & Co LLP, Statutory Auditor

19 August 20X2

Brown & Co. LLP
Oakham Way
Huddersfield
West Yorkshire
HD7 2MR

A Good Deal Limited

Profit and Loss Account for the Year Ended 31 March 20X2

	Note	20X2 £	20X1 £
Turnover	2	93,646,104	67,010,504
Cost of sales		(58,271,205)	(40,031,162)
Gross Profit		**35,374,899**	**26,979,342**
Administrative expenses		(34,087,088)	(25,466,194)
Other operating income	3	13,688	36,500
Operating profit		**1,301,499**	**1,549,648**
Other interest receivable and similar income	4	2,735	8,807
Interest payable and similar charges	7	(121,737)	(197,117)
Profit on ordinary activities before taxation		**1,182,497**	**1,361,338**
Tax on profit on ordinary activities	8	(539,555)	(510,499)
Profit for the financial year	18	**642,942**	**850,839**

Turnover and operating profit derive wholly from continuing operations.

The company has no recognised gains or losses for the year other than the results above.

There is no material difference between the result reported on an unmodified historical cost basis.

The notes on pages 205 to 217 form an integral part of these financial statements.

A Good Deal Limited

Balance Sheet as at 31 March 20X2

	Notes	20X2 £	20X2 £	20X1 £	20X1 £
Fixed Assets					
Intangible Assets	10		54,000		81,000
Tangible Assets	11		8,106,089		5,813,889
			8,160,089		5,894,889
Current Assets					
Stock	12	10,207,876		7,009,427	
Debtors	13	1,944,724		1,278,606	
Cash at bank and in hand		2,493,676		2,598,495	
		14,646,276		10,886,528	
Creditors: amounts falling due within one year	14	(18,398,043)		(12,938,037)	
Net current liabilities			(3,751,767)		(2,051,509)
Total assets less current liabilities			4,408,322		3,843,380
Provisions for liabilities	16		(315,000)		(240,000)
Net Assets			**4,093,322**		**3,603,380**
Capital & Reserves					
Called up share capital	17		80,000		80,000
Share premium reserve	18		420,000		420,000
Profit and loss reserve	18		3,593,322		3,103,380
Shareholders' funds	**19**		**4,093,322**		**3,603,380**

Approved by the Board on 13 August 20X2

A Ryan

Director

The notes on pages 205 to 217 form an integral part of these financial statements.

A Good Deal Limited

Cash Flow Statement for the Year Ended 31 March 20X2

	Notes	20X2 £	20X2 £	20X1 £	20X1 £
Net cash inflow from operating activities	21		2,617,744		3,023,358
Returns on investment and servicing of finance	22		(119,002)		(188,310)
Taxation	22		(990)		(499,508)
Capital expenditure and financial investment		(4,042,948)		(2,388,438)	
Purchase of tangible fixed assets			(4,042,948)		(2,388,438)
Equity dividends paid			(153,000)		(132,000)
			(1,698,196)		(184,898)
Cash outflow before management of liquid resources and financing					
Financing					
Increase in loans and borrowings		1,593,377		-	
Capital element of finance lease/HP contract rental payments		-	1,593,377	(11,531)	(11,531)
Shareholders' funds			**(104,819)**		**(196,429)**

Reconciliation of net cash flow to movement in net debt

	Note	20X2 £	20X1 £
Decrease in cash in the year	23	(104,819)	(196,429)
Cash (inflow)/outflow from (increase)/decrease in debt and lease financing		(1,593,377)	11,531
Change in net funds resulting from cash flows		(1,698,196)	(184,898)
Net debt at start of the year	23	(3,050,475)	(2,865,577)
Net debt at the end of the year	23	**(4,748,671)**	**(3,050,475)**

The notes on pages 205 to 217 form an integral part of these financial statements.

A Good Deal Limited

Notes to the Financial Statements for the Year Ended 31 March 20X2

1. Accounting policies

Basis of preparation

The financial statements have been prepared under the historical cost convention and in accordance with applicable accounting standards.

Turnover

Turnover represents amounts chargeable, net of value added tax, in respect of the sale of goods and services to customers.

Amortisation

Amortisation is provided on intangible fixed assets so as to write off the cost, less any estimated residual value, over their expected useful economic life as follows:

Goodwill   5 years straight line basis

Depreciation

Depreciation is provided on tangible fixed assets so as to write off the cost or valuation, less any estimated residual value, over their expected useful economic life as follows:

Short leasehold properties	Straight line over the life of the lease
Shop fixtures and fittings	20% per annum on written down value
Store opening costs	Straight line over the life of the lease, from opening
Computer and office equipment	20% per annum on cost or 20% per annum on written down value

Goodwill

Goodwill is the difference between the fair value of consideration paid for an acquired entity and the aggregate of the fair value of that entity's identifiable assets and liabilities.

Positive goodwill is capitalised, classified as an asset on the balance sheet and amortised on a straight line basis over its useful economic life. It is reviewed for impairment at the end of the first full financial year following the acquisition and in other periods if events or changes in circumstances indicate that the carrying value may not be recoverable.

Stock

Stock is valued at the lower of cost and net realisable value, after due regard for obsolete and slow moving stocks. Net realisable value is based on selling price less anticipated costs to completion and selling costs.

Deferred taxation

Deferred tax is recognised, without discounting, in respect of all timing differences between the treatment of certain items for taxation and accounting purposes, which have arisen but not reversed by the balance sheet date, except as required by FRS19.

Deferred tax is measured at the rates that are expected to apply in the periods when the timing differences are expected to reverse, based on the tax rates and law enacted at the balance sheet date.

Foreign currencies

Profit and loss account transactions in foreign currencies are translated into sterling at the exchange rate ruling at the date of the transaction. Monetary assets and liabilities denominated in foreign currencies are translated into sterling at the closing rates at the balance sheet date and the exchange differences are included in the profit and loss account.

Operating leases

Rentals payable under operating leases are charged in the profit and loss account on a straight line basis over the lease term.

Operating lease incentives are recognised on a straight line basis, as a reduction of the rental expense over the shorter of the lease term and the period of the first rent review where market rentals will be payable.

Purchases subject to reservation of title

Goods purchased subject to reservation of title are treated as purchases, and any corresponding liabilities are included in creditors, in the same manner as goods which are not subject to reservation of title. Some trade creditors may therefore be secured, but the amount involved cannot reasonably be quantified.

Employer Financed Retirement Benefit Scheme (EFRBS)

During the year, the Company established an employer financed retirement scheme for the benefit of its officers, employees and their wider families, A Good Deal Limited Employer Financed Retirement Benefit Scheme (the Scheme).

In accordance with UITF32 'Employee Benefit Trusts and other intermediate payment arrangements' the Company does not include the assets and liabilities of the Scheme on its balance sheet to the extent that it considers that it will not retain any future economic benefit from the assets of the Scheme and will not have control of the rights or other access to those future economic benefits.

Financial instruments

Financial instruments are classified and accounted for, according to the substance of the contractual arrangement, as financial assets, financial liabilities or equity instruments. An equity instrument is any contract that evidences a residual interest in the assets of the company after deducting all of its liabilities.

2. Turnover

The total turnover of the company for the year has been derived from its principal activity wholly undertaken in the United Kingdom.

3. Other operating income

	20X2	20X1
	£	£
Rent receivable	13,688	36,500

4. Operating profit

Operating profit is stated after charging

	20X2 £	20X1 £
Property rents	9,047,924	7,823,001
Hire of other assets – operating leases	73,261	82,157
The audit of the company's annual accounts	20,000	13,000
Auditors' remuneration – non-audit services	3,500	1,335
Loss on disposal of tangible fixed assets	39,297	1,901
Depreciation of fixed assets	1,711,451	1,288,976
Amortisation of goodwill	27,000	2`7,000
Employer Financed Retirement Benefit Scheme contribution	1,000,200	–

5. Particulars of employees

The average number of persons employed by the company (including directors) during the year, analysed by category, was as follows:

	20X2 No.	20X1 No.
Sales	1,437	1,100
Warehouse	90	75
	1,527	1,175

The aggregate payroll costs of these persons were as follows:

	20X2 £	20X1 £
Wages and salaries	13,195,392	9,650,974
Social security costs	830,785	615,388
Employer Financed Retirement Benefit Scheme contribution	1,000,200	–
	15,026,377	10,266,362

6. Directors' remuneration

The directors' remuneration for the year was as follows:

	20X2	20X1
	£	£
Directors' remuneration (including benefits in kind)	26,000	26,000
Employer Financed Retirement Benefit Scheme	1,000,200	–

The aggregate of remuneration and amounts receivable under long term incentive schemes of the highest paid director was £13,500 (20X1 – £13,500), and a contribution of £1,000,200 (20X1 – nil) was made to an employer financed retirement benefit scheme on their behalf.

During the year the Company, in order to motivate and incentivise its officers and employees, established an employer financed retirement benefit scheme for the benefit of the Company's officers, employees and their wider families. A Good Deal Limited Employer Financed Retirement Benefit Scheme ('the Scheme') £1,000,200 included above relates to the Scheme contributions made during the year.

7. Interest payable and similar charges

	20X2	20X1
	£	£
Bank interest payable	108,962	206,681
Other interest payable	12,775	–
Finance charges	–	(9,564)
	121,737	197,117

8. Taxation

Analysis of current period tax charge

	20X2 £	20X1 £
Current tax		
Corporation tax charge	445,000	540,000
(Over)/under provision in previous year	19,555	(4,501)
UK corporation tax	464,555	535,499
Deferred tax		
Origination and reversal of timing differences	75,000	(25,000)
Total tax on profit on ordinary activities	**539,555**	**510,499**

Factors affecting current period tax charge

The tax assessed on the profit on ordinary activities for the year is higher than (20X1 – higher than) the standard rate of corporation tax in the UK of 28.00% (20X1 – 28.00%).

The differences are reconciled below.

	20X2 £	20X1 £
Profit on ordinary activities before taxation	1,182,497	1,361,338
Standard rate corporation tax charge	331,099	381,175
Expenses not deductable for tax purposes (including goods)	5,706	14,930
Capital allowances for period in excess of depreciation	(98,679)	7,615
Depreciation and loss on disposal of non-qualifying assets	202,978	135,379
Prior period (over)/under provision	19,555	(4,501)
Rounding differences	3,896	1,417
Revenue items eligible for capital allowances	–	(516)
Total current tax for the year	**464,555**	**535,499**

9. Dividends

	20X2 £	20X1 £
Paid	153,000	132,000

10. Intangible fixed assets

	Goodwill £
Cost	
As at 1 April 20X1 and 31 March 20X2	135,000
Amortisation	
As at 1 April 20X1	54,000
Charge for the year	27,000
As at 31 March 20X2	81,000
Net book value	
As at 31 March 20X1	54,000
As at 31 March 20X2	81,000

11. Tangible fixed assets

	Short leasehold land & buildings £	Fixtures & Fittings £	Motor vehicles £	Store opening £	Computer & office equipment £	Total £
Cost						
As at 1 April 20X1	1,074,357	8,533,143	9,901	374,512	708,351	10,700,264
Additions	468,224	2,973,098	–	492,259	109,367	4,042,948
Disposals	(76,828)	–	–	–	–	(76,828)
As at 31 March 20X2	1,465,753	11,506,241	9,901	866,771	817,718	14,666,384
Depreciation						
As at 1 April 20X1	250,132	4,095,532	2,759	–	537,952	4,886,375
Eliminated on disposals	(37,531)	–	–	–	–	(37,531)
Charge for the year	127,031	1,408,744	1,785	98,943	74,948	1,711,451
As at 31 March 20X2	339,632	5,504,276	4,544	98,943	612,900	6,560,295
Net book value						
As at 31 March 20X1	1,126,121	6,001,965	5,357	767,828	204,818	8,106,089
As at 31 March 20X2	824,225	4,437,611	7,142	374,512	170,818	5,813,889

12. Stocks and work in progress

	20X2 £	20X1 £
Stocks	10,207,876	7,009,427

13. Debtors

	20X2 £	20X1 £
Trade debtors	536,689	117,024
Amounts owed by connected companies	323,692	314,530
Other debtors	73,388	176,058
Prepayments and accrued income	1,010,955	670,994
	1,944,724	1,278,606

14. Creditors: amounts falling due within one year

	20X2 £	20X1 £
Bank loans and overdrafts	7,242,347	5,648,970
Trade creditors	7,616,562	5,679,226
Corporation tax	1,004,556	540,991
Social security and other taxes	315,253	402,246
Other creditors	316,489	205,060
Director current accounts	8,891	1,119
Accruals and deferred income	1,893,945	460,425
	18,398,043	12,938,037

15. Security of borrowings

Bank borrowings are secured by a mortgage debenture over the assets of the company.

16. Provisions for liabilities

	Deferred tax provision £
As at 1 April 20X1	240,000
Deferred tax provision charged to the profit & loss account	75,000
As at 31 March 20X2	315,000

Deferred tax

Deferred tax is provided at 28.00% (20X1 – 28.00%)

	20X2 £	20X1 £
Accelerated capital allowances	315,000	240,000

17. Share capital

	20X2 £	20X1 £
Allotted, called up and fully paid		
Equity		
Ordinary shares of £1 each	80,000	80,000

18. Reserves

	Share premium reserve £	Profit & loss reserve £	Total £
Balance at 1 April 20X1	420,000	3,103,380	3,523,380
Transfer from profit & loss account for the year	–	642,942	642,942
Dividends	–	(153,000)	(153,000)
Balance at 31 March 20X2	420,000	3,593,322	4,013,322

19. Reconciliation of movements in shareholders' funds

	20X2 £	20X1 £
Profit attributable to members of the company	642,942	850,839
Dividends	(153,000)	(132,000)
	489,942	718,839
Opening shareholders' funds	3,603,380	2,884,541
Closing shareholders' funds	4,093,322	3,603,380

20. Operating lease commitments

	Land and buildings		Other	
	20X2	20X1	20X2	20X1
	£	£	£	£
Within one year	112,083	367,000	28,912	–
Within two to five years	1,219,367	716,500	47,457	75,017
Over five years	8,417,888	6,738,188	–	–
	9,749,338	7,821,688	76,369	75,017

21. Reconciliation of operating profit to operating cash flows

	20X2	20X1
	£	£
Operating profit	1,301,499	1,549,648
Depreciation, amortisation and impairment charges	1,738,451	1,315,976
Loss on disposal of fixed assets	39,297	1,901
Increase in stocks	(3,198,449)	(1,284,305)
(Increase)/decrease in debtors	(666,118)	100,151
Increase in creditors	3,403,064	1,339,98
Net cash inflow from operating activities	**2,617,744**	**3,023,358**

22. Analysis of cash flows

	20X2 £	20X1 £
Returns on investment and servicing of finance		
HP interest paid	–	9,564
Other interest paid	(121,737)	(206,681)
Interest received	2,735	8,807
	(119,002)	(188,310)

	20X2 £	20X1 £
Taxation		
Taxation paid	**(990)**	**(499,508)**

23. Analysis of net debt

	At start of period £	Cash flow £	At end of period £
Cash at bank and in hand	2,598,495	(104,819)	2,493,676
Bank overdraft	(5,648,970)	(1,593,377)	(7,242,347)
Cash and bank net funds	(3,050,475)	(1,698,196)	(4,748,671)
Change in debt	–	–	–
Net debt	(3,050,475)	(1,698,196)	(4,748,671)

24. Related parties

Controlling entity

The company is controlled by the directors who own 80% of the called up share capital.

Related party transactions

At the year end, the company had an interest-free loan outstanding from Learn Limited of £323,692 (20X1 – £313,564). Learn Limited is under the common control of the directors, Mr A Ryan and Mr P Ryan.

At the year end £55,696 was owed from Mr A Ryan (Jnr), a shareholder of the company.

Directors' advances

The following balances owed to the directors were outstanding at the year end.

	20X2	20X1
	£	£
Mr A Ryan	1,455	188
Mr P Ryan	7,436	931
	8,891	1,119

No interest is charged in respect of these balances.

Appendix C

Sample Abbreviated Published Accounts

REGISTERED NUMBER: 12345678 (England and Wales)

Unaudited Financial Statements
for the year ended
31 December 20X2
For
The Company Limited

The Company Limited (REGISTERED NUMBER: 12345678)

Contents of the Financial Statements

For the year ended 31 December 20X2

The Company Limited (REGISTERED NUMBER: 12345678)

Company Information
For the year ended 31 December 20X2

DIRECTORS:	A Smith
	B Brown
REGISTERED OFFICE:	Worlds End Works
	Honley
	West Yorkshire
	AB9 8CD
REGISTERED NUMBER:	12345678

The Company Limited (REGISTERED NUMBER: 12345678)

Balance Sheet
31 December 20X2

	Note	31.12.20X2 £	31.12.20X1 £
CURRENT ASSETS			
Debtors		2,431	6,211
TOTAL ASSETS LESS CURRENT LIABILITIES		2,431	6,211
CAPITAL AND RESERVES			
Called up share capital	2	100	100
SHAREHOLDERS' FUNDS		2,531	6,311

The company is entitled to exemption from audit under Section 480 of the Companies Act 2006 for the year ended 31 December 20X2.

The members have not required the company to obtain an audit of its financial statements for the year ended 31 December 20X2 in accordance with Section 476 of the Companies Act 2006.

The directors acknowledge their responsibilities for:

a   ensuring that the company keeps accounting records which comply with Sections 386 and 387 of the Companies act 2006 and

b   preparing financial statements which give a true and fair view of the state of affairs of the company as at the end of each financial year and of its profit or loss for each financial year in accordance with the requirements of Sections 294 and 395 and which otherwise comply with the requirements of the Companies Act 2006 relating to the financial statements, so far as applicable to the company.

These financial statements have been prepared in accordance with the special provisions of Part 15 of the Companies Act 2006 relating to small companies.

The financial statements were approved by the Board of Directors on 22 March 20X3 and were signed on its behalf by

A Smith – Director

The notes form part of these financial statements.

The Company Limited (REGISTERED NUMBER: 12345678)

Notes to the Financial Statements

for the year ended 31 December 20X2

1. ACCOUNTING POLICIES

Accounting convention

The financial statements have been prepared under the historical cost convention and in accordance with the Financial Reporting Standard for Smaller Entities (effective April 2008).

The company was dormant throughout the current year and previous year.

Dividends

Equity dividends are recognised when they become legally payable. These are recognised when approved by the Shareholders.

2. CALLED UP SHARE CAPITAL

Allotted, issued and fully paid.

Number	Class	Nominal value	31.12.20X2	31.12.20X1
			£	£
1	Ordinary Share	£1	100	100

3. ULTIMATE PARENT COMPANY

The company is a subsidiary of Another Company Limited, which is the ultimate parent company incorporated in England and Wales.

Appendix D

List of Regulators

Advertising Standards Authority The ASA is the independent body set up by the advertising industry to police the rules laid down in the advertising codes. Its website includes annual reports 1997 onwards; research reports; the current editions of the British Code of Advertising, Sales Promotion and Direct Marketing (the CAP Code), and the various other codes relating to radio and television advertising; and a searchable database of recent adjudications.

Bar Standards Board The Bar Standards Board was established in January 2006 to take over and run separately the regulatory function which had hitherto been carried out by the Bar Council alongside its representative work. Content includes the Bar Code of Conduct and the Equality and Diversity Code for the Bar, information on the complaint procedure, consultation papers and press releases.

Care and Social Services Inspectorate Wales CSSIW is the body responsible for regulating and inspecting establishments and agencies which provide social care services in Wales. Links to legislation are provided in the 'Regulations & Standards' section. Other sections have inspectorate reports, annual reports, newsletters, information leaflets, and details of the complaint procedure.

Care Council for Wales The Care Council, set up under the Care Standards Act 2000, is responsible for registering and regulating social workers and social care workers in Wales. Its online register is searchable. The 'Conduct & Practice' section includes codes of practice, the Conduct Rules, and guidance on the complaint procedure. Other site content includes consultations, recent annual reports, newsletters and e-bulletins.

Charity Commission The Charity Commission is the regulator and registrar of charities in England and Wales. Its site has a searchable database of all registered charities, which includes records of their financial histories. Publications include Commission decisions, guidance, annual reports 1999–2000 onwards, and press releases. The links section covers both other organisations and relevant legislation.

Civil Aviation Authority The CAA regulates all aspects of civil aviation in the UK. Its functions include economic regulation, safety regulation, consumer protection, and the regulation of airports, air traffic services, airlines, tour operators and air travel organisers. In relation to air traffic services it also has competition powers. Their site has an Aviation Legislation section with links to the Air Navigation Order 2005 and other relevant legislation. Also available to download is the full text of the loose-leaf publication CAP 393: Air Navigation: the Order and the Regulations, which sets out the provisions of the Air Navigation Order as amended and regulations made thereafter.

Committee of Advertising Practice The CAP is the self-regulatory body which creates, revises and enforces the various broadcast and non-broadcast advertising codes that are administered by the Advertising Standards Authority. The codes and other rules and guidance issued by the CAP may be viewed directly online or downloaded as pdf documents.

Companies House Companies House carries out a number of functions, including registration, relating to limited companies and company records in the UK. Basic company information, a list of disqualified directors, forms and guidance booklets are accessible – some of these being free of charge. More detailed information and a range of other services are available as subscription services.

Competition Appeal Tribunal The Competition Appeal Tribunal (CAT), created by the Competition Act 1998, hears and decides appeals and other applications or claims involving competition or economic regulatory issues. Information and guidance on appeals to the Tribunal includes the text of the Tribunal's rules, practice directions, and judgments 2001 onwards. Note that judgments on the site may be subject to amendment: final versions are published in Competition Appeal Reports, part of United Kingdom Competition Law Reports (Jordan Publishing Limited).

Competition Commission The Competition Commission provides extensive information on the work of the Competition Commission and of its predecessor, the Monopolies and Mergers Commission, which it replaced in

1999. Includes terms of reference, full text reports 1950 onwards, progress reports relating to ongoing inquiries, and news releases.

Council for Healthcare Regulatory Excellence The CHRE, formerly the Council for the Regulation of Healthcare Professionals (CRHP), promotes best practice and consistency in the regulation of healthcare professionals by nine regulatory bodies. This includes reviewing their disciplinary decisions and, where considered appropriate, referring them to the High Court. The website has consultations, reports, and CHRE's annual report to Parliament.

CSCI Professional The Commission for Social Care Inspection is an independent body responsible for the inspection, regulation and review of social care services in England (excluding children's services, which are currently the responsibility of Ofsted). The sub-site of the main CSCI website, designed primarily for social care professionals, provides information on registration, inspection and enforcement; links to Acts and regulations; national minimum standards; and guidance documents. Publications in the 'About CSCI' section include annual reports, inspection reports and consultations.

Department for Business, Enterprise & Regulatory Reform Responsibilities of this department, created in June 2007 primarily as successor to the Department of Trade and Industry, include productivity, enterprise, business relations, company law, energy, competition, consumer policy and employment regulation. Many sections of the site, for example those on the Companies Act 2006 and on competition matters, have information on relevant legislation, with links to texts of Acts, regulations and commencement orders.

Financial Services Authority The FSA is the independent regulator for the financial services industry, which includes banks, building societies, credit unions, insurance companies, friendly societies, financial advisors, stockbrokers, fund managers, mortgage brokers and insurance intermediaries. The 'FSA Library' section of its website contains an extensive range of downloadable documents including rules and regulations, consultation papers, press releases and annual reports. Also on the site are the consolidated FSA Handbook and the FSA's register of financial services firms.

Gambling Commission The Gambling Commission was established in October 2005, under the Gambling Act 2005, to regulate all commercial gambling in Great Britain apart from spread betting and the National Lottery. Its website has news, information and guidance, much of it in the form of downloadable documents.

Gangmasters Licensing Authority The GLA was created under the Gangmasters (Licensing) Act 2004 to curb the exploitation of workers in the agriculture, horticulture, shellfish gathering, and associated processing and packaging industries. There are links to relevant legislation, codes of practice, guidance, newsletters, and information on licensing procedures.

General Chiropractic Council The GCC regulates chiropractors throughout the UK. The site's Publications section has annual reports, fitness to practise reports, newsletters, press releases, standards, and the full text of the Chiropractors Act 1994 and related subsidiary legislation. Details of decisions relating to registration and professional conduct may be found within the Complaints section.

General Dental Council The GDC regulates all dental professionals in the UK. The Dentists Register and Rolls of Dental Auxiliaries are searchable on its website. Also on the site are 'Standards for Dental Professionals' and other guidance documents; the GDC's various Rules; information on complaints procedures; and details of outcomes of recent hearings of the Professional Conduct Committee.

General Medical Council The GMC registers doctors to practise medicine in the UK. As from 1 April 2006 the List of Registered Medical Practitioners, a register of doctors who are eligible to work in general practice in the health service in the UK, is accessible on the website. Relevant legislation, including a consolidated version with amendments of the Medical Act 1983, is to be found in the 'About us' section, and guidance documents, including both current documents and an archive going back to 1963, in the 'Guidance on Good Practice' section.

General Optical Council The GOC regulates dispensing opticians and optometrists and those bodies corporate carrying on business as optometrists or dispensing opticians. Its Register is searchable online. A Legislation section within 'About Us' has the Opticians Act 1989, rules and regulations made under that Act, and codes of conduct. Details of recent disciplinary hearings may be found under 'Hearings' within 'Our Work'.

General Osteopathic Council The GOsC regulates the profession of osteopathy and maintains the statutory register of osteopaths. Select 'About the GOsC' for a link to the Osteopaths Act 1993; the current and previous code of conduct and other guidance; information on the complaint procedure and recent findings; and recent annual fitness to practise reports. The searchable online register is to be found under 'Find an Osteopath'.

General Social Care Council The GSCC registers social care workers in England and regulates their conduct and training. There is a searchable online Social Care Register. The codes of practice for social care workers and employers of social care workers, both of which apply not just in England but throughout the UK, are available as downloads.

General Teaching Council for England The functions of the GTC, the independent professional body for teaching in England, include maintenance of a register of qualified teachers and exercise of a regulatory role over the teaching profession. The Standards and Regulation section includes the Code of Conduct and Practice and details of recent disciplinary orders and decisions.

Health Professions Council The Health Professions Council, established under the Health Professions Order 2001, currently regulates members of thirteen professions, including chiropodists, dietitians, paramedics, physiotherapists and radiographers. The Publications section has both the original and consolidated (with amendments to date) versions of the Health Professions Order 2001, rules, standards and annual reports. The Complaints section has information on the complaint procedure and details of recent fitness to practise hearings.

Healthcare Commission The Healthcare Commission (full legal name: the Commission for Healthcare Audit and Inspection) regulates and inspects both the NHS and the independent healthcare sector, and has responsibility for reviewing formal NHS complaints that have not been resolved locally. There are links to healthcare legislation, and extensive information on its activities, including consultations, reports, surveys, monthly newsletters and other publications. Investigation Reports, including those published by the Healthcare Commission's predecessor, the Commission for Health Improvement, back to November 2000, may be found in the section 'Your Local Health Services'.

Healthcare Inspectorate Wales The Healthcare Inspectorate Wales promotes improvement in the quality and safety of patient care within NHS Wales, and is also, since 1 April 2006, the regulator of independent healthcare in Wales. Publications include healthcare standards and the text of all reviews and investigations which it undertakes. There are links to legislation in the 'About Us' section. The 'Site Index' provides an A–Z index and a 'document map' in addition to a conventional site map.

Housing Corporation The Housing Corporation is the national government agency that funds new affordable housing and regulates housing associations in England. Its 'Regulatory Code and Guidance' is to be found in the 'Regulating' section. Elsewhere there are consultation papers, circulars, research reports and various other publications.

Human Fertilisation & Embryology Authority The HFEA was created in 1991, under the Human Fertilisation and Embryology Act 1990, to regulate safe and appropriate practice in fertilisation treatment and embryo research. Its Code of Practice for clinics, and related documents, are to be found in the 'How we regulate' section. Documents elsewhere, in separate sections aimed at patients, donors and clinical staff, include annual reports, research reports, news items and press releases.

Human Tissue Authority The HTA was set up under the Human Tissue Act 2004 to regulate the removal, storage, use and disposal of human bodies, organs and tissue from the living and deceased. Site content includes a section devoted to transplantation matters, licensing guidelines, codes of practice, details of current and closed consultations, media releases and news stories. Publications include annual reports, leaflets, and a regular e-newsletter. There are links to the Human Tissue Act 2004 and regulations made under it, and to the Human Tissue (Scotland) Act 2006.

Information Commissioner's Office The Commissioner is responsible for data protection and freedom of information. On data protection this site contains the 1998 Act, annual reports 2001 onwards, codes of practice, a searchable copy of the Data Protection Register, consultation papers and press releases. On freedom of information the site contains the 2000 Act in full, documents concerning its interpretation, consultation papers and a timetable for implementation of the Act's provisions.

Legal Services Review This is the site of Sir David Clementi's Review of the regulation of legal services in England and Wales. Besides the Report of the Review, published 15 December 2004, there is general information about the Review and its terms of reference, press notices, a consultation paper dated 8 March 2004, and relevant publications of the Department for Constitutional Affairs and the Office of Fair Trading.

London Stock Exchange Amongst the extensive stock market information on the LSE's site is a 'Rules & Regulations' section, from which the current Rules of the London Stock Exchange may be downloaded. To locate this section select first 'Products & Services' and then 'Membership & Trading'. Also downloadable are the current AIM Rules, most easily accessed via a direct link to the AIM page from the home page.

Medicines and Healthcare Products Regulatory Agency The MHRA was formed in 2003 from a merger of the Medical Devices Agency and the Medicines Control Agency. The site contains information, news and documents relating to the regulation of medicines and medical devices. Within

'Committees' there are sections devoted to associated advisory bodies including the Medicines Commission, the Committee on the Safety of Medicines and the British Pharmacopoeia Commission, containing annual reports and other material.

Ministry of Justice: Claims Management Regulation Regulation of claims management activities was introduced under the Compensation Act 2006 and came fully into force on 23 April 2007. As an interim measure, until the Legal Services Board is established, the regulator is the Lord Chancellor and Secretary of State for Justice. Content includes links to relevant legislation and rules; guidance and policy documents; consultations; and a regular bulletin, which has recently replaced an earlier series of newsletters. There is also a search facility for checking whether or not a business has been authorised.

National Lottery Commission The Lottery regulator's website includes news releases since its inception in 1999, a newsletter, annual reports 2000–01 onwards, and links to relevant legislation.

Northern Ireland Social Care Council NISCC is the body responsible for regulating and registering the social care workforce in Northern Ireland. Select 'A Guide to Registration' not only for information and guidance on registration but also to access the searchable register itself. Content elsewhere includes codes of practice, the Conduct Rules, consultations, and details of the complaint procedure.

Nursing & Midwifery Council The NMC regulates nurses and midwives and maintains a register of qualified nurses, midwives and specialist community public health nurses. The register is searchable online. The site's Fitness to Practise section includes details of hearings and decisions; links to legislation; fitness to practise annual reports; the NMC code of conduct; and circulars.

Ofcom (the Office of Communications) is the regulator for the media and communications industries, having replaced from 29 December 2003 the Broadcasting Standards Commission, the Independent Television Commission, Oftel, the Radio Authority and the Radio Communications Agency. Its website contains information and documents, including policy guidelines, and selected material from the former sites of the five defunct 'legacy regulators'. Select 'Competition Bulletins' on the home page to access current and archived (back to 1996) information on Ofcom's competition and other regulatory enforcement casework.

Office of Fair Trading The OFT is an independent body which promotes and protects consumer interests and ensures that businesses are fair and competitive. General information, help and advice on the site is directed at both consumers and businesses. This includes a series of 'quick guides to competition law' aimed particularly at small and medium sized businesses. Documents reproduced include press releases, reports, consultation documents and recent annual reports.

Office of Rail Regulation ORR's main function is to regulate Network Rail's stewardship of the national rail network. Like several other economic regulators it exercises, concurrently with the Office of Fair Trading, competition powers within its sector. Since 1 April 2006 it has also been the health and safety regulator for the rail industry. Its site has a wide range of information and documents, and links to railway-related legislation.

Office of the Commissioner for Public Appointments OCPA was created in response to the publication in 1995 of the Nolan Committee's first report on Standards in Public Life (Cm 2850). The role of the Commissioner is to regulate, monitor, report and advise on appointments made by UK ministers and by members of the National Assembly for Wales to the boards of around 1,100 national and regional public bodies. Publications on the site include annual reports 1997–98 onwards, a code of practice, a complaints leaflet and other guidance.

Office of the Commissioner for Public Appointments for Northern Ireland The Commissioner regulates the process by which many of the public appointments in Northern Ireland are made. Publications on the site include annual reports 2000–01 onwards, a code of practice, a complaints leaflet and other guidance.

Office of the Commissioner for Public Appointments in Scotland OCPAS was set up in 2004 to regulate and monitor the way in which ministerial appointments are made to the boards of many of Scotland's public bodies. Publications on the site include annual reports 2004–05 onwards, a code of practice, a complaints leaflet and other guidance.

Office of the Legal Services Complaints Commissioner The Legal Services Complaints Commissioner is an independent government-appointed regulator who works with consumers and solicitors to improve the complaint-handling function of the Law Society of England and Wales. The site's Publications section includes guidance and annual reports.

Office of the Scottish Charity Regulator OSCR is the independent regulator and registrar of Scottish charities, equivalent to the Charity Commission in

England and Wales. The Scottish Charity Register may be searched on its site. Also available are annual reports, consultations and other documents. The Guidance section includes links to legislation.

Ofgem (the Office of Gas and Electricity Markets) regulates Great Britain's gas and electricity markets. The legal content on its website includes links to relevant legislation: to access these first select 'About Us', followed by 'Enforcement' and then 'Ofgem's Powers'.

Ofsted (the Office for Standards in Education, Children's Services and Skills) inspects education and training for learners of all ages, except those in higher education institutes and universities. Since 1 April 2007 it has also been responsible for the registration, regulation and inspection of children's social care in England. All of its inspection reports are published on the site. Other sections provide news, forms and guidance, consultations, statistics, and annual reports 1995–96 onwards.

Ofwat is the economic regulator of the water and sewerage industry in England and Wales. It also plays a role under the Competition Act 1998 in promoting competition within its sector. The extensive range of publications available on the site includes guidance leaflets, codes of practice, consultation papers, and its annual reports to Parliament.

Pensions Regulator The Pensions Regulator, created under the Pensions Act 2004, replaced the Occupational Pensions Regulatory Authority (OPRA) on 6 April 2005 as the new regulatory body for work-based pension schemes in the UK. Its site includes information, guidance, policy documents and codes of practice.

PhonepayPlus, formerly known as ICSTIS (the Independent Committee for the Supervision of Standards of Telephone Information Services), is the industry-funded regulatory body for all premium rate charged telecommunications services. The site's 'Publications & Alerts' section includes the PhonepayPlus Code of Practice and guidelines on its interpretation and application. Elsewhere there is information on the complaint procedure and a searchable database of recent adjudications.

Postcomm – the Postal Services Commission – is the independent regulator for postal services in the UK. The site's Legal Framework section has relevant legislation and information on codes of practice. The Policy and Consultations section has both consultation documents and the policy decisions which have followed on from consultations, and these include the texts of some codes.

Press Complaints Commission The PCC is an independent body through which the British press regulates itself. It deals with complaints from members of the public about the editorial content of newspapers and magazines. Documents on its site include the PCC Code of Practice, annual reports 1996 onwards, press releases, and all adjudications (searchable) 1996 onwards.

Royal College of Veterinary Surgeons The RCVS is the regulatory body for veterinary surgeons in the UK, with statutory responsibilities set out in the Veterinary Surgeons Act 1966. The text of the Act is downloadable, and there is information and advice on recent legislative changes of relevance to veterinary surgeons. The Guide to Professional Conduct is reproduced in full, and there is a searchable register of members. Information on the complaints procedure and details of disciplinary proceedings, including findings and judgments, are to be found in the site's Visitors section.

Royal Pharmaceutical Society of Great Britain The RPSGB is the professional and regulatory body for pharmacists in England, Scotland and Wales. There are searchable registers of members, of pharmacy technicians and of premises. Documents on the site include bylaws, rules and regulations, and its Code of Ethics and Standards. To locate recent determinations, select Statutory Committee (and then 'Current and Recent Inquiries') within the Protecting the Public section.

Scottish Information Commissioner This site explains the rights of members of the public, and the responsibilities of public authorities, under the Freedom of Information (Scotland) Act 2002. A list of appeals currently before the Commissioner, and the full text of decisions already issued, are available. The 2002 Act is presented together with guidance regarding the various exemptions to its provisions.

Scottish Social Services Council The SSSC is responsible for regulating and registering the Scottish social service workforce. Its register is searchable online. The 'Registration and Conduct' section has the codes of practice and the Conduct Rules, and there is a link in 'What we do' (in the 'About Us' section) to the Regulation of Care (Scotland) Act 2001, under which SSSC was set up. Other content includes consultations, details of the complaints procedure, and news.

Solicitors Regulation Authority The SRA, launched in January 2007, is the new independent regulator of solicitors in England and Wales. Its website includes contact details, consultations, news, and the new Solicitors' Code of Conduct which replaced the previous rules of professional conduct on 1 July 2007.

Takeover Panel The Takeover Panel is the website of the Panel on Takeovers and Mergers, the regulatory body which administers the City Code on Takeovers and Mergers. Documents on the site include the Code, the Rules Governing Substantial Acquisitions of Shares, current and recent public consultation papers, and annual reports 1969 onwards.

Utility Regulator The Utility Regulator is the informal name of the Northern Ireland Authority for Utility Regulation (NIAUR), which regulates the electricity, gas, water and sewerage industries in Northern Ireland. Like its counterpart in Great Britain, Ofgem, NIAUR also exercises powers within its sector, concurrently with the Office of Fair Trading, under the Competition Act 1998. Publications on the site include consultation papers 1996 onwards and press releases 1997 onwards.

Appendix  E

Sample Budget

Budget 20X1
(Final)

Presented December 20X1

** Budget 20X1

Detailed Operating Statement

	Budget 20X0	Projected 20X0 (Oct 2010)	Budget 20X1	Jan	Feb	Mar	Apr	May	Jun	Jul	Aug	Sep	Oct	Nov	Dec
Total Sales	3,955.00	4,589.40	4,336.00	356.87	356.87	392.56	321.19	356.87	374.72	374.72	392.56	374.72	374.72	392.56	267.65
Working days	244	244	243	20	20	22	18	20	21	21	22	21	21	22	15
Daily sales				17.84	17.84	17.84	17.84	17.84	17.84	17.84	17.84	17.84	17.84	17.84	17.84
Cost of Sales															
Raw Material Costs	1,532.56	2,236.98	1,601.26	131.79	131.79	144.97	118.61	131.79	138.38	138.38	144.97	138.38	138.38	144.97	98.84
Direct Labour Cost	454.56	448.36	461.18	37.96	37.96	41.75	34.16	37.96	39.85	39.85	41.75	39.85	39.85	41.75	28.47
Stock Movement	-	-		19.27	19.27	21.20	17.35	19.27	20.24	20.24	21.20	20.24	20.24	21.20	14.45
Transport / Carriage	166.47	233.98	234.17	15.72	15.72	17.24	14.97	16.08	16.49	16.49	17.24	16.43	16.43	17.19	11.87
Total Cost of Sales	2,153.59	2,641.04	2,488.46	204.74	204.75	225.17	185.09	205.10	214.96	214.96	225.16	214.90	214.90	225.11	153.63
Gross Margin	1,801.41	1,948.36	1,847.54	152.13	152.13	167.39	136.10	151.77	159.76	159.76	167.40	159.82	159.82	167.45	114.02
	45.5%	42.5%	42.6%	42.6%	42.6%	42.6%	42.4%	42.5%	42.6%	42.6%	42.6%	42.7%	42.7%	42.7%	42.6%
Labour %	11.5%	9.8%	10.6%	10.6%	10.6%	10.6%	10.6%	10.6%	10.6%	10.6%	10.6%	10.6%	10.6%	10.6%	10.6%
Overheads															
Selling & Distribution															
Motor	13.73	13.72	15.92	1.26	1.26	1.26	1.26	1.26	1.26	1.26	1.86	1.26	1.26	1.51	1.19
Travel / Entertaining	16.72	17.43	18.48	1.58	3.08	2.88	2.63	1.38	1.28	0.38	0.38	1.43	2.08	1.28	0.08
Advertising	43.09	47.77	14.24	1.56	0.88	0.88	0.88	0.88	1.63	1.63	1.63	1.63	0.88	0.88	0.88
Bad Debts	12.00	11.79	12.00	1.00	1.00	1.00	1.00	1.00	1.00	1.00	1.00	1.00	1.00	1.00	1.00
Commissions	13.50	6.92	6.08	0.51	0.51	0.51	0.51	0.51	0.51	0.51	0.51	0.51	0.51	0.51	0.51
	99.03	97.62	66.72	5.91	6.73	6.53	6.28	5.03	5.68	4.78	5.38	5.83	5.73	5.18	3.67
Administrative Expenses															
Rates	14.49	13.44	13.56	1.27	0.20	0.20	1.32	1.32	1.32	1.32	1.32	1.32	1.32	1.32	1.32
Insurance	26.17	24.07	23.94	1.99	1.99	1.99	1.99	1.99	1.99	1.99	1.99	1.99	1.99	1.99	2.03
Repairs & Renewals	24.00	42.16	31.35	3.87	2.42	3.02	3.18	3.72	1.72	2.40	1.72	3.36	1.72	1.72	2.49
Light & Heat	25.05	24.71	23.62	1.94	1.94	2.13	1.84	1.94	2.03	2.03	2.13	2.03	2.03	2.13	1.45
Health Insurance	6.81	6.16	6.28	0.52	0.52	0.52	0.52	0.52	0.52	0.52	0.52	0.52	0.52	0.52	0.52
Staff Salaries	294.69	322.36	320.84	26.74	26.74	26.74	26.74	26.74	26.74	26.74	26.74	26.74	26.74	26.74	26.74
Bonus Payments	19.94	30.80	32.72	2.73	2.73	2.73	2.73	2.73	2.73	2.73	2.73	2.73	2.73	2.73	2.73
Employers' NIC	31.80	34.11	36.80	3.05	3.05	3.05	3.07	3.07	3.07	3.07	3.07	3.07	3.07	3.07	3.07
Staff Pension	52.06	51.86	58.45	4.87	4.87	4.87	4.87	4.87	4.87	4.87	4.87	4.87	4.87	4.87	4.87
Postage Costs	7.57	6.19	7.45	0.50	0.50	0.73	0.50	0.50	1.23	0.55	0.50	0.74	0.55	0.50	0.55
Stationery	8.07	8.72	8.78	0.54	1.06	0.55	0.55	1.06	0.54	0.55	1.06	0.74	0.54	1.06	0.54
Telephone, Fax, etc	6.00	6.20	6.50	0.55	0.54	0.55	0.55	0.54	0.54	0.55	0.54	0.55	0.55	0.54	0.55
Audit / Accountancy	12.00	12.18	13.20	1.10	1.10	1.10	1.10	1.10	1.10	1.10	1.10	1.10	1.10	1.10	1.10
Legal & Prof Fees	6.60	22.87	6.12	0.51	0.51	0.51	0.51	0.51	0.51	0.51	0.51	0.51	0.51	0.51	0.51
IT Support	19.81	23.06	19.37	1.61	1.61	1.61	1.61	1.61	1.61	1.61	1.61	1.61	1.61	1.61	1.61
QA Costs	3.89	3.25	3.03	0.13	0.13	0.13	0.13	0.13	0.40	0.13	0.13	0.13	0.13	0.13	0.13
Recruitment Expenses	3.60	14.49	1.80	0.15	0.15	0.15	0.15	0.15	0.15	0.15	0.15	0.15	0.15	0.15	0.15
Training	3.00	3.13	6.03	1.38	0.40	1.00	0.40	0.40	0.40	0.40	0.40	0.40	0.40	0.40	0.40
Exchange Differences	12.00	(6.24)	12.00	1.00	1.00	1.00	1.00	1.00	1.00	1.00	1.00	1.00	1.00	1.00	1.00
(Profit/Loss on Disposals)		(1.50)													
Bank Charges	21.21	20.52	23.26	1.92	1.92	1.98	1.92	1.92	1.98	1.92	1.92	1.98	1.92	1.92	1.97
Sundries / Incidentals	16.86	17.76	16.47	1.35	1.06	1.74	1.06	0.86	1.74	0.74	0.86	3.42	1.16	0.74	1.74
	615.63	680.28	671.56	57.72	54.44	55.94	55.74	56.69	56.20	54.83	54.88	58.95	54.57	55.96	55.65

Depreciation															
Freehold Buildings	15.59	15.59	15.59	1.30	1.30	1.30	1.30	1.30	1.30	1.30	1.30	1.30	1.30	1.30	1.30
Patent Costs	–	–	–	–	–	–	–	–	–	–	–	–	–	–	–
Computer Equipment	13.55	11.72	10.91	0.73	0.73	0.73	0.73	0.73	1.04	1.04	1.04	1.04	1.04	1.04	1.04
Plant & Machinery	73.67	64.44	70.39	5.21	5.21	5.21	5.21	5.21	5.21	5.21	6.79	6.79	6.79	6.79	6.79
Fixtures & Fittings	6.79	5.52	7.18	0.60	0.60	0.60	0.60	0.60	0.60	0.60	0.60	0.60	0.60	0.60	0.60
Motor Vehicles	–	2.19	3.27	0.27	0.27	0.27	0.27	0.27	0.27	0.27	0.27	0.27	0.27	0.27	0.27
	109.60	99.46	107.34	8.10	8.10	8.10	8.10	8.10	8.42	8.42	10.00	10.00	10.00	10.00	10.00
Total Overheads	824.26	877.36	845.62	71.73	69.27	70.57	70.11	69.82	70.30	68.03	74.78	70.26	70.30	71.14	69.31
Other Operating Income															
Operating Profit	977.15	1,071.00	1,001.92	80.40	82.86	96.82	65.98	81.95	89.46	91.73	97.14	85.04	89.52	96.31	44.71
	24.7%	23.3%	23.1%	22.5%	23.2%	24.7%	20.5%	23.0%	23.9%	24.5%	24.7%	22.7%	23.9%	24.5%	16.7%
Interest															
Bank/Loan Interest	27.70	24.39	17.29	1.91	1.51	1.57	1.50	1.49	1.42	1.42	1.38	1.31	1.30	1.24	1.23
HP Interest	2.06	0.97	–	–	–	–	–	–	–	–	–	–	–	–	–
	29.77	25.36	17.29	1.91	1.51	1.57	1.50	1.49	1.42	1.42	1.38	1.31	1.30	1.24	1.23
Less Interest Received	29.77	25.36	17.29	1.91	1.51	1.57	1.50	1.49	1.42	1.42	1.38	1.31	1.30	1.24	1.23
Goodwill Amortisation	176.92	176.92	176.92	14.74	14.74	14.74	14.74	14.74	14.74	14.74	14.74	14.74	14.74	14.74	14.74
Profit Before Taxation	770.47	868.72	807.72	63.74	66.61	80.51	49.74	65.72	73.29	75.57	68.98	81.02	73.48	80.33	28.74
	19.5%	18.9%	18.6%												
Taxation	270.40	292.06	259.38	21.16	22.01	26.15	16.35	20.94	23.12	23.78	21.88	25.34	23.18	25.15	10.31
Profit After Taxation	500.07	576.66	548.34	42.58	44.59	54.36	33.39	44.77	50.17	51.79	47.10	55.68	50.30	55.18	18.42
	12.6%	12.6%	12.6%												
Dividends Paid	357.82	255.82	408.34	11.08	11.08	11.08	11.08	11.08	11.08	11.08	11.08	11.08	11.08	11.08	286.46
Retained Earnings for Period	142.25	320.84	140.00	31.50	33.51	43.28	22.31	33.69	39.09	40.71	36.02	44.60	39.22	44.10	(268.04)
COVENANT TARGET	140.00	140.00	140.00												
EBITDA	1,086.75	1,170.45	1,109.26	88.50	90.96	104.92	74.09	90.06	97.88	100.14	107.14	95.04	99.52	106.31	54.71
	27.5%	25.5%	25.6%	24.8%	25.5%	26.7%	23.1%	25.2%	26.1%	26.7%	27.3%	25.4%	26.6%	27.1%	20.4%

*** Budget 20X1

Balance Sheet

	Jan £'000	Feb £'000	Mar £'000	Apr £'000	May £'000	Jun £'000	Jul £'000	Aug £'000	Sep £'000	Oct £'000	Nov £'000	Dec £'000
Gross PP&E	1,723	1,723	1,723	1,723	1,723	1,734	1,734	1,810	1,810	1,810	1,810	1,810
Accumulated Depreciation	945	954	962	971	980	989	997	1,006	1,014	1,023	1,031	1,040
NBV Tangible Fixed Assets	778	769	761	752	743	745	737	804	796	787	779	770
Goodwill	3,446	3,446	3,446	3,446	3,446	3,446	3,446	3,446	3,446	3,446	3,446	3,446
Amortisation	2,045	2,060	2,075	2,089	2,104	2,119	2,134	2,148	2,163	2,178	2,193	2,207
Shares in Subsidiary	-	-	-	-	-	-	-	-	-	-	-	-
	1,401	1,386	1,371	1,357	1,342	1,327	1,312	1,298	1,283	1,268	1,253	1,239
Long Term Assets	2,179	2,155	2,132	2,109	2,085	2,072	2,050	2,102	2,079	2,055	2,033	2,009
Cash	141	252	307	385	438	525	613	596	416	531	587	406
A/C Receivable	806	797	824	786	772	805	832	858	858	849	866	753
Other Debtors/Prepayments	48	46	44	48	46	44	46	44	42	40	38	36
Inventory	985	965	944	927	908	887	867	846	826	805	784	770
Current Assets	1,980	2,060	2,119	2,145	2,163	2,262	2,358	2,345	2,142	2,226	2,275	1,964
A/C Payable	(363)	(423)	(377)	(359)	(347)	(364)	(371)	(380)	(381)	(374)	(381)	(329)
Bank Loans & Overdrafts	-	-	-	-	-	-	-	-	-	-	-	-
Term Loan < 12 months	(155)	(155)	(155)	(142)	(129)	(116)	(103)	(90)	(77)	(64)	(51)	(38)
Mortgage < 12 months	(50)	(50)	(50)	(50)	(50)	(50)	(50)	(50)	(50)	(50)	(50)	(50)
Payroll Accruals (PAYE)	(25)	(25)	(25)	(25)	(25)	(25)	(25)	(25)	(25)	(25)	(25)	(25)
Other Creditors (VAT + Accruals)	(133)	(91)	(121)	(120)	(88)	(112)	(131)	(108)	(133)	(155)	(122)	(115)
HP Creditor	-	-	-	-	-	-	-	-	-	-	-	-
CT Payable	(313)	(335)	(361)	(378)	(399)	(422)	(446)	(471)	(201)	(224)	(249)	(259)
Current Liabilities	(1,039)	(1,079)	(1,089)	(1,073)	(1,038)	(1,089)	(1,126)	(1,124)	(867)	(892)	(879)	(817)
Net Working Capital	941	981	1,030	1,072	1,125	1,173	1,232	1,220	1,275	1,333	1,396	1,148
Total Assets - Current Liabilities	3,120	3,136	3,162	3,181	3,210	3,245	3,282	3,322	3,354	3,389	3,429	3,157
Term Loans > 12 months	(26)	(13)	(0)	-	-	-	-	-	-	-	-	-
Computer Loan	-	-	-	-	-	-	-	-	-	-	-	-
Commercial Mortgage	(308)	(304)	(300)	(295)	(291)	(287)	(283)	(279)	(275)	(270)	(266)	(262)
Total Long Term Debt	(334)	(317)	(300)	(295)	(291)	(287)	(283)	(279)	(275)	(270)	(266)	(262)
Deferred Taxation	(40)	(40)	(40)	(40)	(40)	(40)	(40)	(40)	(40)	(40)	(40)	(40)
Provision for Liabilities & Charges	-	-	-	-	-	-	-	-	-	-	-	-
Net Assets	2,746	2,779	2,823	2,845	2,879	2,918	2,959	3,003	3,039	3,078	3,122	2,854
FINANCED BY :												
Ordinary Shares	(100)	(100)	(100)	(100)	(100)	(100)	(100)	(100)	(100)	(100)	(100)	(100)
Revaluation Reserve	(150)	(150)	(150)	(150)	(150)	(150)	(150)	(150)	(150)	(150)	(150)	(150)
Retained Earnings - Prior Years	(2,464)	(2,464)	(2,464)	(2,464)	(2,464)	(2,464)	(2,464)	(2,464)	(2,464)	(2,464)	(2,464)	(2,464)
Retained Earnings - Current Year	(32)	(65)	(108)	(131)	(164)	(203)	(244)	(289)	(325)	(364)	(408)	(140)
Total Shareholder's Equity	(2,746)	(2,779)	(2,823)	(2,845)	(2,879)	(2,918)	(2,959)	(3,003)	(3,039)	(3,078)	(3,122)	(2,854)

*** Budget 20X1

Cash Flow Forecast

	Jan	Feb	Mar	Apr	May	Jun	Jul	Aug	Sep	Oct	Nov	Dec	Total
Retained Earnings before Divis	43	45	54	33	45	50	52	56	47	50	55	18	548
Interest	2	2	2	1	1	1	1	1	1	1	1	1	17
Depreciation	8	9	8	9	9	9	8	9	8	9	8	9	103
Amortisation	15	15	15	15	15	15	15	15	15	15	15	15	177
Cash from Operations	67	70	79	59	70	75	76	81	71	75	79	43	846
Accounts Receivable	19	9	(27)	39	14	(34)	(27)	(26)	0	9	(17)	113	71
Inventory	19	19	21	17	19	20	20	21	20	20	21	14	234
Accounts Payable	(19)	60	(46)	(18)	(11)	17	7	9	1	(7)	7	(53)	(53)
Wages Accruals	7	–	–	–	–	–	–	–	–	–	–	–	7
Other Creditors	(3)	(42)	30	(1)	(32)	25	19	(23)	24	22	(33)	(7)	(21)
Prepaid Expenses	(12)	2	2	(4)	2	2	(2)	2	2	2	2	2	–
Taxes Payable	21	22	26	16	21	23	24	25	(270)	23	25	10	(33)
Cash from Operating Capital	32	70	6	49	13	53	41	8	(222)	69	6	80	206
Cash From Operations	99	140	85	108	83	128	117	89	(151)	144	85	123	1,052
Additions to PP & E	(15)	–	–	–	–	(11)	–	(76)	–	–	–	–	(102)
Disposals	–	–	–	–	–	–	–	–	–	–	–	–	–
Capital & Operating Cash	84	140	85	108	83	117	117	13	(151)	144	85	123	949
pre Finance & Equity Change													
HP Interest	–	–	–	–	–	–	–	–	–	–	–	–	–
Bank/Loan Interest	(2)	(2)	(2)	(1)	(1)	(1)	(1)	(1)	(1)	(1)	(1)	(1)	(17)
Total Interest Payments	(2)	(2)	(2)	(1)	(1)	(1)	(1)	(1)	(1)	(1)	(1)	(1)	(17)
Long Term Debt Repayments	(13)	(13)	(13)	(13)	(13)	(13)	(13)	(13)	(13)	(13)	(13)	(13)	(155)
Computer Loan Repayments	–	–	–	–	–	–	–	–	–	–	–	–	–
Comm Mortgage Repayments	(4)	(4)	(4)	(4)	(4)	(4)	(4)	(4)	(4)	(4)	(4)	(4)	(50)
Dividends Paid	(11)	(11)	(11)	(11)	(11)	(11)	(11)	(11)	(11)	(11)	(11)	(286)	(408)
Net Financing Decrease	(28)	(28)	(28)	(28)	(28)	(28)	(28)	(28)	(28)	(28)	(28)	(304)	(614)
Net Change in Cash	54	110	55	78	53	87	88	(16)	(180)	115	56	(181)	318
Cash Beginning of Period	87	141	252	307	385	438	525	613	596	416	531	587	
Cash End of Period	141	252	307	385	438	525	613	596	416	531	587	406	
CFADS	73	129	74	97	72	106	106	2	(162)	133	74	(163)	
Cumm	73	202	276	373	444	550	656	659	497	630	704	541	
Total Debt	19	19	18	19	19	18	19	18	19	18	18	18	
Cumm	19	38	56	75	94	112	131	149	168	186	204	223	
Cover	385%	537%	490%	497%	475%	491%	502%	441%	296%	339%	344%	243%	
Agreed Bank Covenant Target													**101%**

Appendix F

Sample Health Check Report Form

Health Check Report

Company Name _____

People Interviewed _____

Prepared by _____

Date of Preparation _____

Copies of data inspected (list attached to the report)

Brief Overview of Company / Department

Critical Issues Identified

Organisation & Personnel

Corporate Ownership

Insurance

Property

Intellectual Property

Litigation

Taxation

Profit & Loss and Cash Flow

Balance Sheet / Board Meetings

Sales

Competition

Products, Services & Clients

Profit & Overhead Management

Others

Prioritised Action List

What	When	Who

Copy of Data Inspected

Insurance	Policies	Statements	HR	Financial	Various

Appendix G

Glossary of Finance and Investment Terms

Accrued expenses These are expenses due but for which no invoice has yet been received. They may include expenses such as employee wages owed prior to payday, utility charges not yet billed, interest due but unpaid, etc.

Accumulated depreciation This represents the sums accounted for to reflect the decline in useful value of a fixed asset due to wear and tear from use, or obsolescence. This number is added to each period and thus is 'accumulated'.

Administrative expense Management salaries, office staff payroll, office expenses, rent, phones, utilities, etc.

Asset Something of value that is owned by or owed to an organisation.

Asset turnover ratio The asset turnover ratio is a good measurement of how well the organisation uses its assets. This ratio is calculated by dividing total assets into net sales. The higher this ratio is, the better the organisation is at using assets to generate sales revenue.

Balance sheet A balance sheet shows the company's financial condition at a specific point in time. The asset side is equal to the side containing liabilities and shareholders' funds. The sides 'Balance'.

Balance sheet equation The balance sheet equation states that the assets of the company must be equal to the claims against the company. The claims are what is owed plus what is left for the owners after deducting what is owed from the assets. Assets = Liabilities + Shareholders' funds.

Bid The price being offered by a potential buyer for a share.

Blue chip The shares of stable, profitable, and well known companies that have a long history of steady revenues and dividend payments.

Bond A bond represents a debt that is owed by the issuer of the bond to the owner of the bond.

Broker An individual or firm that acts as an intermediary between a buyer and a seller.

Bull An investor who expects the price of a share or the general share market to increase in value.

Bull market A long period of rising share prices.

Buy-and-hold strategy Holding shares for long periods in the belief that the shares will appreciate in value in the long term. This strategy minimises transaction costs and avoids selling on temporary declines.

Buyback A business's repurchase of its own shares.

Call An option that permits the owner of the call to purchase a certain asset at a specified price until a certain date.

Capital Wealth in the form of money or property, owned, used, or accumulated in business by an individual, partnership, or company. Wealth, in whatever form, used or capable of being used to produce more wealth.

Capital gain The amount by which the proceeds from the sale of an asset exceed the asset's cost.

Capital gain tax A tax on the capital gain from assets that are sold.

Cash Notes and coins. Money readily available that will be accepted as a medium of exchange.

Cash flow statement A cash flow statement shows where cash comes from, what it is spent on during the reporting period and the net increase or decrease in cash owned by the company during this period.

Cash receipts All cash received by the company for the reporting period.

Cash receipts from borrowing Cash received from loans the company has received from lending sources like banks.

Close The last price at which a share trades or the last valuation of a stock price average during a trading session.

Company A business that has its own rights and obligations that are separate from the owners of the business. Sometimes called a 'legal person'.

Convertible security A share that is convertible into a different security. For example convertible preferred share may be converted into ordinary shares.

Cost of sales What it costs to produce a product or service. The amount of material, labour and any other production costs directly attributable to producing the product or service.

Coupon The annual rate of interest paid on a debt security as calculated on the basis of the security's face value.

Creditors The amount that the company has been invoiced but has not yet paid. This is money owed to its regular business creditors from whom it has bought goods and services.

Current assets Cash and those assets which will be turned into cash in the near future – within the next year.

Current liabilities All debts that are due within 12 months.

Current ratio The total current assets divided by the total current liabilities. This is a good measure of the company's ability to pay its debts in the immediate future. 2 to 1 is considered a positive ratio.

Current yield The rate of return to be earned from an investment's expected annual cash payment and the investment's current market price.

Debt to equity ratio Total liabilities divided by total shareholders' equity. The ratio of how much money is borrowed versus how much is invested. This is helpful in determining whether or not the company has too much debt to easily pay back.

Debtors Amount invoiced to customers and due from them but not yet collected.

Deed An official document which, when delivered, transfers ownership of an interest in property.

Deferred tax The amount of taxes that eventually must be paid despite temporary tax incentives given by the government.

Depreciation and amortisation Depreciation is the decline in value of an asset due to its being used. Amortisation is the decline in value of an intangible asset such as a patent.

Discount The amount by which the market value of shares or a company bond is below its par or face value.

Diversification Spreading money invested and risks among different and/or unrelated types of companies or investments. Thus if one investment or group of investments goes down in value the others need not necessarily follow and could even be increasing in value.

Dividend A payment from profits that is distributed to shareholders.

Earnings per share ratio Net income divided by the number of shares of a company participating in the profits. This gives a good indication of the earnings ability of a company.

Equity The financial interest that the shareholders own in the company.

Financial ratios Ratios constructed using the various numbers found on financial statements. They are used to estimate the financial strengths and weaknesses of a company.

Financial year A financial year is defined as a period consisting of 12 consecutive months, 52 consecutive weeks, 13 four week periods or 365 consecutive days after which the accounting period is closed. A financial year does not always start and end on a calendar year.

Fixtures and fittings The fixtures and fittings (e.g. signs, shelves, tables and chairs etc.) owned by a company.

Float The initial sale of shares to the public by a company that has been privately held.

Gross margin Sales minus cost of sales. It's called 'Gross' because it does not take into account other types of expenses which must be calculated before 'net profit' is calculated.

Income tax This is the amount of money that the government charges the company for profits that it makes.

Income taxes payable Money owed to HMRC but not yet paid.

Increase or decrease in cash for the year The net increase or decrease in cash owned by the company from the beginning of the reporting period to the end. Cash receipts less cash payment.

Inflation An increase in the amount of money and credit in relation to the supply of goods and services.

Initial Public Offering A company's first offering of shares to the broad public.

Institutional investor An organisation that invests large amounts of money. Examples are a bank trust department, an insurance company, or a venture capital or private equity fund.

Intangibles Assets having no physical substance yet having substantial value to the company. An example would be a patent or an exclusive.

Interest Money paid for the use of money and expressed as a percentage rate per unit of time. For example, 10 % per year paid for the use of £1,000 is £100 per year interest.

Investment Money or other forms of wealth or energy placed into a business, property, shares, bonds, etc. for the purpose of obtaining a return usually in the form of income or a profit.

Investment banker A firm that provides assistance to organisations who are in need of raising funds to finance their activities.

Investment company A firm that pools and then reinvests funds that have been invested by individuals.

Investor An individual or group that puts money into business, property, shares, bonds, etc. for the purpose of obtaining an income or profit. (Includes Angels and Angel Syndicates.)

Leverage The purchase or sale of shares using borrowed funds or credit with the expectation of earning substantial profits.

Leveraged buyout The acquisition of a company by a group of investors using mostly borrowed funds that are secured by the assets of the company being acquired.

Liabilities All the debts and legal obligations for which a business owes and must pay.

Liability Any debt or legal obligation that is owed and must be paid for or any claim on the assets of the organisation.

Liquidation Sale of all the assets of a company. This is done if and when the company becomes insolvent. The assets are sold and the proceeds used to pay off creditors.

Liquidity The degree to which there is a large amount of cash or assets that are readily converted into cash.

Long-term liabilities All debts owed that are due long-term (over one year).

Market price The price at which a share trades in the listed market.

Market value The price at which a share is bought or sold. The value of the investment at the time of purchase or sale as proven by the fact that the price asked results in a sale.

Mortgage The pledging of property to a creditor as security for the payment of a debt.

Net profit The amount of excess after all expenses have been deducted from sales. This is what is available to pay the company's investors or re-invest in operations for expansion.

Net worth The value of all assets less the amount of money owed on the assets.

Opening The beginning of a share trading session.

Operating expenses This is the total of other expenses, other than the direct cost of sales, incurred in getting a product or service sold and delivered to the customer. It is usually divided into selling expenses and administrative expenses.

Operating profit Gross profit minus the operating expenses. This figure shows what the company is making or losing prior to expenses not directly involved with making and delivering the product or service, such as interest.

Option A contract that allows a person or group to either purchase or sell an asset at a specified price until a specified date.

Ordinary shares A class of shares that has a low priority to share in the assets of a company in the event of liquidation.

Other income/expense This is money earned or expenses incurred by the company with actions not directly involved in making or delivering the product.

Par value A share's stated value as printed on the share certificate. Sometimes called face value.

Portfolio A group of investments held by an investor. For example, a mix of shares, bonds, property, gold etc., all taken together, would make up a portfolio of investment.

Pre-emption right The right of a shareholder to maintain proportional ownership of a firm by acquiring a portion of new shares that are being sold to others.

Preference shares Shares of business ownership that give the owner of the shares priority (over ordinary shareholders) with respect to dividends and to assets in the event of liquidation.

Premium The amount by which the market value of a preferred share exceeds its par value.

Prepaid expenses Payments for items that will not be immediately used and are therefore not charged immediately as an expense. For example, six months' worth of office supplies are purchased and at the end of the reporting period only two months' worth have been used. The additional four months' worth are a prepaid expense.

Price/earnings ratio Current market price of a publicly traded company divided by the earnings per share. This is an indicator of how the company is valued by the stock market relative to its ability to earn.

Profit and loss account A financial statement that measures the performance of a business over a period of time.

Profit before tax This is the amount of excess of sales over expenses on which the company must pay taxes.

Property, plant and equipment Those assets that are used over and over again in order to manufacture a product, display it, warehouse it or transport it.

Prospectus A formal document containing relevant facts concerning an issue of shares.

Proxy Written authorisation to act or vote for a shareholder.

Public limited company (PLC) A business with shares of ownership that are traded on the stock market.

Put An option that gives the owner the right to sell a particular asset at a specified price until a given date.

Ratio A ratio is the relation in number or degree between two things. For example £200 in earnings related to 100 shares is 200 divided by 100 or £2 earned for each of the 100 shares. The earnings per share ratio is thus expressed as 2/1.

Redemption The realisation of a share by the shareholder's issuer.

Retained earnings or reserves Retained earnings accumulate as the company earns profits and re-invests or 'retains' profits in the company.

Selling expenses Advertising, promotional materials, sales commissions, sales-related travel and entertainment, trade shows, etc.

Shares Shares of ownership of a company.

Speculator An individual who is willing to take large risks in order to earn above-average returns. Speculators generally hold shares for a relatively short period of time.

Spread The difference between the bid and the offering price for a share.

Stock is composed of three classes of materials: raw materials to be used in the product, goods in the process of being manufactured and finished goods ready for shipment to the customer.

Tender offer An offer to purchase shares from investors.

Title A right to ownership of property.

Total assets All the asset figures added together produce the balance sheet item called total assets.

Total equity Total value of the shareholders' equity including share capital and retained earnings.

Total liabilities Current and long-term debt added together.

Voting shares Shares that give the owner of the share the right to vote.

Working capital Current assets less current liabilities. Called 'working capital' because it is the capital that has been put to work in the business and has taken the form of stock, debtors, cash, etc.

Yield The rate of return on an investment.

Zero coupon share A share that is issued at a large discount from face value and that makes no periodic interest payments.

Index

Comprehensive. Authoritative. Trusted